In China, the decade from 1979 to 1988 witnessed among economists and policymakers an unprecedented willingness to depart from the traditional dogmatic interpretations of socialism and to enter into a discourse aimed at promoting economic reforms and development. Robert C. Hsu, in *Economic Theories in China, 1979–1988*, systematically explores the substance and logic of the evolution of the most vital economic-reform theories prevalent in China during those years (before the recent slowdown). He also examines and assesses the delicate interaction between these theories and the practical policies of the Chinese government.

Hsu's analysis covers the debates over exactly how to combine the market mechanism with socialist planning. Chinese economists argued about how to diversify the ownership system, how to implement price–wage reforms, how to invigorate state-owned enterprises and make them more efficient, and how to develop China's agriculture, industry, and foreign trade. Though Hsu critically dissects the diversity of views and describes the shortcomings that will affect future economic policies and theories, he primarily affirms the new dynamic character of China's economics.

This is the first study in English of economic theories of the reform decade in China and the first to comment on the relationship between theoretical and institutional changes. It will be of interest not only to economists, but also to political scientists and China scholars from many other disciplines.

Economic theories in China, 1979–1988

Economic theories in China, 1979–1988

ROBERT C. HSU

Clark University

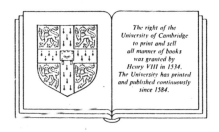

The right of the
University of Cambridge
to print and sell
all manner of books
was granted by
Henry VIII in 1534.
The University has printed
and published continuously
since 1584.

CAMBRIDGE UNIVERSITY PRESS

Cambridge
New York   Port Chester   Melbourne   Sydney

Published by the Press Syndicate of the University of Cambridge
The Pitt Building, Trumpington Street, Cambridge CB2 1RP
40 West 20th Street, New York, NY 10011, USA
10 Stamford Road, Oakleigh, Melbourne 3166, Australia

© Cambridge University Press 1991

First published 1991
Printed in the United States of America

Library of Congress Cataloging-in-Publication Data
Hsu, Robert C.
Economic theories in China, 1979–1988 / Robert C. Hsu.
p.   cm.
Includes bibliographical references and index.
ISBN 0–521–36567–8
1. Economics – China.   2. Socialism – China.   3. China – Economic
policy – 1976–   I. Title.
HB126.C4H835   1991
338.951′009′048 – dc20   91–8622
                                                                    CIP

British Library Cataloguing in Publication Data
Hsu, Robert C.
Economic theories in China, 1979–1988.
1. China. Economics. Theories
I. Title
330.951

ISBN 0–521–36567–8 hardback

This book is dedicated to Chinese economists and other in-tellectuals, who are China's best hope for modernization.

Contents

Preface

Since its conception, this book has taken more than ten years to complete. I became interested in Chinese economics and in writing such a book when I first visited China in 1978. In that year, *Jingji Yanjiu* (Economic Research), the leading Chinese economics journal, resumed its publication after years of suspension during the Cultural Revolution. I greeted its publication with great delight and expectation, and have followed its subsequent issues and those of other journals ever since. Soon after 1978, however, a paradox became clear to me. On the one hand, I firmly believed that, in view of China's long history of intellectual accomplishments, Chinese economists would have much to contribute to world economics in terms of profound theoretical insights and incisive analyses of economic issues. On the other hand, it was obvious that many articles in Chinese economics journals in the late 1970s and early 1980s were superficial and dogmatic, unworthy of the term "economic analysis." The disparity between the two was puzzling to me.

This paradox, or rather my attempt to explain it, has helped to shape the structure of this book, for the vast literature of post-1979 Chinese economics cannot be examined without a central analytical perspective. My working hypotheses that serve as this analytical perspective are that the evolution of Chinese economics can be viewed as the unfolding of an incessant interplay between the Marxist ideology and functional economic analysis on the one hand, and between economic theory and practice on the other hand; and that, whatever intellectual stimulation it had initially given to Chinese scholars, the Marxist ideology became a severe constraint on the development of economics in China once it was adopted as the state ideology or dogma. Due to that state ideology, whose validity cannot be questioned, many unexamined and unfounded beliefs have passed for profound theoretical insights or proven principles and as evidence of the superiority of socialism. This has greatly impeded the development of Chinese economics in spite of the great talent of numerous Chinese economists. The reform decade of 1979–88 saw the gradual loosening of this ideological constraint and the development of more pragmatic interpretations of Marxism, which were necessary to justify reforms. Seen from this perspective, the evolution of economic theories during the decade reflects the declining role of the Marxist ideology and the growing importance of functional economic analysis in China for the sake of promoting economic reforms. This book studies how that evolution has come about.

The book has three major components. The first one is my synthesis of major Chinese economic theoretical views as stated in published materials. For this purpose, I have used over the years the Chinese collection at the Yenching Library of Harvard University. I have also relied heavily on a personal collection of major Chinese materials, funded in part by the Faculty Development Fund of Clark University in various years. Finally, in the summers of 1988 and 1989, I was privileged to use the excellent library of the Institute of Economics, the Chinese Academy of Social Sciences (CASS), in Beijing. My research in China in both years, as well as my international travel in 1988, was funded by a grant from the U.S. Committee on Scholarly Communication with the People's Republic of China (CSCPRC), the National Academy of Sciences. My international travel in 1989 was funded by Clark University. I am grateful to both CSCPRC and Clark University for their financial support and to CASS for hosting my research in China.

The second component of the book consists of additional ideas that were obtained from formal interviews and informal conversations with many leading Chinese economists in the summers of 1988 and 1989. These interviews and conversations were extremely useful in providing background information, including views that have not been published, and in orienting my research to what Chinese economists themselves regard as important. I am most grateful to Huang Fanzhang, a former deputy director of the Institute of Economics, CASS, and currently a research director at the State Planning Commission. He was most generous in helping me in both summers to set up interviews. In regard to those I interviewed, I owe my greatest debt of gratitude to Liu Guoguang, a vice president, CASS, and a pioneer in China's economics; Dong Fureng and Zhao Renwei, honorary director and director, respectively, of the Institute of Economics; Jiang Yiwei, former director of the Institute of Industrial Economics; Zhang Zhuoyuan, director of the Institute of Finance and Trade Economics, CASS; and Wu Jinglian, executive director of the Research Center for Economic, Technological, and Social Development, the State Council. It is a great honor to have interviewed them, for they are among the most distinguished economists in China, as this book makes clear.

Other leading economists I interviewed include the following: Tang Zongkun of the Institute of Economics and a former executive editor of *Jingji Yanjiu*, a publication of the institute; Zhou Shulian, director of the Institute of Industrial Economics; Li Jingwen and Qi Jianguo, director and deputy director, respectively, of the Institute of Quantitative and Technical

Economics; Qin Qiming, senior researcher of the Institute of Rural Development; He Jianzhang of the Institute of Sociology; Liu Gang, Qian Shiming, and Yuan Enzhen of the Shanghai Academy of Social Sciences; Jiang Xuemo and Ye Gang of Fudan University, Shanghai; and He Wei, Wei Jie, and Wei Xinghua of the People's University, Beijing. I also visited the China Enterprise Management Association in Beijing, where I was warmly received by several scholars. To all of them go my sincere thanks.

The third component of the book consists of personal comments on Chinese economic theories and policies. I owe my Chinese colleagues my frank views of their theories; this is the least I can do to repay their kindness and openness to me. I have tried to take advantage of useful Western theoretical insights in my comments. In Chapter 6 I have also commented on China's political system for two reasons. First, economics and politics cannot be separated in China (see Chapter 1). Second, I am privileged to have witnessed the stirring pro-democracy movement in Beijing in May 1989 and to have shared Chinese citizens' shock and sorrow in the aftermath of the June 4 massacre. These extraordinary events, unprecedented in China's history, reflect one dimension of China's political economy that cannot be ignored in a study such as this one.

This book is a critical study of selective Chinese economic theories of the reform decade that, in my view, were either important to the reforms (for example, guidance planning, discussed in Chapters 2 and 3) or are of particular analytical interest. For the latter, I have included, for example, the concepts of workers' self-management (Chapters 1 and 3), socialist consumer sovereignty (Chapter 2), fund socialism (Chapter 3), and labor accumulation (Chapter 4), even though only a small minority of Chinese economists have discussed them. I regard these as examples of Chinese economists' contributions to the economic thoughts of the world that should be made known to the West and elsewhere. Naturally, all the errors in the book are my responsibility. Also, my comments on China's political system in Chapter 6 are entirely personal views that were prompted by the extraordinary events of May–June 1989 in China. The Committee on Scholarly Communication with the People's Republic of China, the National Academy of Sciences, which sponsored my research in China in 1988 and 1989, does not necessarily share my views.

Earlier versions of parts of Chapters 1, 2, and 3 have been published as articles in the following: Robert C. Hsu, "Economics and Economists in Post-Mao China: Some Observations," *Asian Survey,* Vol. 28, No. 12, December 1988, pp. 1211–28 (copyright 1988 by the Regents of the University of California); Robert C. Hsu, "Conceptions of the Market in Post-Mao China: An Interpretive Essay," *Modern China,* Vol. 11, No. 4, December

1985, pp. 436–60 (copyright 1985 by Sage Publications, Inc.); and Robert C. Hsu, ''Changing Conceptions of the Socialist Enterprise in China: 1979–1988,'' *Modern China*, Vol. 15, No. 4, October 1989, pp. 499–524 (copyright 1989 by Sage Publications, Inc.). I thank the copyright holders for permission to adopt liberally the published materials.

I also want to thank Roger Van Tassel for his encouragement over the years, as well as Tom Gottschang, Don Shakow, and an anonymous reviewer for reading the manuscript and giving very helpful comments. Finally and most importantly, I want to thank my family – Sharon, Nancy, and Steven – for their continuous support and understanding. They have been deprived of so much of my time and attention during my years of work on the book.

Robert C. Hsu

Worcester, Massachusetts
May 1990

CHAPTER 1

Introduction and overview

Since late 1978 when China's new leadership adopted modernization as its new development objective, many economic reforms have been introduced. These include the agricultural production responsibility system, the dissolution of the rural communes, the emergence of a small but energetic private sector, more free markets, industrial management reform, financial and tax reforms, and the "open door" foreign trade and investment policy.

In terms of the number of people whose lives have been affected, China's economic reforms are by far the most important reforms that have ever occurred in the socialist countries, outranking the Soviet reforms of the late 1960s and late 1980s and the Eastern European reforms of the 1960s and 1970s. And it is not just the Chinese who have been affected. Many foreign entrepreneurs from the West and Japan, and many investors from Hong Kong and even Taiwan, have been attracted to the newly opened China market. There is no doubt that, whatever the ultimate success of the reforms, future historians will look back at the ten years from 1979 to 1988 as the decade of Chinese economic reforms. Furthermore, whatever the future course of China's politics, the reforms will leave their indelible imprint on the future of the Chinese economy.

In parallel with the reforms, which have been well studied by Western scholars, there have been important changes in China's economic theories – in the way Chinese economists interpret socialism and envision the operation of China's socialist economy – that have not been systematically studied by the outside world. Old doctrinaire beliefs that were the foundation of the earlier economic policies and system have been increasingly criticized and discarded. Old ideological taboos have been breached. New interpretations of the tenets of Marxism and socialism have emerged. Western analytical concepts and techniques have been introduced and utilized. Academic debates ("let one hundred flowers bloom and one hundred schools contend"), after years of absence, have been encouraged. As a result, an unprecedented number of economics journals and books have been published

For a list of abbreviations of the sources cited in the text and in the references, see pages 178–9.

and economics research institutions established, attesting to the new importance of economic theorizing.

This book studies the development of China's economic theories in the 1979–88 period, including the substance and the logic of their evolution, the extent of their analytical advances, and the nature of their shortcomings. These are important to study for a number of reasons. First, these discussions are the theoretical underpinnings of the policy changes and institutional reforms. Hence they reveal the justifications, the dynamics, and the inherent limitations of China's reforms and development. Differences in the debates reveal the reservations that some economists have on policy issues, thus portending the potential problems that might be encountered in policy implementations. Furthermore, the visions of Chinese economists throw light on the future course of the economy, and the limits of their debates reflect the extent of academic freedom in China as defined by its political reality. In short, theory and practice, to use two popular Marxist terms, interact to shape the course of the economy, and the Chinese insistence on the unity of theory and practice makes it important to understand its theory.

The changes in government policies and economic theories in China following the suppression of the pro-democracy movement in June 1989 are beyond the scope of this study. Suffice it to say that progress in market-oriented reforms has been halted and pro-market discussions have been discouraged. These developments confirm the importance of political constraints on academic discussions in China, as explained in the next section. They also make 1979–88 the logical time period for studying China's reform theories.

In the following chapters, we examine Chinese economic theories in specific areas – the market under socialism (Chapter 2), the ownership of the means of production, the socialist enterprise and planning balances (Chapter 3), development strategies (Chapter 4), and prices and wages (Chapter 5). These do not exhaust all the economic topics that Chinese economists have discussed, but they are the most important reform-related topics. They are also closely interrelated. We discuss the trends and the nature of the analytical advances and limitations in these areas, as well as the interplay between economic analysis and the Marxist ideology that invariably characterizes the process of analytical advance in Chinese economics. At the conclusion of the book (Chapter 6), the fatal flaw of China's reforms, namely, the lack of fundamental political change, is discussed in light of the pro-democracy movement and the Tiananmen Square massacre in 1989.

In this chapter, the salient characteristics of China's economics as a whole are discussed so that individual economic theories can be put in proper perspective. In addition, we discuss the extent of economists' policy influence and the nature of academic freedom in China. These form the political-intellectual context in which economic theory and practice interact and in which advances in economic theories are made.

Economics in China

Economics in China is much broader in scope but much more loosely structured than its Western counterpart. It includes not only economic analysis in the sense of logical inference and causal analysis but also ideology and pseudoanalysis, ideology being defined here as the unexamined beliefs in the tenets of Marxism/socialism and in the presumed superiority of socialism over capitalism. In other words, economics in China includes what Western economists would call positive economics, normative economics, and sheer speculation or wishful thinking. This is true both before and after the late 1970s, although the role of positive economics grew considerably in the 1980s. As currently constituted, Chinese economics has three distinct branches or areas: the two major conventional branches of diagnostic economics and functional economics and the relatively new but developing branch of technical economics.[1] In the following, the nature of these branches and the interactions among them are discussed.

Diagnostic economics, which steadily declined in importance during 1979–88 but has regained importance since June 1989, is concerned with deciphering the "true" nature of Marxism and socialism, with interpreting what is consistent with it, and, on the basis of this, with expounding the presumed characteristics of the socialist economic system and the "objective laws" of the system's operation and development. These ideals of socialism were often used before the late 1970s as the standards to criticize the performance of capitalist countries and the revisionism of other socialist countries. In the post-Mao period, variations in China's conditions from those of industrialized countries as observed by Marx have been taken into account to derive conclusions more suited to China's conditions ("socialism with Chinese characteristics"). Discussions on socialist commodity production, the law of value, the law of planned development, the theory of the primary stage of socialism, and so forth belong to this branch.

Of the various tenets of Marxism, Chinese Marxists consider historical materialism and the dialectical method to be the central ones, applicable to any historical situation and to any economic issue. To Chinese Marxist scholars, these are not just a matter of Marxist ideology; they are also a

---

[1] Lin (1981: 6) first made the distinction between the diagnostic and functional branches in Chinese economics. Feuchtwang and Hussain (1983) make the same distinction. Presumably, they would place technical economics within functional economics.

matter of the "correct" perspective and methodology; even the natural sciences, they believe, can benefit from the dialectical method. However, as Heilbroner (1980: 42) has pointed out, indiscriminate application of the dialectical approach by Marxists has reduced the potentially useful idea of contradiction to a meaningless tautology because "if all of nature is contradictory by assumption, nothing is gained by pointing to the contradictory aspect of any particular element within it." In this author's view, this has been the case with Chinese Marxist economists. For example, the pricing of export products can be usefully discussed in terms of the price elasticity of foreign demand and of domestic and foreign supply, and so on, without invoking the dialectical concept. It seems meaningless to discuss the issue in terms of the "dialectical relationship" between high and low export prices, especially in one of the nation's leading management journals (*JJGL*, 1987, No. 5: 43–4).

A Marxist theory that has profoundly influenced Chinese economics is the labor theory of value. This theory is considered analytically invalid and operationally meaningless in the West, but it has been the theoretical foundation of China's price theory and price–wage reform discussions up to recent years (see Chapter 5). Other socialist beliefs that have been an important part of China's diagnostic economics until recently are the traditional beliefs in the superiority of state ownership and state planning (see Chapter 3). These beliefs were inspired more by past Soviet theory and practice than by Marx and Engels.

In a broader sense, the spirit of diagnostic economics extends far beyond these Marxism-related topics and pervades much of China's economics. In discussing virtually any economics topic, it is customary (or obligatory?) for Chinese economists to cite Marx and Engels or Lenin for ideological and analytical support. Diagnostic economics, therefore, is heavily ideological; it is concerned with both the pursuit of Marxist topics proper and the application of proper Marxist values and perspectives. It serves as the ideological foundation of economics, and provides the communicative bridge between economics and other social sciences and philosophy. And most important, to those economists who have paid proper respect to it, diagnostic economics helps provide a sanctuary when the political wind shifts and the ax falls. For this reason, prudent economists have learned to pay lip service to it even if they do not believe in it.

Functional economics is concerned with the policies and methods of planning and managing the economy; it discusses concrete policy measures to achieve specific ends or to solve specific economic problems. For example, the issue of centralization versus decentralization in planning, the organization and control of industries, government revenues and enterprise finance, the pricing and procurement of agricultural products, and so on are the concerns of this branch. Thus functional economics is policy-oriented economic analysis.

With increasing exceptions in recent years, functional economics in China tends to suffer from a shallow empiricism because the issues and orientation of the discussions closely mirror the government's short-term policy concerns, and, more important, because there is no overarching analytical framework to guide the evaluation of empirical results and policy alternatives. In Western economics, pivotal concepts such as the benefit–cost ratio, the rate of return, maximization–minimization, allocative efficiency, and others provide the pillars of an overarching analytical framework that unifies analysis in diverse areas of economics and that guides empirical studies and policy evaluation. Functional economics in China has no such framework. Instead, it typically adopts a pros-versus-cons weighing approach in which the analyst attempts to explore and weigh the positive and negative sides of an issue; it is in the "dialectic nature" of things that all issues have their positive and negative aspects. Although this approach can be very sensible, resembling at its best intuitive social benefit–cost analysis or intuitive marginal analysis, it lacks precise analytical concepts, consistent evaluative criteria, and objective quantitative methods. Consequently, the balance of its analytical scales is easily tipped by the weight of prevailing government policies. In other words, functional economics often consists of fact-finding studies without having objective criteria for selecting and assessing the "facts." Hence it often degenerates into "testimonial"-type case studies in support of government policies.

This does not mean, however, that functional economics is totally unstructured and that the analysis is conducted on the basis of the individual economist's whims and idiosyncrasies. Within its shallow empiricism, there is a certain characteristically Chinese analytical approach or style that loosely guides the posing of questions, the unfolding of discussions or the consideration of the pros and cons, and the proposing of solutions. This is the Chinese analytical proclivity to place economic issues in a "relational" context for discussions. The objective of resolving a problem or conflict is usually expressed as "to handle properly the relationship" between the parties or subjects concerned, and a policy failure is not the failure of socialism per se but is regarded as the result of the failure to handle a particular relationship well.

This analytical proclivity is in part socialist in origin and in nature because traditional socialist planning and management necessitate the specification of the vertical relationship between the state, the production unit, and the individual, or between the "whole" and the "parts," as the Chinese often put it. But it can be argued that the Chinese cultural tradition has also predisposed the Chinese to this relational mode of thinking, and that the diversity of the Chinese economy and the complexity of China's power politics have increased the need for such an approach. In any case, beyond the basic socialist categories, the Chinese have developed many other "relationships" – relationships that are both fundamental and trivial, operational and rhetorical, vertical and horizontal – as the organizing framework for discussions.[2] This organizing principle has provided Chinese economists with a loose but common analytical mode and has brought a certain contextual order to China's functional economics. The lack of objective criteria for evaluating alternatives remains, but its adverse consequences are reduced to some extent.

Partly as a result of this hierarchical, relational emphasis or mode of thinking, most Chinese economists are accustomed to viewing economic issues in the larger context of the multilayered political economy. This perspective has also enabled them to discuss situations of "externalities" without having had the benefit of this analytical concept until recently. In addition, lacking the analytical distinction between "partial equilibrium" and "general equilibrium" – a useful distinction in Western economics that nevertheless has permitted too many Western economists to cocoon themselves in their favorite niches of partial equilibrium analysis – Chinese economists perforce have to include the interaction between the parts and the whole in a manner that resembles general equilibrium analysis in spirit if not in rigor. All of this is done in an intuitive and often nonquantitative way; nonetheless, it constitutes a compensating strength that brings structure and coherence to Chinese functional economics, partially making up for what it lacks in analytical rigor, objectivity, and precision.

Consequently, there is no sharp distinction between macroeconomics and microeconomics in Chinese economic analyses, in contrast to the Western practice. As some perceptive Chinese economists, particularly Yu Guangyuan (1984), have pointed out, economic issues necessarily involve both macro and micro dimensions, and often also meso (intermediate between macro and micro, as used by Yu) dimensions, in such a relational framework. However, given the traditional socialist emphasis on state interests, planning priorities, and so on, Chinese economists have long regarded macro objectives as the foundation of micro activities, the very opposite of the Western emphasis on the micro foundation of macroeconomics. It is only since the mid-1980s that this situation has begun to change because of the reformist emphasis on enterprise autonomy (see Chapter 3).

[2] Horizontal relationships include those between consumption and accumulation, between enterprises, between coastal and inland areas, between heavy industry on the one hand and agriculture and light industry on the other hand, between the majority Han and the ethnic minorities, and so forth.

The imperatives of modernization have also given rise to a new area of economics, *technical economics*. The term, in a narrow sense as used by Baark (1981), refers to the economics of technology policy. In a broader and more meaningful sense as used here and by Dernberger (1982: 569), it encompasses econometrics, forecasting, input–output analysis, linear programming, the economics of energy and other resources, project feasibility studies, and others that are developed in the West. Although some elements of technical economics existed before 1978, they were quite insignificant. With the post-Mao modernization drive and the initiation of academic exchanges with the West, technical economics has taken on new importance. Significant developments in this area in the post-Mao period include the following: Econometric methods are increasingly used in research projects; the Institute of Quantitative and Technical Economics, the Chinese Academy of Social Sciences, has been established as a high-level research institute; mathematical models were used in making the Seventh Five-Year Plan (1986–90); the first regional input–output model in China – the Beijing 1985 model – was developed in 1987; national input–output tables were made for 1981 and 1983; and the 1987 tables are in preparation.

One major characteristic of technical economics is that it uses quantitative methods that are ideology-free and that can be used in different economic systems for different purposes, even though uninformed high officials in China speak of "quantitative economics with Chinese characteristics" (*SLJJJSJJ*, No. 1, 1988: 5–6). However, there are preconditions to be met before technical economics can flourish in a socialist country. First, as Baark (1981: 999) notes, the economics of technology policy cannot be very meaningful unless the prices that are used are meaningful and reflect the supply and demand situation of the resources used. The same is true with other elements of technical economics. The irrational nature of China's price structure, a product of its past policies and ideology, thus imposes a constraint on the utilization and development of technical economics in China. In addition, the fact that most of China's leading economists are not familiar with this branch of economics means that it will take some time before a stimulating intellectual environment can be created for its growth in China. Currently, there is only one major economics journal, *Shuliang Jingji Jishu Jingji Yanjiu (Quantitative and Technical Economics)*, that is devoted to technical economics. A small number of articles in technical economics are published every year in China's leading economics journals by young economists, but these articles are rarely if ever cited or commented on by prominent economists. Partly for this reason, the quality of these technical–economic studies is still very uneven. It is expected, however, that technical economics will become increasingly important and sophisticated in the future if economic reforms, modernization, and academic exchanges with the West are continued and as more young economists enter the field.

Finally, technical economics in China is poorly integrated with the other two branches of economics. This can be seen in the fact that many theories in diagnostic and functional economics are presented not as hypotheses to be rigorously tested, but as propositions backed by little more than rudimentary statistics. In addition, policy discussions are rarely backed by quantitative studies of policy implications.[3]

The relationship between the diagnostic and functional branches is important and revealing. Because functional economics deals with the operational aspect of the socialist economy, it has to maintain a certain harmony or balance with diagnostic economics if China's economics as a broad body of thoughts and analyses is to be internally consistent and integrated and to serve as a meaningful guide to actions. Consequently, diagnostic economics, reflecting the ideology of the times, serves as the ideological foundation of functional economics and assesses or certifies the latter's consistency with socialism. Within the broad limits of ideological compatibility, however, diagnostic economics cannot guide functional economics in its choice or assessment of alternatives.

In the evolution of Chinese economics since 1949, a certain tension or imbalance between the two branches has periodically existed, as Oxford economist Lin (1981: 6) observes. Lin further asserts that, sooner or later, the tension between the two will lead to efforts to restore the balance either by changing the diagnostic branch (e.g., by reinterpreting Marxism) or by changing the functional branch (e.g., by discouraging reformist ideas). This conception of the evolution of Chinese economics views the tension within economics as the motor force of change, propelling economic theories to a new phase of harmony. Presumably, this harmony comes about through a

---

[3] Given the structure of Chinese economics, as discussed earlier, it is not surprising that Chinese economists tend to view Western economics from the same structural perspective. For example, in a conference on economic-reform theories held in August 1987, Chinese economists agreed that they should strive to absorb the "scientific components" of Western economic theories. In doing this, the "essence-oriented theories" *(benzhi lun)* of Western economics should be rejected, but its "operation-oriented theories" *(yunxing lun)*, such as how the commodity economy or large-scale production functions, should be studied for possible insights, and its "method-oriented theories" *(fangfa lun)*, such as input-output analysis, should be learned for application to China's conditions *(GMRB, Aug. 28, 1987: 1)*. In other words, Chinese economists regard Western technical economics and part of its functional economics as scientific, but not its diagnostic economics with its claims of capitalist superiority. Whatever the merits of this view, it does reflect the structure of China's economics itself, which is deeply ingrained in the outlook of Chinese economists.

process of integrative interactions between the two branches, that is, through debates, revisions, and reconciliations, sometimes with one branch dominating, sometimes the other. At least that is this author's interpretation of Lin's hypothesis. A few Chinese authors have occasionally implied that this is indeed the way their economic theories have evolved.

This author's views are eclectic: Changes and internal integration in Chinese economics can come from both internal and external sources. The internal source has already been described. Incremental, evolutionary changes may come about this way. For more drastic or basic changes, the stimulus or impetus tends to come directly from changes in the political environment, or from changes in the political leadership and the accompanying ideological and policy changes. These external changes stimulate or compel compatible changes in both branches of economics, although occasionally the speed of change may differ between the two. The reason is that economists or economic theories in both branches have to be sensitive to the same political environment – to the ideological proclivity of the political leadership and the basic policies it favors – and produce "appropriate" theoretical responses.

The issue is not merely a matter of characterizing the evolution of Chinese economics; it involves the larger question of the nature of academic freedom, and of the role of social scientists in general and economists in particular in a socialist society. This fundamental question can be expressed in terms of the relationship between theory and practice in a socialist society. Chinese scholars and authorities have long stressed the importance of maintaining "unity" between theory and practice as the supreme guideline for academic theorizing and policy actions. To the Chinese, both diagnostic and functional economics belong to the realm of theory, and economists engaged in them are "theoretical workers." Thus, a "theory" can concern itself with issues as abstract and intractable as the nature of socialism or as mundane as the distribution of vegetables in the cities. The realm of practice includes actual policy making, problem solving, the implementation and the results of policies, and the reality of the economy in general.

The unity of theory and practice as an ideal suggests that theory should inform and enlighten practice and that practice should enrich and validate theory, thus resulting in a harmony between the two. In reality, however, given the power politics of socialism in China, the unity, where it does exist, is often reached in a different way. It is primarily the political leaders and their ideology that determine economic practice and set the tone and limits for economic theory, thereby producing unity between theory and practice on the one hand, and harmony between the diagnostic and functional branches within economics on the other hand. The reason is obvious. Political leaders have the power to give political awards, to make or change academic appointments, to influence editorial policies and the direction of theoretical discussions, and, if necessary, to ostracize or persecute dissident academicians and to suspend "antisocialist" or "counterrevolutionary" publications.

Thus, during the Cultural Revolution period, the radical leaders' ideology completely dominated economic theory and determined economic practice. In fact, functional economics was virtually nonexistent because only ideological correctness and diagnostic economics were considered important. During the relatively liberal period under study, reform-minded Zhao Ziyang – who was China's premier in 1983–7 and the general secretary of the Communist Party in 1987–9 – permitted reformist economists to exert wide influence. Nevertheless, China's theoretical workers were often exhorted by the authorities to "catch up" with the advances in reform practice, that is, to come up with theories and suggestions that would justify and perfect the reforms. Under such circumstances, "conservative" economists who favor traditional central planning increasingly found themselves ignored and their views unpublishable. Conversely, after the massacre in June 1989, the pendulum seems to have swung back and "bourgeois" promarket views seem to have been muted as of early 1990. Whether one calls the political leaders' ideology and economic views and policies part of theory or of practice – for these Marxist categories are no longer adequate – they have profoundly influenced economic theories and the limits of academic freedom ever since the founding of the Republic in 1949.

Let us illustrate, with a few important examples, the close relationship between diagnostic and functional economics, as well as the influence of political leaders' ideology on both of them. For instance, when economic policies failed, as they did during the Cultural Revolution, how did Chinese economists explain ex post facto the failure? If, as diagnostic economics claims, socialism is superior to capitalism and is capable of planned and balanced development to avoid the "anarchy" of the market (see Chapter 3), why is China's history of economic development since 1949 littered with imbalances, rigidities, and policy reversals? Furthermore, how can post-Mao economic reforms be justified when they incorporate such capitalist practices as market incentives and private businesses?

Chinese economists' answers to these questions are important and revealing. At the level of diagnostic economics, a long-standing explanation of past economic failures is Mao's "learning error" or "socialist tuition" thesis that the learning of socialism is a long and arduous process – witness how long the capitalist countries have been learning capitalism and still can't do it right – and that China is still learning socialism and making mistakes in the process, thus "paying tuition for learning socialism." In spite of the deemphasis on Mao's ideology since his death, this thesis was frequently resorted to in the post-Mao period, particularly in the early

1980s, to explain the tortuous course of the Chinese economy since 1949. At the level of functional economics, the learning errors are variously interpreted to be the errors of not having handled properly some important relationships in the economy mentioned earlier. In particular, economists in the early 1980s argued that China's past planning and management *methods* were too rigid. They did not adequately take into account the "material interests" of the production units and of individuals as opposed to those of the state, and did not give the former enough autonomy to mobilize their incentives and initiatives; hence the need for reforms in these areas if China's modernization is to succeed.[4]

Given the post-Mao leadership's decision to reform the past planning and management practices, China's functional economics has been engaged in designing and assessing various reform measures and in evaluating the results of implementation. For its part, diagnostic economics has examined and justified these reforms as consistent with socialism under China's concrete conditions at an early stage of socialism ("socialism with Chinese characteristics"). In this regard, the rise of the theory of the "primary stage of socialism" has been very important; it became the major theoretical thrust of China's diagnostic economics in the late 1980s. The theory posits that the traditional yardsticks of socialism as given in the classical Marxist literature are developed for "mature" socialism. Because China adopted socialism as a semifeudal and semicolonial country with a low level of development, it is only in the initial or primary stage of socialism. Hence the criteria of socialism for China need to be modified in light of China's conditions. Policy measures and systemic characteristics such as commodity production for the market, the existence of a small private sector, reliance on the profit incentives in enterprise management, and so on are consistent with socialism at an early stage as long as they promote productivity and thus help to develop socialism. From this perspective, a serious error in the past was the leftist belief that China could skip the primary stage and practice full socialism immediately. The result was that, as with a child wearing an adult's hat and thus covering the eyes and ears, the flexibility and efficiency of the economy were severely restricted (*ZGSHKX*, 1988, No. 3: 50). The primary-stage theory, therefore, is consistent with Mao's learning error thesis.

Thus the theory of the primary stage of socialism has three essential components: the stage of development concept, the concept of China's uniqueness, and the expected productivity increase through reforms. The idea that China is in the primary stage of socialism was first broached in 1981 at the

---

[4] Other explanations given by Chinese authors in general in the 1979–88 period include (1) the "leftist deviation" in ideology and policies, as shown by the gang of four, and (2) the vestiges of feudalism, which led, among other things, to the rule of personality cult rather than the rule of law and to the subordination of economic units to political leaders.

Sixth Plenary Session of the 11th Central Committee of the Chinese Communist Party. In 1982, at the 12th National Party Congress, Deng Xiaoping stressed China's uniqueness by advocating the building of socialism with Chinese characteristics. These two concepts together constitute the general theoretical justification for reforms. It is left to functional economics, using the pros-versus-cons approach, to ascertain that specific reform measures are indeed conducive to productivity increase and that the advantages outweigh the possible disadvantages. In October 1987, at the Thirteenth National Party Congress, the theory was formally incorporated into the official ideology of the Chinese Communist Party, a shown in then party general secretary Zhao Ziyang's speech to the Congress.

The role that the political leadership has played in the rise of this theory illustrates dramatically the influence of political leaders' ideology on economics, as discussed earlier. Before the formal adoption of the theory, various economists had touched on the substance of various aspects of the theory to justify specific reform measures, as can be seen in the following chapters. However, they did not utilize the concept systematically as the unifying theme in justifying post-Mao reforms in general. After the Communist Party Congress formally adopted the theory as its reform ideology – and certainly reformist party economists participated in formulating it – the theory became virtually overnight the new creed in China's diagnostic economics, and indeed in all the social sciences. Liu Guoguang, a vice president of the Chinese Academy of Social Sciences, declares that the "primary-stage theory should be used to guide research in various areas of social sciences in order to deepen our research" (*GMRB*, Jan. 2, 1988; 1). In fact, the primary-stage theory has since then overshadowed classical Marxism as the major ideological yardstick in China's diagnostic economics by which the consistency of various reform measures with socialism is to be assessed. Some Chinese authors have even attempted to expand it into a general stage theory of socialism.

In this manner, both diagnostic and functional economics are subject to the same external political influence and coexist in a harmonious equilibrium in the post-Mao period. Generally speaking, however, it is easier for functional economics than for diagnostic economics to change because the latter often involves basic changes in long-held beliefs. For example, in recent years, a number of Chinese economists have advocated the introduction of alternative forms of ownership – workers' ownership, enterprise ownership, shareholding ownership, and so on – to replace or modify state ownership of the means of production (see Chapter 3). Although state ownership produced many problems in the past, as pointed out by many economists at the level of functional economics, the deep-seated belief that state ownership is essential to socialism has made it difficult for China's diagnostic economics to justify alternative forms of ownership. Similarly, since 1985 a growing number of small state-owned enterprises has been leased to private individuals for management. Touted as the "separation of the two rights" (ownership right and management right), this management arrangement has been supported by many economists on pragmatic, functional grounds to minimize administrative interference in enterprise management (see Chapter 3). However, as the leased enterprise prospers and the lessee's income becomes as much as eight times higher than that of his or her average employee, the consistency of enterprise leasing with socialism becomes hotly debated. A discussion campaign was launched in mid-1987 in the press on whether the "family name" of leasing is socialism or capitalism.[5] Thus, on basic systemic issues such as these, functional economics has been ahead of diagnostic economics in catching up with the reform practice. Sooner or later, however, and barring extremist political interventions such as those that occurred in June 1989, diagnostic economics will be influenced by functional concerns if economic problems are to be solved. In fact, the primary-stage theory of socialism itself is an ingenious diagnostic response to the need for reforms, and with its blessing, an increasing number of economists in the late 1980s accepted "socialist mixed ownership" and growing income inequality as compatible with socialism at the primary stage (see Chapters 3 and 4).

The distinction between diagnostic and functional economics does not mean that Chinese economists necessarily specialize in one branch or the other, or that economic theories clearly belong to one branch or the other. On the contrary, most economic theories contain elements of both, and many economists move between ideological rumination and functional analysis constantly and with ease, as if oblivious to the differences between them. Even in endorsing market-oriented reform measures, many economists have cited Marx and Lenin for support, as if invoking the Marxist spirit while prescribing the market machine. Thus ideology and analysis interact at various levels of Chinese economics – between economics and the dominant ideology of the political leadership; between diagnostic economics and functional economics; and within the thinking processes of individual economists themselves.

Economists in China

Because the scope of economics is broad and imprecise, so is the definition of economists or "economic workers," as they are often referred to in China. It includes not only academic economists at teaching and research

[5] See various issues of *Jingji Ribao* (Economic Daily), starting on June 12, 1987.

institutions but also economic researchers, advisers, writers and commentators affiliated with government organizations and the press, and bureaucrats directly involved in economic policy making and implementation. Dernberger (1982) classifies them into academic economists, applied economists, and technical economists. In this classification, applied economists work in the government's economic bureaucracy. Halpern (1985a) classifies them into academic economists and economic bureaucrats. In this simplified classification, economic bureaucrats are broadly understood to include government economic officials, advisers, researchers, and commentators who are routinely engaged in making, implementing, assessing, or expounding official economic policies. Also, these two classifications do not correspond to this study's classification of Chinese economics into diagnostic, functional, and technical branches because academic economists can teach and do research in any branch of economics.

Economists, social scientists, and party theoreticians who are engaged in expounding or examining the theoretical aspects of economics are referred to by the Chinese as economic "theoretical workers" or members of the "theoretical circle." Thus economic theories are not the exclusive domain of professional economists. Nor is prior professional training in economics necessary for one to become an economist; many economists are self-taught or learned their craft on the job. Consequently, the level of competence in economic analysis is very uneven among Chinese economists. Many of them, particularly the older ones, are weak in quantitative methods. Also, many of them, particularly the economic bureaucrats, are generalists in the sense that their previous training or career experience may have been in part organization, general government administration, or even the military. It is misleading, therefore, to characterize all economists in China as specialists, as Halpern (1985a) does, even if their current positions or responsibilities fall within a narrow area of economic affairs.

It was stated previously that the impetus for basic changes in economic theories in China has typically come from outside of economics – from political leaders, their ideologies and economic policies, or from changes in the political environment. This does not mean, however, that Chinese economists do not influence policies in any way, and that their theories merely echo the leaders' views and rationalize prevailing official policies. Here it is important to distinguish between two concepts: the basic policy line or orientation and the policy measures that are designed to incorporate and carry out the policy line. The *policy line* is determined by the political leader(s) and reflects his (their) fundamental ideology or basic views as to how things should be done in pursuing socialist development in China. The leaders' basic policy line is rarely questioned openly, except in a period of political change or instability, and even then the questions are normally voiced by potential political challengers, and not by economists as such except after the political change.

On the other hand, *policy measures* can be changed relatively easily as long as the changes are consistent with the basic policy line. Therefore, policy measures can be discussed and even criticized by economists. For example, Deng Xiaoping's basic policy line of "economic reforms without bourgeois liberalization" is not to be challenged by economists, but the details or the mechanics of the reforms such as the design, scope, timing, and sequence of specific changes, as well as the consequences of the changes, can be discussed by economists as long as they are not "antisocialist." In other words, the leaders' policy line sets the limits within which economic discussions take place. This is the context in which Chinese leaders' conception of academic freedom is to be understood (more on this later).

Consequently, aside from performing their normal duties, such as teaching, research, or economic administration, many economists also perform the important function of assessing and influencing policy measures. They can do this in two ways. The first is to participate directly in decision making as advisers or in other capacities. As Halpern (1985a) has documented, economists have participated in government decision making at least since the mid-1950s, but the meaningfulness of their participation – that is, their effectiveness in terms of affecting the outcome – has fluctuated over time in a cyclical manner, reflecting the cyclical nature of political changes and of attitudes toward economists in China. Thus in the 1955–7 period, economic bureaucrats participated extensively and meaningfully in decision making; during the Great Leap Forward (1958–9), both economic bureaucrats and academic economists participated, but less effectively. In the early 1960s, both groups participated. During the Cultural Revolution, the academics were left out. In the post-Mao period, both groups participated meaningfully.

Naturally, direct participation in policy making has always been limited to a relatively small number of trusted and prominent economists both in and out of academe, but its importance increased considerably in the post-Mao period. For example, since 1980 in the State Council as well as in every ministry of the Council, there have been economists from inside and outside the government bureaucracy who advise the policy makers directly. On many occasions the latter are said to have taken their advice seriously, at least more so than previously.

Indirectly, economists can influence economic thinking and policy making by publishing in the media, as well as in professional journals and other publications, and by participating in professional conferences. Although all these forms of participation existed in the 1950s and early 1960s, the number of professional publications and conferences was much larger in the

1980s. This type of participation performs a number of useful functions for the government and the society at large. First, in a nonauthoritarian way, it can educate or prepare the public or the relevant economic sector for a forthcoming policy measure or legislation. Chinese discussions of economic issues are typically conducted like a campaign, with great intensity within a certain time period, ranging from several months to a few years, during which a large number of economists comment on a particular economic issue or proposal. They may justify the proposed new measure or legislation as consistent with socialism/Marxism, or support it on pragmatic grounds, or explore its theoretical or practical implications or potential problems. Toward the end of the discussion campaign, national conferences on the issue are often held in which a large number of theoretical workers and economic bureaucrats may participate and in which a consensus or a number of major conclusions emerge. Similarly, nationwide essay contests on the topic are often sponsored by official newspapers and professional journals to promote theoretical "blooming and contending" in the "correct" direction. Since the contests are open to everyone, it is not surprising that many of the winning essays are written by government economists who reflect government views. Also, nationwide "knowledge contests" on reform issues are occasionally held to propagate the "correct" knowledge. Thus, what starts out as an exploration of an issue invariably ends with a managed consensus or a predominance of views that are supportive of government positions.

Nevertheless, in the post-Mao economics literature as well as in official policy discussions, invariably there are some economists who express different views or reservations, or who point out potential pitfalls in a proposed new measure. In this way, before a new policy measure is introduced or a new law is promulgated, the public or the concerned economic units are well informed about it. The reservations expressed help officials in charge of implementing the measure to become aware of potential problems. For this reason, Dernberger's (1982: 575) characterization of Chinese economic research as "little more than ex-post rationalization of the facts" is not entirely accurate, at least not for the 1979–88 period. After a change has been introduced, the press and the professional journals may continue, at least occasionally, to publish articles about it, discussing the extent of the progress that has been made or the problems that may have developed. These tend to be ad hoc fact-finding studies, and the methods of analysis are often crude, as discussed earlier. Nevertheless, these follow-up studies explore the causes of the problems that have developed and offer suggestions for improvement. In this manner, economists perform the function of *limited* policy evaluation. Possible criticisms of the policy line, where they exist, are carefully couched in terms of the adverse consequences of various policy measures.

In these ways, academic freedom is practiced within limits and in a controlled environment, as was the case during the 1950s, although the limits in the post-Mao period until June 1989 were broader and more flexible. However, as the experiences of 1957 and 1989 indicate, the limits can change very quickly, depending on the decisions of a few political leaders. This variability in the limits of academic freedom over time, aside from and perhaps more than the existence of the limits at any one time, cannot but put a damper on the willingness of many economists to voice criticisms.

Ironically, precisely because the limits of debates were broader and more flexible in the 1979–88 period, confusions and contradictions also arose as to how far economists could go in voicing criticisms. Formally, the government adopted the "double-hundred policy" of encouraging debates and a diversity of views ("let one hundred flowers bloom and let one hundred schools of thought contend"). However, in late 1983, during the height of the "anti–spiritual pollution" campaign – a conservative backlash against Western cultural influences due to the "open door" policy – Liu Guoguang, a leading reformist economist and then director of the Institute of Economics, the Chinese Academy of Social Sciences, felt obliged to condemn "spiritual pollution in economics" (*JJRB*, 8, 1983: 3). In 1986, Dong Fureng, another leading reformist economist who succeeded Liu as the director of the Institute of Economics, along with several other prominent economists, declared that the double-hundred policy should be implemented under the guidance of Marxism (*JJYJ*, no. 7, 1986: 3–21), thus echoing a point made earlier by then Premier Zhao Ziyang. Also, as mentioned earlier, Liu Guoguang, currently a vice president of the Chinese Academy of Social Sciences, stated in early 1988 that the primary-stage theory of socialism should be used to guide research in social sciences. Such is the vulnerability of Chinese academic freedom to subtle shifts in the political environment and to cues in political leaders' pronouncements. Needless to say, the authorities did not define what constitutes the spiritual pollution in economics or the correct interpretation of Marxism. In fact, Marxism itself is being reinterpreted to support the reforms, as mentioned earlier, making the limits of academic freedom vague and unpredictable.

It should not be concluded from the preceding discussion, however, that Chinese economists have thus become a homogeneous lot; on the contrary, there are many shades of differences among them. According to various leading economists this author interviewed before June 1989, the great majority of Chinese economists are in favor of reforms. A small minority are staunch supporters of the traditional system of central planning and control; several economists at the People's University in Beijing are known to be traditionalists because of their career background and the influence of the

Soviet economists who taught at the university in the 1950s. Another small minority, typically the younger ones, are privately in favor of the Western capitalist system. Of the great majority, a small minority favor reforms according to the Eastern European or the Hungarian model of market socialism (see the next section); the rest support China's reform strategy of developing socialism with Chinese characteristics. This classification of Chinese economists, although imprecise, is no doubt accurate, as only authoritative insiders can know, since opponents of reform and of socialism cannot easily have their views published.

The theoretical orientation of those who still favor traditional central planning has become more sophisticated over the years and contains an element of modern economics. Led by Wu Shuqing – a vice president of the People's University until his appointment as the new president of Beijing University after the Tiananmen Square massacre in 1989 – these traditionalists believe that a socialist economy at the primary stage such as that of China, is a "shortage economy" because of the low level of productivity development. Therefore, the market mechanism cannot be relied on to operate efficiently, and planning has to be the main allocative mechanism, with the market playing a secondary role.[6]

Even among economists who support reforms with Chinese characteristics, one can discern various differences, some of which are institutionally based, affecting the research emphasis, and others theoretically based, leading to policy differences. In terms of institutionally based differences, economists affiliated with the State Council or its ministries and commissions are understandably preoccupied with concrete policy issues and typically do not discuss abstract theoretical issues such as allocative efficiency, the "socialist consumer sovereignty," and enterprise objective function. And a case can even be made, as some Chinese critics have pointed out, that some government economists do not genuinely understand, and are not committed to, market-oriented reforms, but simply devise and propagate policy measures favored by political leaders.

On the other hand, research economists at various institutes of the Chinese Academy of Social Sciences and academic economists at the major universities tend to be much more theoretical in orientation and broader in their scope of inquiry. In particular, economists at the Institute of Economics (IE) and the Institute of Industrial Economics (IIE) of CASS have long been at the leading edge of theoretical innovations. In the 1950s and early 1960s, reformist economists such as Sun Yefang of IE first advocated the

---

[6] This theme is espoused by Wu Shuqing in a number of unpublished conference papers. For a comprehensive synthesis of the views of the traditionalists at the People's University, see Wu Shuqing and Hu Renwu (1987). A popular political economy textbook that reflects relatively conservative views is Jiang Xuemo (1988a).

reform of industrial planning and management by giving the enterprise greater autonomy. In the post-Mao period, Liu Guoguang himself has been a pioneer in the advocacy of "guidance planning" to combine planning with the market mechanism and in the discussions of development strategy (see Chapters 2 and 4). Other leading reformist economists such as Jiang Yiwei, a former director of IIE, have advocated a system of enterprise-based "economic democracy" that goes beyond the conventional workers' self-management to form the basis for political democracy (see Chapter 3). Dong Fureng, the honorary director of IE, has been a leader in ownership reform discussions and currently advocates socialist mixed ownership (see Chapter 3). Zhou Shulian, director of IIE, has theorized about the "rational socialist enterprise," with important insights (see Chapter 3). Zhang Zhouyuan, director of the Institute of Finance and Trade Economics, has been a leader in China's price discussions (see Chapter 5). In addition, a growing number of economists at these institutes have been exposed to Western economic theories and have been among the first to adopt some Western analytical concepts to aid their analyses.

In terms of theoretically or policy-oriented differences, Harding (1987: 80–3) has distinguished between radical reformers and moderate reformers who differ in the speed and extent of market-oriented reforms they advocate and in their commitment to socialist planning. Although this classification is correct, it should be pointed out that by 1987–8, the great majority of reformist economists were in favor of market-oriented reforms; the government, they believed, should influence the economy through indirect macro instruments, and not by the traditional socialist planning.

Even among the pro-market economists, however, understanding of the nature and requirements of the market mechanism varies greatly. In 1986–8, at least two major schools of thought were contending for policy influence concerning the manner in which and the speed at which further reforms should be carried out. The first school of thought, led by Li Yining, a professor of economics at Beijing University and once a trusted adviser to former party leader Zhao Ziyang, contended that the reform of enterprise ownership should precede price reforms. Li Yining (1986a, 1986b) wanted to transform large and medium-sized state enterprises into joint-stock companies in which the state, the enterprise, and the enterprise workers would hold stock and participate in decision making through a board of directors. He argued that only after this reform was implemented would the enterprise and the workers have the autonomy and incentives to operate efficiently in a competitive market environment, and that only then would the price reform be effective. The second school of thought, led by Wu Jinglian of the Academy of Social Sciences and concurrently the director of a research center of the State Council, emphasized integrated or coordinated reforms of the price system, the enterprises, and the macro management system. It contended that unless these reforms were carried out concurrently and fairly quickly (three to five years for the first phase), reforms in separate areas would not be effective and China would experience serious economic problems. The reasoning was that unless a reformed enterprise could operate in a competitive market environment with rational prices, enterprise reform per se would not be effective and would not lead to efficient allocation of resources in the economy. Price reform was necessary to create the competitive market environment, but price reform alone was not sufficient (Wu Jinglian and Zhou Xiaochuan, 1988). These two schools of thought are popularly referred to as the "enterprise ownership reform" and the "price reform" school of thought (discussed further in Chapter 5).

Finally, at the level of diagnostic economics, there is yet another way to characterize the differences, at least until the mid-1980s, among reformist economists. Although the Chinese themselves do not emphasize these differences, they are relevant and of analytical interest because they reflect fundamental differences in Chinese economists' conceptions of socialism. As discussed in Chapter 3, socialism as a body of anticapitalist critiques and systemic ideals has two related but distinct tenets or themes – the "anti-market-anarchy" tenet, which postulates state planning and control of the economy, and the "anti-capitalist-exploiters" tenet, which promises industrial democracy and workers' self-management ("masters of the means of production"). Ever since the Chinese leaders embarked on economic planning in the early 1950s, the planning-control aspect of socialism has dominated the industrial-democracy aspect of China's socialist development. From this perspective, one can identify two broadly defined schools of thought or socialist sentiments among the reformist economists in post-Mao China. The first, and dominant, school of thought is concerned with proposing ways to make the socialist planning and management system more flexible and efficient or with harmonizing the market with socialism. Economists of this school differ among themselves in the reform measures they emphasize at the level of functional economics – guidance planning, industrial financial reform, enterprise director responsibility system, and so on – but not in the priority they give to the socialist ideal of planned or state-guided development over that of industrial democracy. The second school of thought, disillusioned with the results of past state planning and control, stresses the latter ideal and has proposed ways to translate that theoretical promise into reality. These include the proposals to give workers self-management and to replace state ownership with workers' ownership or enterprise ownership so that ownership right and management right will be unified. The most eminent leader of this school, Jiang Yiwei (1980a, 1988), proposes a system of enterprise-based, bottom-up economic democracy at the enterprise, industry, and national levels, which will serve as the foundation for socialist political democracy.

Thus, at the level of diagnostic economics, the first school of thought subscribes to the prevailing reformist interpretation of socialism, whereas the second school adheres to or builds on a fundamentalist interpretation of a separate tenet of socialism. Although the second school of thought is not accepted at the policy level, it is accepted within the limits of academic freedom because its ideological foundation is impeccable. This is a rare example in Chinese economics of a situation in which a respectable theory in its diagnostic branch does not echo or influence policy practice. The majority of reformist economists, while paying homage to this venerable but long-neglected aspect of socialism, regard it as impractical and conducive to micro–macro conflicts at China's current stage of socialist development. They support instead the separation of management and ownership ("management contract responsibility system," enterprise leasing by individuals, etc.) and the enterprise "director responsibility system" that gives enterprise managers, not workers, more decision-making power vis-à-vis the state and the enterprise's party committee secretary.

This apparent lack of unity between theory and practice with respect to the second school of thought cannot be thoroughly understood without reference to the nature of economics and of academic freedom in China. As discussed earlier, these are shaped by one *unchanging* characteristic of China's political economy – the fact that party leaders are able to emphasize a certain aspect or interpretation of socialism that best suits their policy objectives, and to promote as well as to draw policy suggestions from the development of theories that are compatible with that interpretation, thereby producing unity between theory and practice. These theories consequently become the mainstream in economics. Within this mainstream, there may be a great diversity of views on the best means to attain a given policy objective, as was the case during the 1979–88 period. The double hundred policy of encouraging theoretical blooming and contending applies primarily to this level of functional economics. Outside of this mainstream, economic theories based on alternative interpretations of socialism have limited or no influence on policy practice. They may not be acceptable for publication, as was the case during the Cultural Revolution, or they may be publishable within the limits of academic freedom, as was the case in 1979–88, all depending on the temper of the times. In this sense, economists in the 1979–88 period enjoyed an added degree of academic freedom by China's standards, although they had little or no policy influence for theories outside the mainstream. But those economists and other social scientists who do not support the leaders' policies or accept the supremacy of the Communist Party are regarded as the source of spiritual pollution and bourgeois liberalization and have no place in this socialist conception of academic freedom, whatever the time period.[7] It is in this political–intellectual environment that China's economic theories have evolved in the post-Mao period.

Reform theories with Chinese characteristics

Within the limits of academic freedom as discussed previously, Chinese economists in the 1979–88 period developed, in their functional economics, a large and impressive variety of alternatives for all major institutional changes. This diversity of views was unprecedented in China and possibly also in the entire socialist world. As will be detailed in the following chapters, their wide-ranging proposals and debates included the different ways to combine the market with the plan (see Chapter 2), to modify the ownership system and to reform the management of the state-owned enterprises (see Chapter 3), to develop various sectors of the economy (see Chapter 4), and to reform the price–wage system (see Chapter 5). Furthermore, contrary to popular belief, their ideas and proposals were largely indigenous in origin and were not transplants from other socialist countries. Naturally, some of them were similar to those that have been discussed in other socialist countries. This is not surprising; given the basic socialist ideology and organization, there are only so many ways to rearrange or recombine a given set of policy and institutional variables; this by no means proves that the ideas are consciously borrowed from abroad. In fact, the majority of Chinese economists are not familiar with the details of Eastern European economic theories and reforms. As of mid-1989, the first and only comprehensive survey of Eastern European economic thought – that of Hong Yingxing, Zhou Xiaohan, Jin Bei, Hu Yongming, Zhu Zhengming, and Lu Jianren (1988) – was written by six then graduate students in economics and was not published until 1988. Thus most Chinese economists could not have consciously drawn on the Eastern European experiences or theoretical insights. Nor did they want to; as early as 1982 the Chinese political leadership asserted, and most Chinese economists concurred, that the Chinese have to find out for

[7] For example, many young Chinese intellectuals view the "democratic socialism" of Western Europe as a superior alternative to China's version of socialism. However, because democratic socialism rejects Marxism and the leadership of the Communist Party, it is not acceptable to the Chinese authorities. Consequently, the official Chinese press has never published the views of supporters of democratic socialism. On the other hand, detailed critiques of democratic socialism have been published (*GMRB*, Apr. 21, 1987: 3). The official Chinese justification for this unequal treatment of the two sides of an issue is that the double hundred policy is not an objective in itself, but rather a means for the development of "socialist sciences and culture" (*HQ*, No. 4, 1987: 5; No. 6, 1987: 3–5). Hence the implementation of the policy has to be consistent with socialism (i.e., with the prevailing interpretation of socialism).

themselves the types of reform that suit China's conditions and thereby develop socialism with Chinese characteristics.

It is true that, since the early 1980s, an increasing number of Chinese economists have studied the reform experiences of Eastern European countries, particularly Hungary. They have also studied the writings of some prominent Easter European economists, such as Kornai, Brus, Lange, and Sik. However, in 1984, a delegation of economists who visited Hungary concluded that Hungarian policy practices "cannot be indiscriminately copied" because of the great differences in conditions between the two countries, although the Hungarian experience did have useful lessons for China (*JJYJ*, No. 3, 1984; 22). This statement is consistent with Halpern's (1985b: 97) observation that the Hungarian experience influenced the Chinese less in the content of reforms than in the strategy of their implementation.

In the realm of economic theorizing, Chinese economists have adopted certain analytical concepts and categories used by some Eastern European economists – particularly Kornai's (1980a, b) "shortage economy" and "soft budget constraint" and the classification he made during his 1985 visit to China of different adjustment and control mechanisms of an economy (*JJYJ*, No. 12, 1985: 3–6) – and these have been useful tools in Chinese discussions, as we see in Chapters 2 and 3. However, the Chinese have generally concluded that the applicability of the Eastern European economic models to China is limited because of their exclusive concern with *small* socialist countries that are very different from China. For example, the intermediate-level government between the central government and the state-owned enterprises is very important in the Chinese economy but is absent in these countries. In addition, up to 1989, Eastern European countries had not introduced, and their economists had not discussed, ownership reform. This topic became increasingly important in China's reform theories in the late 1980s as new types of nonsocialist ownership were introduced in China (see Chapter 3).

Polish economist Brus and Czechoslovak economist Sik visited China in 1980 and 1981, respectively, and lectured on the need for coordinated, systemwide reforms. Sik, in particular, stressed the importance of introducing market prices and reportedly persuaded the Chinese leadership to consider implementing a price reform in the early 1980s. As part of the preparation, the Price Research Center of the State Council was established to calculate equilibrium prices (discussed further in Chapter 5). However, the reform was aborted because of opposition from people who stressed the importance of planned prices under socialism (*JJYJ*, No. 2, 1989: 13). In other words, ideologically China was not ready for Brus's and Sik's ideas in the early 1980s, as Chapters 2 and 5 make clear. During 1986–8, Chinese economists increasingly supported market prices and coordinated reforms, not because of Eastern European theoretical influence, but because China's own experiences and problems increasingly make such a development inevitable. The names of Brus and Sik are rarely mentioned in the Chinese economics literature since the mid-1980s, unlike that of the Hungarian economist Kornai.

Kornai's (1980a) theory of socialist shortage economy – that the planned socialist economy is inherently a shortage economy, where the shortage is systemic and chronic – has become relatively well known in China since the mid-1980s.[8] It has sharpened Chinese economists' understanding of the problems of prereform Eastern European socialist economies and has given them insights into the problems of China's own prereform economy. In addition, it has ironically given a small number of traditionalists an analytical tool with which to argue against the dominance of the market mechanism, as mentioned earlier. However, several Chinese economists have argued that its relevance to China's reform theory and practice is limited. In particular, Wu Renhong (1988: 6–7) points out the following limitations of the model in relation to China's post-1979 economy: (1) It assumes a high level of capacity utilization, whereas in China the utilization level is low. (2) It assumes a labor shortage, which is not valid in China. (3) It assumes that price signals are not operative, whereas in China the dual-track price system (see Chapter 5) has affected investment and production decisions. More generally, Kornai's various theories are considered by Hong Yinxing et al. (1988: 363–5), who have produced the only comprehensive study of Eastern European economic theories in China, as innovative but weak in the following areas: (1) He does not deal with the deeper underlying factors that shape the socialist economic system; hence he does not foresee socialist reforms. (2) He does not study in depth socialist enterprise organization and market structure. (3) He superficially regards the major differences between economic systems as lying in the adjustment method – that is, administrative adjustment versus market adjustment – and does not consider more essential differences. Note that all these are areas that have proved to be important to Chinese economic theories, as discussed in the following chapters.

On the other hand, Chinese reforms are not conscious attempts to emulate the capitalist countries, and Chinese economic theories are not rationalization for such emulation, although Western press reports have often

---

[8] Kornai (1980a) argues that the planned socialist economy is a shortage economy because of the way its enterprises respond to incentives of the system. Socialist enterprises are rewarded by planners for rapid output expansion, not for minimizing production costs and making profits. Enterprises incurring losses remain in business because state subsidies are available. Because of this "soft budget constraint," socialist enterprises do not have the incentive to economize on the use of inputs in their drive to increase output, thus leading to chronic shortages of inputs in the economy. There is also a shortage of desired consumer goods, but this is not as observable as the shortage of inputs because consumers are constantly adjusting to it by making substitutions.

given such a misleading impression. Even journals as well informed as the *Economist* (Aug. 27, 1988: 21) have discussed the course of reforms in China in such simplistic and misleading terms as the "choice between communism and capitalism." It is true that in discussing various economic issues in recent years, Chinese economists have drawn on Western economic concepts and theories. This is consistent with a long history of "Western studies for Chinese use," but it by no means implies that the Chinese accept the underlying purposes of the Western theories. As explained earlier in connection with diagnostic economics, and as elaborated on in the following chapters, Chinese reform theory and practice amount to a reinterpretation of socialism, but not the abandonment of it in favor of capitalism. This can be seen most clearly in the cases of market reform and ownership reform. As is discussed in Chapter 2, the Chinese have permitted a greater role of the market in the economy, and Chinese economists have discussed various ways to combine the market with the plan. However, as Chinese economists have argued, commodity exchanges and the market are not the monopoly of the capitalist countries. Furthermore, the Chinese conception of the "perfect market" is a regulated market subject to the guidance of the state. It should not be confused with the Western ideal of a "perfectly competitive market" that is free from government intervention. As to ownership reform, it is shown in Chapter 3 that, although Chinese economists favor a socialist mixed ownership system in which various forms of ownership coexist, most of them regard it as important that public ownership occupies a leadership role in that system. Consequently, they do not favor large-scale privatization of public enterprises.

For these reasons, the eventual success or failure of China's reforms should not be evaluated in terms of whether the reforms have made China more capitalist-like, as many Western observers have done, but in terms of whether the Chinese have succeeded in achieving their own objective of making Chinese socialism more flexible and efficient. And theoretically, there are many ways to achieve that goal, as the wide variety of Chinese economic theories suggest. Consequently, a wide range of outcomes are theoretically possible in China's economic reforms, and the final outcome will depend on what proves to be workable under China's actual conditions. From this perspective, the evolution of Chinese economic theories in the 1979–88 period, like the course of Chinese economic reforms in the same period, is an unfolding process of trial and error, of finding out what is workable in China, given its limited options and its multitude of constraints and problems. For this reason, it is appropriate to characterize Chinese economic theories, as well as China's reform practices in the 1979–88 period, as largely the product of China, as reform theories with Chinese characteristics.

CHAPTER 2

The market under socialism

Although China's economic reforms in 1979–88 cover all areas of the economy, the central underlying strategy or orientation is to combine socialism with the market mechanism in order to impart greater economic incentives and flexibility to the economic system, thereby raising productivity in all sectors of the economy. This introduction of the market mechanism into a society that has been hitherto ideologically hostile to it is no easy task. For it to succeed, fundamental attitudinal changes have to be brought about and the market-oriented changes have to be theoretically justified. On the surface, the Chinese seem to have accomplished this quite well. In the mid-1970s, the market was considered to be the embodiment of capitalism and the antithesis of socialism; even minor rural market activities and peasant sideline production for local markets were criticized as the "tails of capitalism." By 1982, the dominant attitude toward the market had been transformed, so much so that the 1982 state constitution declares that the state "ensures the proportionate and coordinated growth of the national economy through overall balancing by economic planning and the supplementary role of regulation by the market" (Article 15). In 1984, it was announced that most state-owned enterprises would be given autonomy to produce in accordance with the market rather than with mandatory plan quotas.[1]

Many questions naturally arise. Are the changes in the Chinese attitude toward the market as rapid and thorough as they seem? What do Chinese economists and policy makers mean by the term "market"? Are the market mechanism and planning compatible, and how do the Chinese propose to combine them? These are some of the important questions that will be examined in this chapter.

---

[1] The decision was first given in the "Provisional Regulations on Greater Decision-Making Powers for State-Owned Industrial Enterprises" issued by the State Council on May 10, 1984 (*RMRB*, May 12, 1984). It was finalized in the "Decision of the Central Committee of the Communist Party of China on Reform of the Economic Structure" adopted on October 20, 1984 (*RMRB*, Oct. 21, 1984).

Commodities and the market

In Western economics, the term "market" denotes the mechanism of free supply–demand interactions to allocate resources – products, labor, capital funds, foreign exchanges, and the like; hence the terms "product market," "labor market," "capital (or money) market," and "foreign exchange market."

The Chinese conception of the market is much narrower than this. It starts with the proposition that the market exists only for "commodities," which are exchanged through the medium of money at their "values" in accordance with the "law of value."[2] Furthermore, until the mid-1980s, it was unanimously held that under socialism, labor is not a commodity, and neither are state-owned natural resources. Therefore, no markets exist for labor and natural resources. On the other hand, agricultural products sold by the peasants to the state, as well as consumer goods produced by both collectively owned and state-owned enterprises, are commodities. As to the means of production or capital goods produced by state enterprises, Chinese views have changed much since the late 1970s. Previously, following the orthodox Soviet views propounded by Stalin (1952),[3] Chinese scholars generally believed that the means of production under socialism are not commodities. Rather, they are all state owned, and their distribution is merely an internal allocation between departments of the giant state industrial entity (Gao Zhihua, 1980: 8). For this reason, the socialist economy is basically not a commodity economy. In other words, the Chinese conception of the market before the late 1970s was generally that of a limited product market that excluded capital goods.

There were, of course, exceptions to this view. Before 1956, the Chinese generally accepted Stalin's view without reservation. Between 1956 and 1959, as the Chinese leadership began to drift away from Soviet tutelage, Stalin's orthodoxy began to be challenged in parallel with Khrushchev's

---

[2] In a nutshell, the law of value posits that the value of a commodity is determined by the amount of "socially necessary labor" expended on its production and that commodities are exchanged in the market at equal value. Consequently, Chinese discussions of commodities are inexorably mixed with discussions of whether the law of value operates under socialism. See Chapter 5 for more details.

[3] The orthodox Soviet view is given by Stalin (1952). Stalin's view, reflecting the general consensus of the economic debates of the 1920s in the Soviet Union, was that the law of value was alien to the socialist economy but was unavoidable in the sphere of circulation because the collective sector coexisted with the state sector and there was a need for exchanges between the two. In the sphere of production and transfer within the state sector, planning was supreme and the law of value had no role to play. See, for example, Clausen (1983: 67), and Zimbalist and Sherman (1989: 235–9).

de-Stalinization in the Soviet Union. A number of authors contended that the means of production, in spite of their state ownership and allocation, are commodities for various reasons: (1) The producers of the means of production have to be compensated by the state in accordance with the amount of labor spent in production, just like other producers of commodities in other sectors. (2) The enterprises treat one another as independent economic units, and the means of production allocated have to be accounted for in enterprise accounts, being treated by the enterprises themselves as commodities (Zhang Zhuoyuan and Li Xiuzhen, 1985: 366–9, 375–8). (3) The enterprises, being conscious of their separate identities, regard the exchanges of the means of production among themselves as the transfer of ownership (Yu Guangyuan, 1959: 39). Some other authors stressed the commodity nature of the means of production because they wanted prices to be determined on the basis of their values (Zhang Zhuoyuan and Li Xiuzhen, 1985).

In 1961–2, Yu Fengcun (1962: 51–3) supported the view that the *commodity nature* of commodities arises out of the division of labor in the economy because goods produced for self-consumption cannot be commodities, whether under socialism or capitalism; and that the nature of ownership merely explains the *social nature* of commodities; therefore, commodities are compatible with socialism and communism. This view was not widely shared and did not go unchallenged.

During the Cultural Revolution decade (1966–76), academic discussion of the subject abated as academic publications were suspended and many intellectuals were persecuted. It can only be inferred from post-Mao publications that the majority of what might be called nonradical economists during the period continued to accept the orthodox view. In the remaining highly politicized publications of the period, the "gang of four" or the "Shanghai school" argued that commodity production existed under China's socialism as a vestige of the old society, and that it differed little from capitalist commodity production. This would inevitably lead to the emergence of a new capitalist class. In order to prevent this from happening, socialist commodity production and exchange had to be restricted and controlled by the dictatorship of the proletariat (Christensen, 1983: 76–81; Zhang Zhuoyuan and Li Xiuzhen, 1985: 369–70). The argument was, of course, politically motivated. Ideologically, the market was anathema to the radical gang of four.

In the post-Mao period the commodity issue was resurrected, and the discussions went through several phases. In the immediate post-Mao period, much of the discussion was devoted to repudiating the radical views (Christensen, 1983: 82–90). From late 1978 on, Chinese scholars turned their attention to the refutation of Stalin's thesis and the affirmation of the positive role of the market under socialism. Hu Qiaomu (1978), an eminent party theorist, first signaled the new trend by asserting that the law of value does in fact regulate production in the state sector, that commodity production and circulation will continue under socialism for a long time, and that they are compatible with socialist planning. Between 1979 and 1981, the compatibility of socialism with commodity production and the market was increasingly reaffirmed. Feng Baoxing, Wan Xin, and Zheng Dajian (1979) argued that the means of production exchanged under socialism are commodities in that (1) they possess the intrinsic nature of commodities, namely, a use value and an exchange value; (2) they or their values are contained in consumer goods, which are recognized as commodities; (3) they should be exchanged on the basis of equal exchange, just like other commodities; and (4) from the point of view of ownership, state enterprises in fact treat one another, rather than the state, as the de facto owners of the means of production. Variations on the same theme abound in the Chinese literature.

Liu Guoguang and Zhao Renwei (1979: 47) and other authors approach the issue from a different angle. They contend that commodities and the market are compatible with socialism because the antithesis of socialist planning is not the market but spontaneity and anarchy in production, and that the antithesis of the market economy is not the planned economy but the "natural economy," that is, the subsistence economy. The differences between the socialist economy with public ownership of the means of production and the capitalist economy with private ownership are that market activities under the former can be consciously controlled to promote socialist development, whereas those under the latter are marked by spontaneity and anarchy. Therefore, the market is not and should not be the monopoly of capitalist economies. These views are now widely accepted and have become an essential part of China's economic theories.

In the early 1980s, two strands of thought developed in different directions. The first strand argued for the expansion of commodity production and greater enterprise autonomy in China. According to it, the scope of commodity production in a country such as China should be expanded because China adopted socialism while still an underdeveloped, semifeudal, and semicolonial capitalist country; its economy is still dominated by the "natural" economy of small, self-sufficient producers, and its level of productivity is still very low. Therefore, socialist China must stimulate commodity production "as the only means to build a powerful material base for socialism" (Jiang Yiwei, 1980: 61); otherwise, economic development would be impeded by the persistence of "feudal behavioral traits." To expand commodity production, some authors stress the need to give enterprises more autonomy to produce for the market. Others stress the salutary effects of partial individual ownership of the means of production in raising productivity and output, as was the case with agriculture in the early 1980s (Zheng Bangcai, 1984; see also Chapter 3).

The second strand of thought, dominant in 1982–3 and developed as a reaction against some changes in the economy, stressed the planned nature of the socialist economy. As Riskin (1982: 316–19) observes, Chinese reformist market theorists were initially naive about the market mechanism. They stressed the advantages of stimulating flexibility, incentives, and efficiency without realizing the market mechanism's capacity to contradict social objectives. Thus when the conservatives reacted unfavorably to the reformist theories (see the next section), discussions turned to the need and the ways to combine the market and the plan properly in order to make them complement, rather than contradict, each other. As a result, since 1982–3, Chinese scholars have increasingly stressed that the socialist economy is not just a commodity economy but is a *planned* commodity economy. Thus, although the concept of the market has been broadened, it has also been qualified.

A result of this development is that Chinese economists have also become increasingly aware of the "market imperfections" and the need to introduce complementary institutions such as contract law, patent law, market regulations, and so on if the market mechanism is to function well and to be consistent with social objectives. This is discussed in the following sections.

An important turning point was reached in the mid-1980s when the concept of the market was greatly broadened to include the capital market, the labor market, and the technology market. Associated with this have been extensive discussions on whether labor power is a commodity under socialism. This issue has become important to the Chinese because of the reform to give enterprises more autonomy, including the power to hire and even to fire their own workers in order to increase labor productivity.

Never before in China has it been suggested that labor power can be a commodity under socialism. In 1980, reformist economist Jiang Yiwei (1980a; 67) reiterated the traditional view that labor power as a commodity is "totally nonexistent in a socialist commodity economy." That view is based on the Marxist belief that, under socialism, laborers are the masters of the means of production and the employer–employee relationship no longer exists; hence labor power is not a commodity. Since 1985–6, however, a growing number of economists have argued otherwise. For example, He Wei (1987c: 5) of the People's University in Beijing, although not denying that the means of production are publicly owned under socialism, argues that in China's current stage of development, laborers and the means of production are not "unconditionally unified," but are unified through the "exchange of labor power as a commodity." The reason is that although laborers collectively own the means of production, the individual laborer "owns nothing but his own labor" and has to sell his labor to make a living. Consequently, labor power is a commodity.

Another reformist view argues that the difference between capitalism and socialism lies not in whether labor power is a commodity, but in who appropriates the surplus value. Under capitalism laborers have only one status, and they neither own the means of production nor appropriate the surplus value. Under socialism, laborers have a dual status. On the one hand, they own nothing and have to sell their labor power; on the other hand, as members of the public ownership system, they own the surplus product they produce. Hence they are simultaneously employees and part of the employers. Because the means of production that workers collectively own can be sold and bought as commodities under socialism, so logically can labor power be sold and bought as a commodity (He Wei, 1987c: 5–6).

An eclectic view is given by Dong Fureng (1986b), then director of the Institute of Economics, the Chinese Academy of Social Sciences. He argues that whether or not labor power is a commodity under socialism depends on the specific institutional arrangement for the employment of labor. Under China's traditional system of unified allocation of labor, labor is allocated by the state at wages set by the state; neither the enterprise nor the worker has any choice about each other. Therefore, the employment relationship between enterprise and workers does not involve commodity exchange of labor power. Under the new labor contract system, the terms of employment are voluntarily agreed on by the two parties; therefore, it involves a commodity exchange of labor power for wages, which is a mutually beneficial and nonexploitive relationship. Under the capitalist system, the same commodity exchange in the labor market is exploitive because the "surplus product" is appropriated by the capitalists for their benefit only. This is the crucial difference between socialist labor and capitalist labor as a commodity.

The debate was still going on as of mid-1989. Interestingly, by 1988 Jiang Yiwei himself has revised his view considerably. He argued that whether or not labor power is a commodity under socialism depends on the concrete circumstances. During China's primary stage of socialism, a minor element of private ownership is appropriate and labor power is a commodity if it is in private employment. In his ideal system of labor self-management, all workers share the profits and losses of the enterprise and their labor power is not a commodity. Under the shareholding ownership system, which Jiang Yiwei also advocates (see Chapter 3), stock-owning workers are part owners of the enterprise, and it would be inappropriate to say that they sell their own labor power to themselves as a commodity. This does not preclude the existence of a labor market under socialism, however. In a socialist labor market, jobs can be exchanged for their "use values" (i.e., personal preferences, etc.) without entailing the buying and selling of labor power as a commodity (author's interviews, July 27, 1988, and May 20, 1989).

There have also been interesting discussion about the capital or money market. Because this is related to the issue of the ownership of the means of production under socialism and has important implications for the conceptions of socialism, it is discussed in Chapter 3. It is important to point out here, however, that as the concept of socialist ownership changes, it inevitably modifies the concept of the socialist commodity economy as well. By 1986, Chinese economists had come to view public ownership as the dominant but not the only form of ownership in the socialist commodity economy (*JJYJ*, No. 6, 1986, 6:17–18). As discussed in Chapter 3, Chinese conceptions of socialism have also undergone fundamental changes.

Thus, from the late 1970s to 1986–8, the Chinese conception of the socialist market was broadened from a limited product market to one that includes various factors of production; in Marxist parlance, it is a commodity economy. At the same time, however, the nature of the socialist commodity economy was qualified to be a *planned* commodity economy. This qualification reflected lingering ideological reservations about the market, as well as Chinese economists' efforts to integrate and harmonize the market and the plan under socialism, as discussed in the next section.

One final comment on this issue is in order. To outsiders, the recurrent Chinese debate on the commodity nature of the socialist economy and the ongoing debate on whether labor power is a commodity under socialism would seem metaphysical and sterile, tantamount to ideological hairsplitting in their laboriousness and meaninglessness. However, the issue is certainly not trivial in China's context, for its political and economic implications are enormous. It is only when this commodity hurdle has been cleared and the ideological ground prepared that the use of the market mechanism can be legitimized and pursued in earnest.[4]

Nevertheless, from a non-Marxist perspective, one cannot but view the need for such recurrent ideological ground clearing or for the reinvention of the commodity as unfortunate and its protracted and laborious course as extremely costly in terms of the valuable resources devoted to it. And one cannot but ask: Why does it matter so much? In addition, one cannot but have mixed feelings about the future of market-oriented discussions in China. On the one hand, one may feel that whatever has been accomplished to date is extremely fragile, for in China what grows out of an ideology can always be blown away by the same ideology, by the shifting wind of its interpretations, as shown by the fate of Chinese economic theories during the Cultural Revolution. Thus the suppression of the pro-democracy movement in 1989 does not augur well at all for the continuation and further

---

[4] For the same reasons, similar debates have taken place in other socialist countries, as Clausen (1983: 53) and other authors have pointed out.

development of market-oriented theorizing in the foreseeable future. On the other hand, one may argue that in the longer run, the advances in ideas made during 1979–88 will be enduring in China, and that further progress will be made in the future. The reason is that as long as the Chinese leadership desires economic development and cooperation with the West, further market-oriented reforms will be needed, which will require deeper understanding and further justification of the use of the market mechanism (discussed further in Chapter 6).

The market and the plan

From according new legitimacy to socialist commodities and the market, the Chinese have proceeded to explore the proper scope of the market under socialism. The issue is the extent to which and the manner in which the market is to be combined with planning to regulate production and distribution. This issue arises because, although the Chinese accept the commodity nature of the socialist economy, most economists also want government planning or guidance to play a role in the commodity economy. Between 1979 and 1988, dominant Chinese views on the ways to combine the market and the plan have gone through four periods of change: 1979–83, 1983–4, 1984–6, and 1986–8. In the following, the major changes in these periods are outlined.

The first and most significant conceptual development occurred in 1979–80 when, as a reaction to the problems of past planning practices and emboldened by the euphoria of political change, a number of leading economists published their ideas on combining the market with socialist planning. He Jiangzhang, Wang Jiye, and Wu Kaitai (1980) advanced the "permeation" thesis, in which the market and the plan permeate each other. Liu Guoguang (1980) envisaged the two as "rubber-glued" together. These two views are similar in essence – that the market and the plan should not be separated – and in their reasoning. The reasoning is that the plan needs to be consistent with and supported by the market to make it flexible and conducive to incentives, whereas the market needs to be guided by the plan to ensure the unity of interests among the state, the collective, and the individual under socialism (Liu Guoguang and Zhao Renwei, 1979: 53). Thus the plan and the market are complementary, correcting each other's imperfections. This perspective became widely accepted by reformist economists in the early 1980s as the ideal, a feasible one, of China's economic reforms. This is a watershed in the evolution of China's post-Mao economic thought.

Many veteran planners and top party cadres, however, disliked this talk of the market; they wanted to "reform" the legacy of the chaotic Cultural

Revolution and return to the "golden age" of the 1950s. This sentiment, never far beneath the surface, came into the open in late 1981 and led to the rise in 1981–2 of the conservative view that is critical of the pro-market reformers. For example, You Lin (1981) divides the economy into two sectors, according to the importance of the products, and wants important products to be planned by the state in terms of production, prices, and distribution; minor products should be regulated by the market. In refutation, pro-market reformers argue that in this model, the two regulatory mechanisms as well as the two sectors are separated and uncoordinated, and that the model will not work because each sector will ignore the needs of the other. Hence the problems of rigid planning and blind production will reappear in the planned sector and the market sector, respectively (Zhao Renwei, 1985a; 479).

In light of China's subsequent experience in combining the market with government planning, it is clear that the permeation and rubber-glued models are simplistic and naive about the market mechanism, but they are also bold and innovative in China's context in 1980, coming just a few years after the end of the Cultural Revolution. On the other hand, the two-sector model would shift China back to the system of the 1950s, with the planned sector dominating the economy. In fact, the two-sector model had its origin in the 1950s. As early as 1956, Chen Yun, a veteran planner and a reform advocate in the 1950s, argued that the Chinese economy should have three forms of management: (1) state planning and control of the bulk of industrial and agricultural products; (2) a "free market" for articles of daily use under various degrees of state guidance; and (3) free markets for minor local products, with no state control. In the guided market, production would be "carried on freely, with the changing conditions of the market as its guide and within the scope prescribed by the state plan," and the producers would be given plan targets "merely as figures for reference" (Chen Yun, 1986: 12–13; Lardy and Lieberthal, 1982: 20–1). Chen Yun also called the state-planned sector the "state market" and, when coupled with the guided market, the "unified socialist market." Thus the term "market" was used by Chen Yun in two senses – first, as the totality of production and distribution, whether planned or otherwise, and second, as the mechanism of supply–demand interaction that determines the production and distribution of specific products. The first usage introduces an element of tautology; the market and the plan are, by definition, compatible. The second usage reflects Chen Yun's view that planning can be supplemented with the market as the regulatory mechanism of the economy.

As part of the conservative backlash against the pro-market economists, Chen Yun reiterated in early 1982 his priority for reforms – "planned economy in the main and market regulation as the supplement" (or "the big plan and the small market,'' in a popular paraphrase) – which was popularized by the government in early 1982 into a policy slogan (*RMRB*, Jan. 26, 1982: 1). As a result, proponents of the permeation model and of the socialist commodity economy such as Liu Guoguang and He Jianzhang were criticized in government circles (He Jianzhang, author's interview, July 15, 1988). Subsequently, Liu, He, and other leading "radical" reformist economists such as Sun Yefang and Wu Jinglian were pressured into expressing support at a forum for this conservative emphasis on planning (*RMRB*, Feb. 22, 1982: 5; *ZGCMB*, Feb. 13, 1982: 2). This conservative backlash continued through the anti–spiritual pollution campaign of 1983 in which pollution in economics was also criticized. Pro-planning government economists such as Deng Liqun, Wang Renzhi, and Gui Shiyong become more influential in government councils as market-oriented theorizing became temporarily muted in published materials (He Jianzhang, author's interview, July 15, 1988).

In spite of the conservatives' attempts to restore the planning system of the 1950s, it was no longer possible to do so in the early 1980s because the problems of past central planning were well known, and because the impressive results of the rural reform had strengthened the leadership's commitment to, and power to implement, additional market-oriented reforms. Thus, starting in late 1983, discussions on ways to combine the market with the plan were renewed; there were also related discussions on how socialist planning itself can be made more flexible and effective so that it will be compatible with reforms. The discussions centered on whether or not the scope of mandatory planning should be reduced and that of guidance planning expanded, as He Jianzhang (1979) proposed.

Mandatory planning (zhiling jihua) is the orthodox type of socialist planning, with compulsory targets for production and distribution. Most Chinese economists have concluded that excessive mandatory planning produces rigidity and disincentives, and therefore that mandatory planning should be limited to the major macro proportions and balances of the economy, and to the production and distribution of essential products and the key enterprises that produce them. Here the role of the market is minimal. *Guidance planning (zhidao jihua)* is a more flexible type of planning, concerned with the micro activities of most enterprises, with the key enterprises excepted.[5] These enterprises should have much autonomy in their production for the market. They should be given guidance plans by the planners that contain suggested targets. These targets are not binding, and the enterprises can

---

[5] There have been disagreements among Chinese economists on the proper scope for guidance planning and for mandatory planning (see Chapter 3 and Hsu, 1986).

adjust them in accordance with changes in the market or in supply conditions. Thus, in guidance planning, the market mechanism plays a dominant role and planning a minor and indirect role. Although there was much debate on the nature and methods of guidance planning and mandatory planning, as surveyed by Zhao Renwei (1985a: 485), by October 1984, when China's leaders decided to reform the urban industrial sector, Chinese economists had widely accepted guidance planning as the best way to combine the market with planning in order to raise the productivity of enterprises and to make production more attuned to market demand (discussed further in Chapter 3).

In addition, it was generally agreed that the use of economic levers (prices, taxes, credit, interest rates, state purchase orders, etc.), supplemented by a new legal framework (contract law, patent law, bankruptcy law, etc.), was the best means to steer enterprises toward the plan's targets. By changing the economic levers, the state could induce enterprises to produce more of the products that were needed by society but had low profit rates, or to produce less of the products that were not important to society but had high profit rates. Some economists were of the view that the economic levers should also be applied to enterprises under mandatory planning.

The October 1984 decision of party leaders to reform urban industries is regarded by Chinese economists as another important turning point in China's market-oriented reforms. As a result of that decision, economists' theoretical discussions of the market entered a new phase because now it could be taken for granted that the reformed economy would be predominantly market-oriented. Ideologically, it was now officially proclaimed that the socialist economy was a planned commodity economy and that the commodity economy needed to be expanded in China. In addition, it was held that the commodity economy was also a market economy; hence the experience of the capitalist countries concerning the market might provide useful lessons. This decision led to a rapid decline in the scope of mandatory planning and a rapid expansion in that of guidance planning in the economy (see Chapter 3).

In addition, a new way of combining market flexibility with planning in some sectors of the economy was introduced. Previously, both Chen Yun's "big plan and small market" and pro-market economists' "guidance planning versus mandatory planning" represented a particular type of dual system. The economy was conceptually divided into two separate sectors in which planning and the market mechanism, respectively, predominate. As an integral part of this dualism, state-set prices would prevail in the planned sector, and floating prices (flexible within state-set limits) and free prices would prevail in the other sector. In 1984–5, however, a different type of dual system was introduced to further expand the role of the market. For many industrial materials previously covered by mandatory planning, a certain level of output was subject to plan quotas at low controlled prices; excess output over and above the quotas could be sold in the market at higher market prices. The same two-tier price system also applied to grains – lower purchase prices for state contract purchases and market prices for the additional output sold in the market.

This method of combining planning and the market in the same industries was introduced to facilitate the transition to a predominantly market-oriented system following a thorough price reform (see Chapter 5). Conceptually, this dual system presumed that planning and the market mechanism within the same industries would be compatible and complementary, as did the advocates of the permeation and rubber-glued models in 1979–80. As is shown in Chapter 5, this was not the case in practice, and many problems resulted from it.

The 1986–8 period saw the continuation of the same trend to combine the market with the plan. One significant development was that a central idea, which was implicit in the discussions of the previous periods, was made explicit in this period so that it became firmly established and widely accepted. The idea is that the market and the plan are compatible under socialism because they are merely two alternative methods of adjusting and developing the economy, and thus can be adopted and combined in accordance with the conditions of the economy. Hence a socialist economy is also a market economy, and a capitalist economy can also be a planned economy according to this view. The following statement by Gao Shangquan (1988: 23), then a deputy minister of the State Commission for Restructuring the Economic System, gives the clearest official exposition of this view:

Regulation [of the economy] through either planning or market is a method and not a fundamental attribute of the social system. Both methods can be turned to good use under the economic conditions of public ownership. . . . In general, both planning and market regulations are managerial processes; neither is identified with a special society, nor do they conflict with each other.

In more sporty terms, Jiang Yiwei of the Institute of Industrial Economics, the Chinese Academy of Social Sciences, likens both planning and the market to basketball rules and economic systems to ball teams. The same rules are to be observed by all teams, capitalist and socialist alike. It is the nature and organization of the teams – that is, the ownership and production relations – that distinguish the socialist teams from the capitalist ones. For example, the Japanese team may have hired players; the boss may scold or beat up(!) the players if the game is not played well. The Chinese team would have none of these attributes because it is the players' own team. The outcome of the competition would determine which system is superior; as a result, changes (reforms) within either team may be made (author's interviews, July 26, 1988, and May 20, 1989). As of mid-1989, most Chinese economists agreed with Jiang Yiwei and Gao Shangquan that both socialist and capitalist systems can utilize planning and the market as the adjustment mechanisms of the economy, and that it is the nature of ownership of the means of production that is the hallmark of an economic system, even though they have no consensus as to the best form of socialist ownership (see Chapter 3).

This is certainly a very narrow and simplistic view of the market (and of Japanese sports). There are various problems with such a view. First, it assumes that the market mechanism and government planning are merely system-neutral techniques that are separate from and external to the economic systems. As is explained later, this assumption is not valid. Second, it assumes that the Chinese government possesses the extraordinary skills that are required to finetune the economy by combining the market with planning in various proportions in accordance with the economy's needs – skills that even the developed countries do not possess. Third, it assumes away any possible incompatibility between the two mechanisms to be combined.

Such an approach has been criticized by other scholars as well. Kornai (1980b: 156) characterizes this approach, which has also existed in Hungary, as a naive "supermarket shopping" approach to economic systems in which disparate items are taken from different shelves as one wishes. He argues that such an approach will not work in socialist reform and that in real life an economic system has to be considered a "package deal," with all its good and bad features taken together. Kornai may have overstated his case – because, taken literally, his package deal approach permits no reforms in any economic system and no possibility of a successful mixed economy – but his statement does contain a valuable insight. Along the same line, Prybyla (1986: 23) contends that techniques of the market system cannot be used disjointly. "They must be applied as a system, their organic interconnections unbroken"; otherwise, "they either atrophy or work in a perverse way."

Prybyla implies, correctly in this author's view, that market-oriented reforms in a socialist economy can be workable and that a socialist mixed economy can be viable if and only if the essential organic interconnections of the market system are introduced and fostered together, and are safeguarded against arbitrary infringement by the government. These organic interconnections include the depoliticization of economic activities, the safeguarding of personal liberty and property rights, and the existence of a free, competitive environment. From this perspective, the Chinese conception of the market and of planning as merely managerial techniques for adjusting the economy misses an essential dimension of the market mechanism and is, therefore, not conducive to the creation of the necessary market environment.

In conclusion, during the decade 1979–88, Chinese economists increasingly accepted the market as an important element of the socialist economy. However, as of mid-1989, they tended to view the market mechanism as merely a policy tool, although an important one, in the government's tool box for fixing the economy, and not as an inherent and important attribute or dimension of the living economic system itself that requires compatible support systems to be healthy and effective. This *mechanical* conception of the market, as opposed to Prybyla's *organic* one, is too narrow for understanding the market mechanism. It suggests that many Chinese economists have not yet fully appreciated the spirit of the market mechanism in their discussions of the market and planning, even though some of them have advocated "coordinated reforms" in connection with the price reform (see Chapter 5).

Market competition

The legitimization of the market and the increasing autonomy of enterprises will not necessarily improve the performance of enterprises unless the market is truly competitive. As the experiences of China and other countries have shown, a market that is monopolized by the state invariably causes complacency and inefficiency; this is precisely one of the economic ills that reformist economists want to eliminate. Consequently, Chinese economists have been stressing the importance of promoting competition in the market. One way to achieve this is to create "multiple channels of distribution," permitting producers in different sectors of the economy – state-owned enterprises, collectively owned enterprises, individual households, and even private enterprises – to compete in the same market and thus end the past practice of state monopoly in most industries.

This new attitude toward market competition represents a fundamental change in the Chinese conception of socialist enterprises. Previously, following Lenin, Stalin, and other Marxist writers, the Chinese had believed that the interenterprise relationship under socialism is characterized by fraternal cooperation and socialist emulation for the purpose of pulling the backward up to the level of the advanced – the very antithesis of capitalist competition for profits by destroying one's rivals. Competition and socialism were therefore thought to be incompatible (Sun Shangqing, Chen Jiyuan, and Zhang Er, 1979: 62).

In 1979, several Chinese economists started arguing that competition is the logical accompaniment of commodity production, and hence that there can be socialist competition as well as capitalist competition. Socialist competition differs from the capitalist version in that the former is under the guidance of the plan, whereas the latter is anarchic and causes polarization between the rich and the poor. Socialist *competition* differs from socialist *emulation* in that, in the long run, the former leads to the elimination of chronically inefficient enterprises. Consequently, socialist competition strengthens the plan's guidance of enterprises because it provides economic prodding and pressure to the enterprises (Liu Guoguang and Zhao Renwei, 1979: 52–3; Sun Shangqing et al., 1979: Wu Tongguang, 1979; Zhu Jiaming, 1979).

As can be expected, the advocacy of socialist competition encountered opposition. Jin Mingjun (1979), for example, argues that competition is harmful to socialism because (1) it will bring about anarchy and imbalances in socialist production; (2) it will corrode cadres' and workers' socialist thought; and (3) it will fundamentally change the "socialist mutual relationships" between the state and the enterprises and between enterprises. However, these opponents of socialist competition are a shrinking minority, given the past ills of enterprise complacency and the momentum of reforms.

Subsequent supporters of socialist competition mostly elaborated on the same theme. Competition under socialism is desirable because it will prod the inefficient enterprises to catch up; it will force them to pay closer attention to the consumers' demands and thus correct the past problem of the divorce of production from social needs; and it will eliminate inferior products and enterprises that are costly to society. And all of them emphasized that socialist competition should be subject to the guidance of the plan; it is not to be spontaneous and anarchic, nor should it adversely affect the plan's targets. Otherwise, market competition will degenerate into "pernicious competition."

The proviso that competition should be subject to the plan's guidance is so important to the Chinese that, in actual policy practice as well as in theoretical discussions, it often outweighs the objective of enterprise efficiency itself. This can be seen in the following examples.

The first example relates to China's cigarette industry, which has large, modern plants in the cities as well as many small plants in rural areas. Since the early 1980s, because of their profitability and their contribution to local tax revenues, the small plans have proliferated in tobacco-producing areas, established by the rural collectives or local governments outside the state's plan. This has led to price competition in the industry, which has adversely affected the profits of the large state plants and the state's revenue. The small plants have also reduced the supply of raw materials to the large plants, causing the latter to produce below capacity. Although these small plants are usually protected by local protective measures and tend to be technically inefficient, they may have competitive advantages in the form of lower wage and transportation costs. Nevertheless, Chinese authors have invariable criticized the small plants for engaging in "blind production," for "upsetting the plan," and for "the small squeezing out the large" and "the inefficient squeezing out the efficient."[6] In short, they considered the competition to be anarchic and urged more central planning and control.[7] As a result, the State Council issued a directive in mid-1983 against such unauthorized price reduction (*JJRB,* July 8, 1983). In September 1983, the government decided to monopolize the production and distribution of cigarettes in the country and ordered the closure of many small plants established outside the state plan (*RMRB,* Oct. 6, 1983).

A second example relates to export price competition. In 1983, when some exporting units competed for foreign markets by reducing prices, they were censured for hurting state export earnings while benefitting themselves and foreigners. It was argued that, in these cases, the enterprises involved should consider the broader "social benefits" or consequences of their actions and refrain from hurting their fellow enterprises and the state (*RMRB,* Aug. 27, 1983: 3). In other words, the *competitive relationship* between enterprises should be subordinate to and guided by the *planned relationship* between the state and the enterprises. Thus, competition is desirable only within the limits of state interests; otherwise, it becomes "pernicious competition."

As China has become increasingly involved in foreign trade, enterprises engaged in exports have become increasingly competitive with one another. Consequently, they have been criticized by Ge Hui (1986) and others for engaging in pernicious competition, that is, being competitive with fellow Chinese exporters but not with foreign rivals, thus benefitting primarily the foreigners. They have been urged to become "cooperative allies" in order to deal with foreign rivals who are backed by "monopolies." Cooperative allies have common economic interests and should compete with each other in qualities, services, management, and product reputation, but not in price cutting (Ge Hui, 1986: 35–6).

---

[6] Obviously, "efficiency" here is used to mean technical efficiency, not economic or allocative efficiency, which includes cost and price considerations. Because the latter concept is broader and more pertinent to the functioning of the market mechanism, it is clear that many Chinese economists in the early 1980s did not fully appreciate the implications of the market mechanism.

[7] Alternatively, Xue Muqiao (1981: 13) suggests that, to avoid the wastes of duplication and anarchic competition between the small and the large, small local producers should be permitted to have their excess materials processed by large state plants and to share the latter's profits. He also recommends the formation of cooperative undertakings between large state enterprises and small local ones under state guidance. These are essentially suggestions for various degrees of vertical cooperation or integration. However, transportation costs and the impact on interenterprise and interregional competition have not been taken into account.

The idea that socialist competitors can and should cooperate with each other is not limited to exports, although it is more pronounced there. In fact, a recurrent theme in the Chinese discussions of competition, especially in the early 1980s, was that socialist competition, unlike the capitalist type, is not antagonistic; socialist enterprises cooperate with and assist, as well as compete with, one another. This ideologically inspired proposition, still supported by some economists in 1986, "logically" led to another proposition: that socialist enterprises, unlike their capitalist counterparts, will not withhold technical information from one another because they do not produce for private profits; therefore, the diffusion of new technology under socialism can be expected to be more rapid than under capitalism. This, it was argued, is another manifestation of the superiority of socialism. Whatever the validity of this proposition in the past, there have been numerous complaints since the early 1980s that many enterprises are refusing to share their technical secrets, or are giving out inferior technology while retaining the superior one for themselves.[8] The reasons are that enterprises since the early 1980s have been able to retain part of their profits and that there is increased competition in the market.

Chinese responses to this problem of "technological blockade" are characteristically both ideological and pragmatic. In the early 1980s, some authors continued to insist that in technological diffusion there is no inherent conflict of interest between socialist enterprises – socialist enterprises are "not only objects of competition, but also comrades of mutual help" – and suggested more "socialist education" as the answer (*GMRB*, Mar. 20, 1982; *RMRB*, Mar. 2, 1980). By 1984, however, most authors had become more hard-headed and advocated vigorous enforcement of the 1984 patent law to protect the interests of innovating enterprises. The concept of the "technology market" – the idea that it is appropriate to charge a price for the transfer of technology between socialist enterprises – also emerged as a result. Thus, rhetoric aside, the Chinese clearly acknowledged by 1984 that socialist enterprises do have legitimate self-interests that are incongruous with egalitarian socialist sharing ("everybody eating from the same public pot"), and that those interests need to be protected by a short-term restriction of competition and the granting of short-term monopoly profits if innovation is to be encouraged in the long run.

In Western economics, there are other legitimate grounds for government intervention to restrict market competition: (1) "natural monopolies," such as public utilities, in which the economies of scale are important; (2) the existence of "externalities" that make the producers' costs and benefits different from those of the society; and (3) "infant industries" that need to be

---

[8] See, for example, *RMRB*, Mar. 2, 1980; May 28, 1981; Sept. 25, 1982; Jan. 7, 1984; Mar. 15, 1984; *GMRB*, Feb. 23, 1983; Mar. 20, 1982; *JJRB*, Jan. 1, 1983.

protected from foreign imports until they mature. With the exception of the concept of externalities in the mid-1980s, the Chinese have not introduced these concepts to justify state restriction of competition. This is, of course, easy to understand. In a market economy, competition is the ideal, and therefore every instance of government restriction of competition needs to be justified. In post-Mao China, it is market competition itself that needs to be justified, and it is therefore sufficient, or indeed imperative, to delineate the proper scope of competition in terms of state guidance and the prevention of anarchy. Presumably, natural monopolies will be among the key enterprises subject to mandatory planning, and enterprises with externalities can always be controlled and infant industries protected in the name of safeguarding state interests and preventing anarchy. The Chinese conception of market competition, therefore, is both narrow and flexible – narrow in scope and flexible in what can be exempted from it.

Finally, an essential prerequisite for a competitive market is the availability of market information to both producers and consumers. Chinese authors' approaches to this issue were again both ideological and pragmatic, especially before the mid-1980s, indicating that the attitudinal changes that are necessary for successful market-oriented reforms were incomplete. A small minority of socialist fundamentalists, especially in the early 1980s, contended that because socialism has eliminated "management secrets and bourgeois prejudices of private capitalism," and because the masses can thus be mobilized for statistics gathering and control, socialism "provides superior conditions for complete, regular and extensive statistics." Thus there will be "tremendous superiority in statistical work in terms of incentives and organization" under socialism (Tian Jianghai and Zhang Shuguang, 1981: 33). Following this line of "reasoning" (or wishful thinking), statistical problems – including statistical falsifications at the lower levels of government that have long plagued China's planning in the past – are *by definition* nonsocialist; they are the result of failing to learn or to take full advantage of socialism rather than an inherent failing of the socialist system of planning itself. This is an example of the pseudoanalysis in diagnostic economics discussed in Chapter 1.

Counterposed to this group are the majority of Chinese economists who recognized the existing inadequacy of statistical and market information and recommended various corrective measures. They supported the enactment of the 1983 law on statistical work, which delineates the responsibility for this work at various levels and provides penalties for falsification of data. They also urged the government to make market surveys and forecasts, which would be the basis for making guidance plans for enterprises. These surveys and forecasts, they said, should be frequently updated and made available to the enterprises. However, some authors argued that the lack of comprehensive market information has caused some enterprises to engage in blind production. They recommended strengthening of state planning and control and slowing down of the introduction of guidance planning because "conditions are not ripe" for it (*JJRB*, June 21, 1984: 2).

One final issue related to competition concerns bankruptcy. Can socialist enterprises go bankrupt under competition, just like capitalist firms? Not according to the long-held belief in China; lack of bankruptcy under socialism was held to be another manifestation of the superiority of socialism over capitalism. This has been a self-fulfilling prophecy in China because the government has stood ready to subsidize any failing enterprise. According to one estimate, as many as one-quarter of state-owned enterprises in China incur deficits every year (*RMRB*, Oct. 10, 1986: 5). However, before 1986, none of these were permitted to go bankrupt for fear of the unemployment that would result from it.

It should be pointed out that not all enterprise deficits result from mismanagement and inefficiency. Some losses are called "policy-based losses" because of the state's policy of deliberately setting low prices for some products. Grains distributed by state grain bureaus, energy, and some basic industrial materials belong to this category (see Chapter 5). In addition, there are other institutional factors beyond the enterprises' control that have contributed to their losses – for example, the traditional state employment system, which made it impossible for managers to fire incompetent personnel.

The desirability of allowing chronically unprofitable enterprises to go bankrupt was first broached around 1983 on the grounds that it would save the state's resources in the long run (*JJRB*, Oct. 31, 1983). By 1985, it had become the state's policy to promulgate a bankruptcy law, and discussions to support it became vociferous. At the level of diagnostic economics, it was argued that bankruptcy is not unique to capitalist countries but is common to all commodity economies in which market competition prevails, (*BR*, No. 10, Mar. 11, 1985: 25). In a curious twist of logic (or perhaps socialist psychology), the previously feared unemployment of the workers of the bankrupt enterprises was now portrayed by some authors in a favorable light: By having the workers share the same fate with the enterprise, "the sense of being the masters of the factory will be greatly heightened and the democratic management of the factory improved" (*BR*, No. 10, Mar. 11, 1985: 25; Cao Siyuan, 1984: 46; *RMRB*, Dec. 6, 1986). At the level of functional economics, the majority of economists simply argued that the long-term benefits to society of eliminating the chronically delinquent enterprises far outweigh the short-run losses of state property and the problem of temporary unemployment. In an insight akin to that of Western marginal analysis, Cao Siyuan (1984) argued that bankruptcy need not entail the loss of property to the state; if the assets of the bankrupt enterprises are sold to other enterprises, society will benefit from having the assets used by efficient rather than inefficient enterprises.

From a larger perspective, other economists argued that bankruptcy cannot be an effective means to spur enterprise efficiency unless other related reforms – labor insurance system, price reform, genuine enterprise autonomy, and so forth – are undertaken (Cao Siyuan, 1984; Dong Fureng, 1986b). Thus by 1986, the issue had become an integral part of the broader argument for systemwide reforms. In September 1986, the provisional insurance law for unemployed workers (euphemistically called "state enterprise employees waiting for assignment") was promulgated, providing up to twenty-four months of diminishing unemployment compensation to workers of bankrupt state enterprises. In December 1986, the bankruptcy law was promulgated (*RMRB*, Dec. 3, 1986). It can be expected that other related changes will also be introduced.

In summary, since the late 1970s and early 1980s, Chinese economists progressively accepted and promoted market competition as an integral part of the market mechanism to spur enterprise efficiency. They also paid some attention to the legal and informational requirements of market competition. However, they were relatively slow to accept one of the inevitable consequences of competition: bankruptcy. In addition, competition was desired as a means to a specific end but not as an end in itself. Therefore, like the larger market mechanism itself and its price system, market competition had to be subject to the state's guidance. In the hierarchy of state policy objectives in the 1980s, market competition could be and was restricted when it conflicted with higher policy objectives.

The buyers' market

In the first half of the 1980s, there was a lively debate among Chinese economists on whether a buyers' market should be created in China. By "buyers' market" the Chinese mean a market situation in which the quantities of goods supplied slightly exceed the quantities demanded at the prevailing prices. The term is Western in origin and is relatively new to the Chinese, although it has been used by writers in other socialist countries. Some Chinese economists advocate it as a means to promote market competition and consumer choices, and thus to facilitate the introduction of the market mechanism into the economy. Although the proposal is problematic, as discussed later, it represents yet another aspect of the change in attitude toward the market.

Until the late 1970s, Chinese writers and policy makers, following the orthodox Soviet view, commonly regarded the existence of the sellers' market – in which the quantities of goods demanded exceed those supplied at

the prevailing controlled prices – in the socialist economies as a manifestation of the superiority of socialism. It was believed that it was the rapid
growth of consumer purchasing power, unmatched by that of the capitalist
economies, that caused the excess demand or shortage. The lack of competition inherent in the sellers' market led to various problems that are commonly found in all controlled economies, such as the neglect of consumer
interests, poor quality, a surplus of unwanted goods in the midst of general
shortage, and the development of black markets. It is in this context that the
proposal to create the buyers' market arises.

Huang Fanzhang (1979) presaged this new school of thought with his
advocacy of "socialist consumer sovereignty." To attain this consumer
sovereignty, he would give state enterprises profit incentives to produce
according to consumer demand. Liu Guoguang (1980) first proposed the creation of a buyers' market in connection with his advocacy of guidance planning to link planning with the market mechanism. His arguments are as
follows. In a sellers' market in China, it is necessary to have mandatory
planning, with planned distribution of products and materials; otherwise,
some buyers will be left without some essential goods. This makes it impossible to introduce the market mechanism, with its benefits of competition
and choices. However, in a buyers' market with a slight excess supply, there
is room for competition, thereby creating the condition for linking the market with the plan. Further, the slight surplus constitutes rational social reserves for the maintenance of macro balances without incurring the wastes
of capitalist overproduction. Liu Guoguang (1983) further argues that a buyers' market would help stabilize the economy and avoid a fiscal deficit and
increases in money supply. He claims that it is easier for the socialist
planned economy than for the capitalist economy to attain a buyers' market
because both production and supply, on the one hand, and purchasing power
and demand, on the other hand, can be controlled directly and indirectly by
the state under socialism. This, to his mind, is another manifestation of the
superiority of socialism. Other proponents of the buyers' market do not go
this far; they merely stress the benefits of competition and choices (Luo
Jingfen, 1980; Wang Cainan, 1983).

From the preceding discussion, it is clear that the envisioned buyers' market is intended logically for the sector under guidance planning. In the free-
market sector, prices fluctuate freely and a buyers' market cannot exist, at
least not for long; in the mandatory-plan sector, planned distribution of
goods makes a buyers' market impossible. It is only in the guidance-plan
sector that prices will fluctuate within a range set by the planners. The price
range may not be low enough for the buyers to buy up all the supply and
thus the surplus.

As is commonly understood, in a buyers' market the quantity of a product supplied exceeds the quantity demanded at the prevailing price, with the excess supply exerting a downward pressure on the price. However, the equilibrium or market-clearing price is not readily reached for various reasons, including market imperfections; otherwise, both the surplus and the buyers' market will disappear. Thus the implication of maintaining a buyers' market in a socialist country under guidance planning is that either the whole range of permissible price fluctuations has to be set above the equilibrium level, or the enterprises are somehow unable to slow down their production or unwilling to lower their prices in order to eliminate the surplus. Of course, the consumers can be prevented from buying up the supply by a new state control of their purchasing power or spending, a possibility hinted at by Liu Guoguang (1983). This will shift the demand schedule downward, causing a temporary excess supply. However, in the absence of price control, market competition will drive the price down toward the equilibrium level and the surplus will disappear.

In other words, the deliberate creation and maintenance of a buyers' market under guidance planning invariably involves the extended use of some form of state control – price control, suppression of price competition, mandatory surplus production, income or spending control, and the like – to cause and perpetuate an artificial disequilibrium in the market. It is difficult to see why this is desirable and how it will facilitate the introduction of market competition and the market mechanism, and why the ability to do this is a manifestation of the superiority of socialism.

Not all Chinese economists share the notion that a buyers' market is desirable. Some have criticized its surplus as wasteful and have correctly argued that an overall balance between supply and demand is more desirable (Jia Lürang and Lin Wenyi, 1981; Jiang Rui, 1983). Zhang Shushan (1981) contends that for many products, the level of reserves or surplus is already excessive in China.

To some extent, the problem with the initial proposal and the ensuing debate may be semantic rather than substantive; it depends on what is meant by a "slight" excess of supply over demand. In its normal course of operation, a prudent market-oriented socialist enterprise may choose to carry a slight amount of excess inventory over and above expected sales, especially if the market is competitive and the consumers' goodwill cannot be taken for granted. This excess inventory is insurance against the unexpected, and its existence does not constitute a buyers' market. Nor does it constitute a buyers' market if the slight surplus is dictated by the state to guard against future shortfalls ("social reserves") and is available for use only on terms set by the state because competition and consumers' choices will not be increased as a result. In short, Chinese economists' case for a buyers' market is lacking in clarity and in substance.[9]

In spite of such analytical ambiguity and deficiencies, the introduction and popularization of the concept of the buyers' market, as with other new concepts, has had a positive effect on the evolution of economic analysis in China. It has enabled economists to bring the problems of a sellers' market into sharper focus and hence to break away from the orthodox socialist ideology, from the unexamined belief in the desirability of the socialist sellers' market. Furthermore, it has contributed to the rise of the broader market-equilibrium analysis. For example, Wen Qian (1986) argues that the ideal socialist market is an "equilibrium market" in which the "strength" of the buyers and sellers is in equilibrium, that is, it is neither a sellers' nor a buyers' market. This equilibrium concept is still crude and nebulous, because it is not clear how this strength is measured, and the equilibrium price is expressed in terms of equality between the market price and the "value" of the product, the latter being a vague and unmeasurable Marxian concept (see Chapter 5). In time, this new view itself will stimulate further advances in the analysis of the subject matter. Such a zigzag process of analytical advance can be expected when every analytical step forward entails the discarding of some bricks of the old ideological foundation; it is certainly consistent with what the Chinese call the "dialectics of development."

Since the mid-1980s, Chinese economists have not debated the desirability of creating the buyers' market as intensively as in the early 1980s because they have been increasingly preoccupied with problems of urban industrial reform and inflation; inflation arises in China mainly because aggregate demand in the economy is outstripping aggregate supply for various reasons (see Chapter 5). Nevertheless, advocates of a buyers' market remain convinced that in a sellers' market in China the government will inevitably use administrative means to allocate resources, thus impeding market-oriented reforms. Their critics argue, however, that given the high growth rate of aggregate demand in China relative to that of aggregate supply, it is unrealistic to hope for the creation of a buyers' market before the end of the century. They conclude, therefore, that further reforms will have to be implemented under the condition of shortage, but that through reforms the shortage should be alleviated (Zhao Renwei, 1987: 6).

---

[9] Some authors, such as Wang Cainan (1983: 28), define "slight" surplus as consisting of (a) necessary social reserves against future contingencies and (b) those products not purchased by buyers because of inferior quality, high prices, or wrong varieties or specifications. This definition is still ambiguous; it takes the existing prices as given. If prices are flexible downward, there is no way to know a priori how much surplus consumers will not buy.

Developing the perfect socialist market

The preceding sections have touched on various facets of the Chinese conceptions of the market between 1979 and 1988. After nearly a decade of discussions, it was logical that various strands of thought would converge at a grand synthesis of the ideal type of market that the Chinese would like to have. Thus in 1986, some economists began to discuss the concepts of the "complete market system" and the "perfect market mechanism" and the measures to attain them. The discussions show that most reformist economists agree on the nature of the ideal socialist market but have differing views on the way to attain it; they also reflect the difficulties that the Chinese are experiencing in developing the market mechanism and in introducing further market reforms. Thus it is instructive to examine them here at the conclusion of the chapter.

In terms of the scope of the market, a complete market system includes not only the product market, the capital market, and the labor market, but also the market for technology, capital goods, production materials, and so forth. Seen in this light, Chinese economists have traveled a great distance since 1979, when product market was the only type of market that was acceptable under socialism.

In terms of the operations of the market, the perfect market mechanism should have the following characteristics:

1. The market should be stable and competitive. Stability means that drastic fluctuations in prices should be avoided. Some authors also argue that this calls for a buyers' market in which supply slightly exceeds demand. Competitiveness means not only "equal competition" in any local market, but also the integration of the national market network without any artificial barriers such as "regional blockades" and monopoly (Jiang Zuopei and Ding Xianhao, 1986).[10]

---

[10] A small number of economists have different views on the desirability of integrating the national market. One view contends that China's provinces should form their own independent markets and take care of their own market development. A second view would also give the provinces much autonomy, and the provinces would interact economically as members of an association of independent states, such as the European Community. These views are based on the belief that small, autonomous markets would be able to limit the interference of the central government, and hence their economies would prosper, as the small economies of Hong Kong and Taiwan have prospered (*GMRB*, Sept. 17, 1988: 3). There are two major problems with these views. First, they have confused the pro-market policies of Hong Kong and Taiwan with the smallness of their local markets. It is the former, not the latter, that are responsible for their prosperity; in fact, it can be argued that

2. The market should be efficient and "normal." This means that market prices, which include interest rates and exchange rates, should reflect both supply and demand, on the one hand, and the "value" of the resources used in production, on the other hand (prices will be discussed further in Chapter 5).
3. The market should be "controllable" by the state for macro objectives. The instruments of control are indirect economic levers and guidance planning, where possible, and direct administrative control and legal actions if necessary.

Thus it is clear that the Chinese conception of the perfect market is very different from that of the West; it is broader in scope but more restrictive in nature. Whereas Western economists regard a perfectly competitive market without government interference as the perfect market, the Chinese regard the state as an indispensable element of the perfect market. Without the state's guidance, market activities will become "spontaneous" and therefore "blind," and enterprise behavior will become "irrational," resulting in anomalies and wastes such as fraud and oversupply. According to some economists, the basic reason for such blindness is that individual producers can see only their own immediate and partial interests, and cannot see the overall market situation and the larger interests of society. Consequently, state guidance is needed to safeguard society's interests and the state's macro objectives.

On the other hand, Chinese economists do not want government officials to become anti-market and interfere unduly in the market. In 1986–8, unreasonable government interference in the operation of the market and in the activities of state-owned enterprises were increasingly regarded by economists as the main cause of China's market imperfections and fragmentation. This interference took the following forms: (1) many local governments prohibited products from outside areas from entering local markets in order to protect local industries; (2) for the same reason, they withheld supplies of local raw materials to large state-owned plants in large cities, although the latter may be more efficient than local ones; and (3) in spite of reforms to give state-owned enterprises managerial autonomy, state officials continued to interfere in enterprise activities, thus preventing them from responding fully to market signals.

Accordingly, in order to develop the perfect socialist market, Chinese economists recommended, on the one hand, measures for the government to promote the market, and on the other hand, ways to eliminate undesirable

the former were adopted in part to compensate for the latter. Second, even if China's regional markets are free from central government interference, they can still be arbitrarily regulated by the provincial and local governments.

government interference in the market. Among the former are the following: (1) the state should provide timely market information and forecasts to enterprises; (2) the state should be vigilant for signs of enterprise blindness in order to adjust and control enterprise activities by appropriate means; (3) a network of laws and regulations needs to be established to enable the government to deal with illegal activities such as fraud, speculative buying and selling, illegal price increases, and breach of contract; and (4) the government should train "modern socialist entrepreneurs" for the perfect socialist market (Zhou Shulian, 1986). It is not clear, however, how the modern socialist entrepreneurs can be trained (see Chapter 3).

There are areas of agreement as well as differences among economists concerning the cause of undesirable government interference in the market and the measures to eliminate it. The majority of economists regard it as the vestige of the previous economic planning system, in which government bureaucrats administratively controlled the economy; as the economic system is being reformed, it will gradually disappear if further reforms are implemented. In particular, the reform to separate government administration from enterprise management should be vigorously implemented. In addition, many economists agree that the current tax contract system – under which local governments are responsible for collecting sales and profit taxes and for delivering a contractual amount of tax revenue to the central government – is responsible for encouraging local governments to protect local industries at the expense of more efficient outside industries; local tax revenues will be increased with more local production once the locality's fixed tax obligation to the central government is fulfilled. Thus reform of the tax system is needed.

Zhou Zhenhua (1988) approaches these problems from a structural perspective. He argues that government distortions of the market mechanism are closely related to two structural characteristics of the Chinese economy. First, the economy is dualistic: An underdeveloped rural sector with surplus labor coexists with a more developed urban sector. Because the urban sector cannot absorb the rural surplus labor, local governments in rural areas are forced to use "unequal competition" – trade barriers, withholding of raw materials for local use, and so forth – to establish and protect inefficient local plants to absorb surplus labor. This impedes the normal development of a competitive market and of modern urban enterprises.

The second structural characteristic is the plurality of interests in the economy. The state, the enterprises, and the individuals have different interests; so do various government branches and various localities. The narrow, short-term interests of various government branches and localities lie in the fragmentation of the national market, that is, in preventing the normal development of an integrated national market. Consequently, the interests of the enterprises and of the individuals are jeopardized, in contradiction to the intention of the reforms.

Zhou's views are perceptive because they touch on some basic and powerful motives that militate against the normal development of the market in China. In addition, he makes it clear that these motives are embedded in the underdeveloped and labor-surplus nature of the Chinese economy and in the power structure of the Chinese polity, and are not merely due to the transitional nature of China's economic system. His "plurality of interests" argument is tantamount to a "conflict of interests under socialism" argument, which directly contradicts the traditional assumption of "congruence of interests under socialism" (see Chapter 3). For policy measures, he recommends readjustments of the "structure of interests," including a greater centralization of state powers and a clear division of tax authority between the central and local governments, as well as various measures to safeguard the autonomy of enterprises.

Beyond these discussions to improve the market mechanism in China, Chinese economists have discussed issues of enterprise ownership reform and price reform that affect the efficiency of the market mechanism. Proponents of the former want to replace or modify the traditional state ownership of the means of production in order to give enterprises and workers more incentives to respond to market signals. They argue that the main actors of the market – workers and enterprises – have to be well motivated through participation in ownership and management before the market mechanism can be effective. Proponents of price reform regard the existing irrational dual-track price system, in which market-determined prices and state-set low prices coexist for many products, as a major imperfection of the existing market itself. They argue that the market mechanism cannot be meaningful and cannot function effectively unless price reform is implemented and most prices are determined by market supply and demand. Because ownership and price reforms involve many other issues, they are discussed in Chapters 3 and 5, respectively.

In conclusion, Chinese economists made great strides and bold innovations in their understanding and advocacy of the market mechanism in the ten years from 1979 to 1988. They accomplished these tasks concurrently as they altered their conceptions of socialism. In the next chapter, we discuss how Chinese economists have changed their views on three major aspects of the traditional socialist economy – the state ownership of the means of production, the lack of autonomy of the state-owned enterprises, and state planning for the economy.

CHAPTER 3

Socialism: Ownership, state enterprise, and planning

As Chinese economists' conceptions of the market have changed dramatically, so have their conceptions of socialism. In fact, the market and socialism are so closely intertwined in the Chinese discussions that one cannot fully understand their attitudes toward one without understanding their attitudes toward the other. Consequently, in discussing the market in Chapter 2, aspects of socialism have been alluded to. In this chapter, changes in the Chinese conceptions of socialism and their implications for the economy are discussed.

Reinterpreting socialism

What is socialism, and what is the nature of the socialist economy in Chinese views? This question is at once simple and complex, depending on the level of answer wanted. At the simplest definitional level, the Chinese, as Marxist-Leninists, have always maintained that socialism as a socioeconomic system is the transitional stage between capitalism and communism, a stage that is superior to capitalism. At a more analytical level, in terms of the economic characteristics of socialism and the bases of its superiority to capitalism, Chinese views have changed considerably in the 1979–88 period. In this regard, two facets of socialism should be distinguished: its normative values or moral ideals and its functional aspects as a political-economic system. The Chinese conceptions of socialism as a set of normative values are inspired by Marx and Engels' classic critiques of capitalism and their visions of socialism. However, before the late 1970s, the Chinese conceptions of socialism as an operational political-economic system were shaped mainly by the wrtings of Lenin and Stalin and by the Soviet model of planning and organization between the 1930s and the 1950s, because Marx and Engels had said little about it. These two facets of socialism have not been clearly distinguished by the Chinese; instead, they were rather wishfully combined by the Chinese in their diagnostic economics to produce the following basic propositions on, or beliefs in, socialism:

1. Socialism is based on public ownership of the means of production. In this way, the basis for the "class exploitation" of capitalism is

53

eliminated; workers are now "masters" of the means of production, and the fetters on the development of "productive forces" are eliminated. Furthermore, state ownership is regarded as the optimal and the highest form of public ownership (Liu Guoguang, 1988a: 24).

2. The socialist economy is a planned economy under the guidance of the state, the antithesis of the capitalist "commodity economy" that produces for the market. This has implications at both micro and macro levels. At the micro level, production by state-owned enterprises will be carried out, not for private profits according to the whims or "anarchy" of the market, but for rational social purposes according to plan targets. At the macro level, the economy will develop in a planned and proportionate manner, without the cyclical fluctuations and ever-worsening crises of capitalist market economies. In addition, growth and productivity of the economy will be higher than under capitalism as wastes and lack of coordination are eliminated (*HQ*, 1980, No. 2: 12–15).

3. The distribution of income in the socialist economy is based on labor, that is, on the amount of "socially necessary labor" contributed by each worker. There is no unearned income based on the ownership of capital and private employment. Therefore, "socialist equality" will prevail. However, due to extreme leftist influence, between 1958 and 1979 the Chinese commonly confused socialist equality in the preceding sense with egalitarianism ("everyone eats from the same big pot"), which amounted to equal pay regardless of labor (Liu Guoguang, 1988a: 34–5).

These traditional Chinese beliefs, and the institutions and policies that are based on them, were increasingly questioned and modified by China's reformist economists in the 1979–88 period. A basic analytical problem with these propositions is that before 1979, Chinese authors generally regarded them not merely as socialist ideals but also as the scientifically proven systemic characteristics ("scientific socialism") that will necessarily prevail in the economy in accordance with "objective laws" once ownership of the means of production is made public and state planning is institutionalized. This failure to distinguish between socialist ideals and socialist reality, or between the normative and positive facets of socialism, is responsible for many fallacies and inconsistencies and is the source of a great weakness in China's economics before 1979, particularly in its diagnostic branch (see Chapter 1).

In the 1979–88 period, as reforms were introduced, modifications in the Chinese conceptions of socialism were increasingly made. As early as 1980,

Jiang Yiwei (1980a: 66–7), one of China's leading reformist economists, asserted that there are two fundamental principles of socialism – public ownership of the means of production and distribution of income according to labor. Other than these, "none of the specific ways of doing things should be regarded as final, but should be examined through actual practice"; and "so long as public ownership is maintained, there can be no violation of socialist principles."

Other economists have similar or slightly different definitions of socialism. For example, with the parallel discussions of commodity production in the socialist economy (see Chapter 2), prominent economists such as Ma Hong (1984), Yu Guangyuan (1986b: 6), and others have repeatedly stressed the importance of commodity production and have included it as one of the basic principles of socialism. But until the mid-1980s, virtually all of them regarded public ownership of the means of production as the foundation of socialism from which the other important characteristics are derived. In addition, many prominent economists argued that whether or not specific economic practices are consistent with socialism needs to be evaluated in the light of China's actual circumstances at its current primary stage of socialist development.

In other words, the criteria of socialism as given in classical Marxism for mature socialism or as practiced in the Soviet Union under Stalin may not be appropriate for China, given China's very different conditions. The widespread acceptance of this argument culminated in the emergence and predominance of the theory of the primary stage of socialism. As discussed in Chapter 1, once that theory was officially sanctioned in late 1987, it opened the way for wide-ranging reinterpretations of socialism. Thus, in the relationship between the state and the enterprise, in the enterprise's response to the market, and in the relationship between the enterprise and its workers, reform practices were interpreted by theorists as being consistent with socialism (socialism with Chinese characteristics). Even the most important pillar of socialism, namely, public ownership of the means of production, was modified in both theory and practice after the mid-1980s to allow for the coexistence of different forms of ownership, as we shall see. Similarly, the principle of income distribution according to labor was modified to allow for a minor element of nonlabor income.

The ultimate criterion of socialism, according to the new view, is what is workable in China's socialist development – that is, what will best develop China's "productive forces" – and not what is laid down in classical Marxism or the Soviet experience. Furthermore, practice is the sole and ultimate judge of what is workable under China's conditions, although practice needs to be clarified, systemized, and guided by theory, which means in reality that theory needs to be developed to justify and refine practice, as discussed in Chapter 1. Because functional economics is concerned with what is workable in practice, it has increasingly overshadowed China's diagnostic economics in 1979–88.

Is this socialism? Are the reforms consistent with the "true" socialist path? A number of Western scholars do not think so and have criticized China's reforms accordingly (Brodsgarrd, 1983a: 55; Solinger, 1983; 1984: 73–106). Their criticisms will certainly be valid if the orthodox criteria of socialism discussed earlier are used. But should they? Should not the definition and contents of socialism change as the economic conditions (stage of socialist development) of a country change or as they vary from country to country? These are no doubt important questions, but they will have to be answered by experts in socialism. From this author's viewpoint, it does not matter at all whether Chinese reform theory and practice are consistent with true socialism so long as they are workable, help improve productivity, and raise the Chinese standard of living.

Another important change in the Chinese conceptions of socialism concerns how the "superiority" of socialism will be realized. As mentioned earlier, before the late 1970s, most Chinese authors equated socialist ideals with socialist practice and thus assumed that the presumed socialist superiority will automatically be realized. After the chaos and hardships of the Cultural Revolution, all but the most obtuse Chinese realized that the reality of socialism as practiced in the past in China is a far cry from the planned and proportionate development suggested by the traditional Chinese conception of socialism. In attempting to explain this disparity, many economists have resorted to the "learning errors" or "paying tuition for learning socialism" thesis of socialist development originally espoused by Mao Zedong in 1956 (see Chapter 1) – that it is a long and arduous process to learn socialism and, hence, that errors are bound to be made in the process (*GMRB*, July 29, 1980: 1; *JJRB*, Aug. 8, 1983: 1). This thesis is certainly consistent with the subsequent primary-stage theory of socialism and has thus transformed the presumed superiority of socialism from an *immediate certainty* into a delayed *future inevitability*.

A more sophisticated or sophistic version of the same theme goes even further and argues that the socialist superiority is an "objective possibility," but that it can be realized only if "objective economic laws and natural laws" are observed in the economy (Jiang Xuemo cited in *JJRB*, Dec. 28, 1988: 3; Zhu Tiezhen, 1980: 45). Furthermore, the operation of these laws varies according to circumstances, making it very difficult to master and apply them. And because socialist China was born of semifeudalism and semicolonialism, the appropriate laws are even more difficult to discover. In other words, socialism is inherently superior to capitalism if it is correctly learned and implemented, but it is very difficult to do so, given the difficult and changing circumstances.

The problem with this argument, which is echoed by many authors in various versions, is that it can always be made to excuse the failings of any economic system. Nevertheless, the acknowledgment of the *conditional nature* of socialist superiority is very important as long as the socialist ideology remains important to the Chinese. It helps Chinese intellectuals to rid themselves of self-blinding dogmatism, which was so unabashedly displayed during the Cultural Revolution, and thus helps to open the way for learning from abroad, particularly from the hitherto "inferior" capitalist countries. In addition, it helps to rechannel many intellectuals' energy from sterile ideological pursuits to more objective studies of the economy, however intractable the "objective laws" and "natural laws" of socialist development.

In the rest of this chapter, important changes in Chinese economists' views on three major aspects of the socialist economy – the nature of socialist ownership, the management of the state-owned enterprise, and the logic of socialist planning – are examined. The issue of distribution according to labor is discussed separately in Chapters 4 and 5, but it is touched on in this chapter in relation to the issue of ownership. It is shown that all of these are part and parcel of China's changing conceptions of socialism as applied to its current stage of socialist development.

Ownership of the means of production

As mentioned earlier, public ownership of the means of production is considered by the Chinese to be the most important characteristic of socialism; it is the "material foundation" of the superiority of socialism. In addition, state ownership has traditionally been considered as the superior form of public ownership. In the 1979–88 period, as China's ownership system underwent changes, questions were raised about these beliefs and about whether alternative forms of ownership are compatible with socialism. There are three major reasons for these developments. First, state ownership as the best form of socialist ownership was increasingly criticized because it had brought about rigid state control of the economy and lack of workers' incentives in the past. Consequently, economists proposed alternative forms of socialist ownership. Second, a small but growing private sector of the economy emerged that showed much vitality. It provided much-needed employment, but at the same time also greatly enriched some individuals. Third, in the 1980s, shares or stocks were issued by various enterprises – stated owned, collectively owned, and privately owned – to enterprise workers and/or to the general public as a new way to raise funds. This made it possible to combine different forms of ownership, thus raising many theoretical questions about the socialist ownership system. This section examines the Chinese debates on these questions.

Public ownership and state ownership

In its actual usage in China, public ownership consists of two categories or levels: "ownership by the whole people" (*quanmin suoyou zhi*) and "collective ownership by the working people" (*laodong zhe jiti suoyou zhi*), that is, ownership by members of a collective or cooperative. The former is considered to be the superior form of public or socialist ownership and, prior to 1979, was invariably equated with "state ownership" (*guojia suoyou zhi*) on the grounds that the socialist state represents all the people and their interests. Collective ownership, which existed in China's rural areas since the early 1950s and occasionally in the cities on a small scale, is regarded as a lower form of public ownership.[1] Before 1979, Chinese theorists generally considered the transformation of collective enterprises into state-owned enterprises as inevitable in socialist development. After 1979, a variety of views developed. A small number of economists still would like to see the transformation. The majority support its continued coexistence with state ownership. Some others believe that both collective and state ownership will evolve into a higher form of "society's ownership by the whole people" (Yan Renchang, 1985: 189–92).

The sanctity of state ownership under socialism was first questioned in 1979 by Dong Fureng (1979) of the Institute of Economics, the Chinese Academy of Social Sciences. He argues that state ownership is only one possible form of ownership by the whole people, and that it has proved to be incompatible with economic flexibility and efficiency because it has brought about rigid administrative control of the economy, especially at the enterprise level. Therefore, he advocates a type of "workers' ownership" in which all workers control and manage the means of production in accordance with their collective interests. In this system, decisions are made

---

[1] Some authors distinguish between "collective ownership" (*jiti suoyou zhi*) and "cooperative ownership" (*hezuo suoyou zhi*) and regard the latter as a lower form of the former. Also, the term "local public ownership" (*difang gongyou zhi*) has been used to refer to rural enterprises set up by the village-township governments. Local public ownership is considered a lower form of public ownership. See, for example, Xue Muqiao (1987). The conventional criterion for assessing an ownership form is the degree of its "publicness," which in turn is regarded as positively related to the development of "production forces." In other words, it is believed that the more public the form of ownership, the more conducive it is to large-scale production and the development of productivity, and therefore the higher the level of ownership. Recent discussions on various forms of ownership have raised questions about this belief.

"democratically" by the workers, and the state plays only a coordinating role. Unlike collective ownership, enterprises do not own the means of production but only make use of them, with much management autonomy. Profits ("surplus product") go to all the workers, not to the enterprises (Dong Fureng, 1979: 25). Operationally, it is not clear how workers are to make managerial decisions; nor is it clear who will be responsible for the possible losses of the enterprises.

As is seen repeatedly in this study, Dong Fureng has been an influential pioneer in many areas of post-Mao economics, and his critique of state ownership has no doubt lent support to the post-1979 movement, in both economic theory and policy practice, toward greater enterprise autonomy, which is a major objective of Dong's reform theories. However, his questioning of the supremacy of state ownership under socialism has met with only limited support, if not outright opposition. The major opposition comes from Jiang Xuemo (1979), a leading conservative professor of economics at Fudan University, Shanghai, who argues along the traditional line that because the means of production belong to the whole people, they can only be managed by an institution that represents the interests of all people, that is, the socialist state; therefore, state ownership is the only feasible form of ownership by the whole people.[2]

There are other views, promulgated in 1979–80, that are more qualified: (1) Although state ownership is not the only possible form of socialist public ownership, it is the logical one in China because of the need for central guidance and management during the early, underdeveloped stage of socialism. (2) State ownership should be the dominant form of socialist ownership, but there can be a minor element of "enterprise ownership" in which the enterprise or the workers own the means of production. (3) A three-level ownership system has also been suggested – ownership by the state, by the industrial branches (or industrial corporations and associations of corporations), and by the enterprises, with enterprise ownership as the foundation (Yan Renchang, 1985: 166–8).

These discussions in 1979–80 did not have much impact on the majority of economists who believed that the ills of state ownership could be cured by management reform to give state enterprises more autonomy without changing the nature of ownership. In fact, this is the direction that China's industrial reform subsequently took, and Chinese economists became in-

---

[2] As of 1988, Jiang Xuemo still held the same view. However, he believed that the benefits of public ownership can be realized only with political democracy. Without democracy, public ownership will not be workable because of incessant state interference in enterprise management, whereas private ownership may be workable, as in Taiwan and South Korea (author's interview, Aug. 17, 1988).

creasingly preoccupied with planning and management reforms in the first half of the 1980s, as is discussed in the next section.

In 1985–7, there was a resurgence of interest in the nature of socialist ownership. There are two reasons for this development. First, various industrial reforms that were expected to cure the ills of state ownership were progressively introduced but did not produce all the expected results (see the next section). Second, concurrently with the implementation of these reforms, alternative forms of ownership emerged in China. As economists began to pay attention to them in the mid-1980s, state ownership also received new scrutiny.

This new round of discussions on socialist ownership was again initiated by Dong Fureng (1985a). He criticizes the prevailing view that management reform can free state enterprises from state interference without ownership changes. He argues that socialist ownership is not a matter of who owns the property in the legal sense, but rather of "production relations" in the political economy, that is, of how well the laborers are linked with the means of production; this is, after all, the basis on which capitalist private ownership is criticized by the Marxists. From this perspective, under state ownership laborers are indirectly linked with the means of production through the intermediary of the state or its various layers of administrators. A better form of socialist ownership would link the two directly, presumably through the "workers' ownership" that he advocated in 1979.

During the 1985–8 period, Dong Fureng was joined by many other economists in criticizing state ownership. Among the most outspoken are Hua Sheng, Zhang Xuejun, and Luo Xiaopeng (1988c: 17–18) of the Chinese Academy of Social Sciences, who criticized state ownership for aggrandizing the state's power to control the society in two ways. First, as the representative of society, the socialist state monopolizes all public jobs and tends to transform itself from society's public servant into its master. Second, it monopolizes the means of production and transforms all citizens into dependent employees of the state. Given these events, they conclude, state administrative interference in enterprises is inevitable.

Disillusionment with state ownership has stimulated much interest in alternative forms of socialist ownership that could replace or modify state ownership. Many theoretical possibilities have been explored, but they center on two major categories: workers' ownership and enterprise ownership. Among the economists who support workers' ownership, Li Weisen (1986) wants to replace state ownership with the "real laborers' ownership" by issuing them "ownership certificates" on the basis of their labor contributions; these certificates can be traded in the stock market, and their values as well as their dividends will fluctuate with the performance of the workers' enterprises. Li considers the current public ownership by the "whole people," that is, state ownership, "illusory" because the state controls everything. Less strident but probably more influential is Jiang Yiwei (1987c), the long-standing advocate of workers' self-management, who wants to make workers "part owners" of the means of production through the ownership of shares. A variant of workers' ownership consists of turning state ownership into "group stock ownership" in which state-owned enterprises would issue stocks to be owned by the state, the enterprise, and the workers according to certain fixed percentages. The enterprise and the workers would receive their shares from the state without compensation because the state is simply returning to them the portions of the assets that are the fruit of their past "labor accumulation" (*laodong jilei*, i.e., the formation of assets through the use of labor power in production; *GMRB*, Nov. 8, 1986: 3).

Another alternative form of socialist ownership advocated by ownership reformers to replace state ownership is "enterprise ownership" (*qiye suoyou zhi*) or "legal person ownership" (*faren suoyou zhi*); it should be distinguished from the traditional collective ownership. As of 1988, at least two versions of enterprise ownership had been discussed. One version, advocated by He Wei (1986, 1988) of the People's University in Beijing, has the following essential features: (1) The funds for establishing the enterprise come from the state rather than from members of the enterprise, as in collective ownership. (2) The property of the enterprise belongs to society, not to the enterprise or its members. Members derive only "labor income" from their use of public property, with the obligation to maintain and expand it. (3) Part of the profits can be used for enterprise accumulation but not for distribution to workers; the rest goes to society as taxes. The enterprises are to be responsible for their losses. (4) Enterprise ownership is the transition from state ownership to Marx's ideal of "free associated individuals," which can be realized only during the highest stage of communism. The transition from state ownership to enterprise ownership can be made by leasing state-owned enterprises to workers.

He Wei considers state ownership to be the root cause of all socialist problems; it is necessary only at the time of the socialist revolution. Enterprise ownership is a type of "ownership by society" (*shehui suoyou zhi*) in which social groups, rather than individuals, are the owners. However, he does not advocate the elimination of private ownership in China under current conditions; he advocates only the restriction of "exploitation" and private consumption. He is certain that private ownership will eventually disappear on its own when the conditions are ripe (author's interview, May 30, 1989).

A second version of enterprise ownership, as proposed by Shen Shouye (1987), allows workers of the enterprise to own the means of production once the initial state investment is repaid with interest by the enterprise.

Thereafter, enterprise profits are to be used for workers' incomes, enterprise taxes, and accumulation. Shen justifies this ownership form and the enterprise's use of profits at both ideological and functional levels, as is typical of Chinese economics. At the ideological level, he argues that in accordance with the Marxian labor theory of value, any increase in value in the production process over and above the initial state investment is created by living labor alone; therefore, profits net of repayment and taxes should be used by workers. At the functional level, he holds that enterprise ownership has many benefits: It makes workers the masters of the enterprise; the separation between enterprise and government is greater; and society benefits from the new vitality of the enterprise, whereas the state is not worse off because the initial investment is paid back with interest. However, basic industries such as railways, mines, highways, mail and communication, and the like remain under state ownership to facilitate state planning and control.

As can be expected, the idea of enterprise ownership has encountered the familiar objection that, because socialist ownership means ownership by the whole people, only state ownership is appropriate because only the state can represent the whole people. In addition, conservative economist Jiang Xuemo (1988b: 34) of Fudan University opposes the replacement of state ownership with enterprise ownership lest the "guiding backbone" of the economy be lost and the economy become "a plate of loose sands." Zuo Mu (1987: 66) contends that large modern enterprises require centralized planning, which in turn requires state ownership. In response, He Wei (1986: 38–9) makes the blunt point that ownership by the *whole* people has never really existed in China under state ownership because the peasants have always been excluded from it. The peasants, who constitute 80 percent of the population, participated in collective ownership only in the past and never exercised any ownership right or participated in any production relations as owners of state property.

Although He Wei is technically correct, neither he nor anyone else has ever questioned the deep-seated belief that the essence or ideal of socialist ownership is "ownership by the whole people," although some authors have complained that this term is too vague. Thus the challenge to state ownership is not a challenge to the ideal itself but to the conventional belief that state ownership is the best way to realize that ideal. In response to this challenge, and in recognition of the fact that state-owned enterprises are still plagued by bureaucratic interference in spite of various management reforms, defenders of state ownership are willing to separate the state ownership right from the management right ("separation of the two rights") by adopting the "management contract responsibility system" in order to increase flexibility in management.

In this contract responsibility system, managers and workers of state-owned enterprises sign a contract to deliver a certain amount of taxes and profits to the state in return for management autonomy and profit incentives. Depending on the terms of the contract, the excess over the quota may be kept by the enterprise, and the deficiency may be made up by it. Although this system falls far short of ownership reformers' ideal of combining management autonomy with the ownership right, it is not very different from the leasing of state enterprises to workers, which is accepted by advocates of enterprise ownership as the means of transition to their new system. The main difference between management contracting and enterprise leasing is that the contractor bears only the risks and receives only the income specified in the contract, whereas the lessee bears more risks and keeps all the net profits.[3]

In 1986–8, the management contract responsibility system was adopted in many medium-sized state enterprises. However, administrative interference in enterprises was not eliminated, and many enterprises did not behave as rationally as was expected (see the next section). This led Guo Jia (1987) to propose a compromise solution. He argues that under the separation of the two rights, enterprises cannot be expected to behave rationally as if they actually owned the means of production. They still have to deal with numerous representatives of the state – administrative superiors, tax officials, financial officials, the banks, party secretaries, planning committees, and so forth – and their management right is inevitably circumscribed. To alleviate these problems, Guo Jia proposes the "contractor's two rights," that is, a complete management right and a certain amount of ownership right for the enterprise. In this system, the state retains the ultimate ownership of the means of production, but the contractor shares the ownership right and has more power over the use and expansion of the means of production.

On the related policy issue of share or stock ownership, supporters and critics of state ownership also adopted positions that are not far apart. Many supporters of state ownership are willing to let state enterprises issue and sell shares to their workers and the public, provided that the state owns the majority of the shares. For their part, advocates of ownership reform support shareholding as a practical way to introduce diversity into the ownership system and to promote a closer link between workers and the means of production (Jiang Yiwei, 1987a; share ownership is discussed further later in this chapter). However, the fact that both sides of the state-ownership debate accept management contracting, leasing, and share ownership on tactical grounds should not be interpreted as the convergence of the two schools of thought on socialist ownership. Rather, it is a case of "sharing the same bed but dreaming different dreams" (*tung chuang yi meng*).

[3] The majority of Chinese economists feel that leasing is more appropriate for small enterprises, whereas management contracting is more appropriate for large and medium-sized enterprises. I have benefited from conversations with Professor Liu Guoguang on this point. See also *JJRB*, Aug. 18, 1987: 3.

Thus, in the late 1980s, the sanctity of state ownership was no longer above challenge, although the ideal of ownership by the whole people had never been questioned. In response, defenders of state ownership broadened their concept to make it compatible with different forms of management and with a minor element of nonstate shareholding ownership. Which point of view will prevail in the future will depend on the results of China's experiments with different forms of management and ownership and on the preferences of the political leadership.

Private ownership

The introduction of private ownership since 1979 is the logical consequence of China's trial-and-error strategy of reform; it is not the fruition of a well-thought-out economic theory or policy on ownership reform. As is well known, Chinese reforms started in 1979 in agriculture in the form of the "household contract responsibility system," in which remuneration to the peasant household is linked to its output. Following the initial success of the responsibility system, in the early 1980s the government permitted more and more peasant households to engage, on their own, in specialized commercial farming and nonfarming activities for the market. The need for household production required, and the incomes from it made possible, individual ownership of minor means of production. As the reform spread to the cities in 1984–5, small private businesses were established, offering diverse services that were not well provided by the state and the collective sectors, and at the same time helping to relieve a serious unemployment problem. As these private activities in both rural and urban areas further expanded, the employment of labor outside the household became necessary. After reformist Zhao Ziyang was appointed the new secretary general of the Communist Party in late 1987, and before June 1989 when the Tiananmen Square massacre took place, the expansion of private ownership was officially encouraged. For example, starting in early 1988 and with Zhao's blessing, a small number of small and medium-sized state enterprises were privitized through auctions (*WSJ*, Feb. 19, 1988: 16). In April 1988, the Seventh National People's Congress formally revised the state constitution to permit the existence and development of privately owned enterprises (Article 11). Private ownership of land, however, is not included in this provision. Chinese economists generally feel that collective ownership of farmland coupled with a long-term lease for farmers who pay rent to the collective is more conducive to the rational use and control of land (*GMRB*, Dec. 3, 1988: 3). The following discussion, therefore, does not apply to it.

In discussing private ownership, most Chinese economists distinguish between private ownership by individual laborers and ownership by private employers. The former exists in the "individual economy" (*geti jingji*); the latter exists in the broader "private economy" (*siren jingji*), which is based on the use of hired labor. The distinction is useful in China's context because the ideological reservations that some economists have about private ownership apply more to the latter than to the former.

Generally speaking, Chinese economists regard private ownership by both individuals and employers as nonsocialist. However, in their view, the existence and growth of this nonsocialist sector does not necessarily undermine socialism and promote capitalism in China at its current primary stage of socialism. There are various reasons for this. At the ideological level, Lin Shuiyuan (1987: 61–2) has given the most detailed rationale. He argues that Marx and Engels did *not* propose the immediate elimination of private ownership after the seizure of power by the proletariat. He cites Engles's views in the *Principles of Communism* (*MEXJ*, Vol. 1: 217, 220–1) to the effect that the proletariat can eliminate private ownership only when the necessary conditions are present – that is, when large quantities of production materials have been created. Before then, Engles would use fiscal measures such as progressive taxes, high inheritance taxes, and compulsory bond purchase to restrict private ownership and would use the competitive power of state-owned enterprises to expand the public sector. Similar measures were proposed in Marx and Engles's *Communist Manifesto* to restrist private ownership, and this was meant to take place in the advanced countries. Therefore, Lin Shuiyuan concludes that in backward economies, flexible handling of private ownership is needed to develop the economy. He further cites the experience of the Soviet Union to support his view. During the War Communism period (1917–20) after the Bolshevik revolution, complete nationalization of enterprises led to disastrous consequences for the economy. In contrast, during the New Economic Policy period (1921–8), a flexible policy that permitted some private businesses led to the economy's rapid recovery.

Expanding on the same theme, Li Xuai (1988: 51) concedes that capitalist "exploitation" is involved in the employment relationship based on private ownership. However, he regards private employment and exploitation, which is considered an element of capitalism, as inevitable and even necessary at the primary stage of socialism because nascent socialism needs to use the remnants of the old society to build itself, as was the case with capitalism in its infancy.

Distinguishing between private ownership and individual ownership, Sun Liancheng and Lin Huiyong (1988) argue that Marx and Engels, as shown in the *Communist Manifesto*, criticized the private ownership system in which the bourgeoisie alone owned the means of production ("partial private ownership'') but not ''individual ownership'' in which everyone owned the means of production and, therefore, could not be exploited by others. The latter is consistent with socialism because Marx envisioned the postcapitalist society as entailing the rebuilding of ''associated social individual ownership'' (*MEQJ*, Vol. 23: 832; Vol. 48: 21).

At the functional level, Chinese economists, using the pros and cons approach, agree that private ownership has both positive and negative effects on the development of socialism, and that the relative importance of these effects changes with the circumstances of the country. For example, according to the consensus reached at a 1986 national conference on the private economy, the private sector contributes to the growth of productivity and thus to the development of the socialist economy in various ways: (1) it supplements and competes with the state sector; (2) it pools idle factors of production for production; (3) it creates employment opportunities; (4) it provides capital accumulation for the state; and (5) it helps train entrepreneurs. The possible harmful effects are (1) the inordinate power of the owners in decision making and in the appropriation of employees' surplus labor and (2) possible speculative behavior and the emergence of the nouveau riche (*GMRB*, Nov. 8, 1986: 3). According to Liu Guoguang (1986a: 19), a crucial factor to take into account in weighing these pros and cons of private ownership is the relative strength of the state sector. In the early 1950s, because socialism was not yet well established and the state sector not yet dominant in China, the growth of the private sector would have been detrimental to the development of socialism; currently, because the state sector is dominant, the benefits of the private sector outweigh its harmful effects.

This line of reasoning illustrates both the strength and the weakness of the pros-and-cons–weighing approach mentioned in Chapter 1, which is characteristic of China's functional economics. The reasoning is intuitive, pragmatic, and sensible, but its policy conclusions can be easily changed to support any policy decisions. Furthermore, it seems to imply that the pros and cons can somehow be compared to determine the proper proportion between private and public ownership for China at its current stage of development. It is in fact impossible to do so short of making a political decision, and no Chinese economist has been foolhardy enough to venture a suggestion.

Many variations on the theme abound in the Chinese economics literature, although the emphasis varies with the individual author. For example, Zhang Xiaoming (1987) stresses the competitive effect of private ownership. He argues that public ownership in China has promoted income equality but has sacrificed productivity and efficiency because public ownership in the past was promoted administratively by the state without the benefit of competition from nonpublic ownership. And because ''without competition, there will be no development," Zhang supports private ownership in order to supplement and compete with public ownership. This has the salutary effect of promoting both efficiency and equality.

The arguments in favor of private ownership have important implications. Because public ownership is still regarded as the foundation of socialism and because private ownership is the antithesis of public ownership, the acceptance of private ownership for the sake of promoting productivity implies that raising productivity is more important than pursuing socialist purity. Naturally, no Chinese economists have put it this way, but a perusal of the Chinese literature does suggest that this "productivity first" attitude is quite widespread among economists. In fact, many economists claim that a high level of productivity – eventually higher than that of capitalism – is the most important manifestation of the superiority of socialism (*JJRB*, July 7, 1987: 3). In any case, it is interesting to note that all Chinese economists characteristically justify the use of private ownership to raise productivity in the name of serving socialism, choosing to ignore the fact that the means used to serve the end may alter the nature of the end itself. A few authors go so far as to consider individual ownership as socialist or semisocialist if it serves the public sector and is subject to state control.

This does not mean that all Chinese economists who now accept private ownership on a limited scale are ready to embrace it permanently on a large scale for the sake of future productivity growth. To some economists, precisely because private ownership is accepted as a means, whereas public ownership is desired as an end, private ownership is expendable whenever it becomes unwieldy. In other words, private ownership is acceptable only to the extent that it remains an appendage of public ownership, supplementing it but never threatening to dominate or overwhelm it.

These two attitudes are not necessarily mutually exclusive at China's current stage of development, but they have very different implications for the future of private ownership in China. One would expect those who emphasize productivity first to favor the permanent existence and even continuous expansion of the private sector, and those who emphasize private ownership as an appendage to view it with suspicion, ready to restrict, discard, or transform it whenever necessary. In fact, Chinese economists' views on the future of private ownership are generally divided between these two positions. Some economists favor "long-term coexistence and mutual competition" between private and state enterprises (*GMRB*, Nov. 8, 1986: 3). Among these economists are those who advocate a type of "socialist mixed economy" (Dong Fureng, 1987; Wu Jixue and Zhu Ling, 1986) or a "semisocialist ownership system" (Dong Fureng, 1985a: 11). On the other hand, other economists, notably Liu Guoguang (1986a: 19), favor "tight supervision and control" of private businesses to curb their "negative influence," and would consider possible conversion of them into cooperative enterprises or joint enterprises with the state.

It is ironic that a reformist economist as prominent as Liu Guoguang, who has long advocated a greater role of the market (as discussed in Chapter 2), should adopt such a position. Yet Liu Guoguang does not seem to realize that, as pointed out by Prybyla (1986: 23), the market does its job best in a "pluralistic, competitive, free-wheeling, free-choice environment." Tight supervision and control and the threat of conversion are the antithesis of this market environment and stifle the very vitality that made private ownership acceptable and even desirable in China in 1986–8. Liu Guoguang (1986a: 20; also personal communication, 1987) further argues that the proper proportions of private and public ownership are best determined by their relative performance in the market through "equal market competition." This proposition is illogical because private businesses under tight supervision and control cannot compete on an equal footing with state enterprises, which enjoy various advantages, including a "soft budget constraint." Thus, the so-called equal market competition is not a fair test of the true or potential strength of private businesses, which the Chinese presumably are eager to find out.

Shareholding ownership

As China's reform spread from agriculture to industry, the need for the mobilization of additional funds and for more flexible ways of industrial management and coordination led to the experiment with the shareholding ownership system. Shareholding was introduced on a small scale in the following situations: (1) individual peasants pooling funds to run private businesses or collective enterprises; (2) existing urban enterprises, state-owned or collectively owned, selling shares to their workers in order to expand or set up subsidiaries; (3) regional governments or enterprises engaging in cooperative activities by setting up joint ventures; and (4) joint ventures between Chinese and foreign enterprises.

Theoretically, shares of collective or state-owned enterprises may be owned by enterprise workers, the general public, the enterprises themselves, or government units. Thus shareholding ownership can create various combinations of different forms of ownership that do not fit the traditional categories, and the growth of shareholding can challenge the dominance of state ownership. In view of this, and given the fact that there is no precedent for successful shareholding ownership in other socialist countries, is the introduction of shareholding in China a sign of retrogression to capitalism?

Chinese economists' views on share ownership are still tentative and divided. As of mid-1989, the discussions were conducted at two levels – at the ideological level to assess its consistency with Marxism and at the functional level to explore the pros and cons and the proper design of the system. These correspond to the diagnostic economics and functional economics distinguished in Chapter 1.

The ideological implications of shareholding were debated between 1985 and late 1987, when the political leadership ruled in its favor. In the debate, both proponents and critics of shareholding resorted to interpreting or reinterpreting Marx's views. Proponents generally invoked Marx's views in *Capital* (Vol. 3, ch. 27) regarding the capitalist joint-stock companies as the "transitional forms from the capitalist mode of production to the associated one"; the capital raised as "social capital" ("capital of directly associated individuals"), as distinguished from private capital; and its undertakings as assuming the form of "social undertakings," as distinguished from private undertakings. From these, they concluded that Marx regarded shareholding ownership as compatible with, or even as a prerequisite for, the establishment of socialist public ownership (Liu Guoguang, 1986a: 22; Wang Senlin, 1986). Furthermore, they stressed that shareholding under China's socialist system differs from that of capitalism in fundamental ways. First, the bulk of the shares are held by state-owned and collective enterprises. Second, the individuals who own shares are workers who "democratically" manage the enterprises; the enterprises are public in nature. Thus, shareholding in China is a new form of social capital that differs from the social capital under capitalism. Similarly, the dividends received by individuals are consistent with the distribution of income according to labor because the money used to purchase shares is labor income, not income based on exploitation, as in capitalism (Chen Zhao, 1985: 63; Wang Senlin, 1986; Zeng Kanglin, 1985: 40).

Critics object strongly to the argument that share income is consistent with distribution according to labor. They point out that, according to the Marxian labor theory of value, only living or present labor that workers provide in the production process can create value. Share funds embody past or dead labor that cannot create new value, and therefore should not be included as labor in the distribution of income, just as capitalists' ownership of the means of production cannot be so regarded. These critics do not deny that material compensation needs to be paid to people who make their funds available to enterprises. However, they argue that such payment arises out of the separation of the ownership and use of funds, and is therefore a reward for loans under both capitalism and socialism and should not be confused with compensation for labor (*GMRB*, Dec. 20, 1986: 3).

A third and more pragmatic view of the issue of income distribution admits that share income, like income derived from private businesses, is "distribution according to funds" but contends that such nonlabor income is "necessary and reasonable" in China's current primary stage of socialism (Jin Xizai and Liu Chunlin, 1987). Because China has different forms of ownership and enterprise management, naturally there will be different forms of distribution – those that are in accordance with labor, as well as those that are not. According to this view, which is becoming increasingly popular, it is better to accept the inevitability of this and to recognize the contribution of shareholding to economic development than to rationalize it as being consistent with distribution according to labor or to oppose it because it is not (Wang Mengkui, 1987). Nevertheless, all authors who hold this view recommend some limits on stockholders' dividends because the dividends do come from the "surplus value," and unless quantitatively restricted, quantitative change can lead to qualitative change and "exploitation" may result (Yan Simao, 1984: 40).

At the functional level, the debate centers on the perceived advantages and disadvantages of shareholding to the economy and to workers. Various issues have been raised, including financial implications and workers' attitudes. Financial implications concern the possibility and results of pooling idle financial resources for investment by the state. Supporters of shareholding ownership argue that share dividends are necessary to attract these resources. The use of these resources will help reduce the government deficit and hence the inflationary pressure (Xiao Zhuoji, 1988). In addition, shareholding ownership will enable the state to establish state investment-development corporations that will own enterprise shares. In this way, state investment activities can be separated from the state supervision of enterprises, which is considered to be desirable in giving state enterprises more autonomy (Jiang Yiwei, 1987b).

On the other hand, skeptics of the system do not think that employees can afford to buy many shares. According to them, in large state enterprises, which are usually capital intensive, employees can contribute at best a very small portion of the capital needed, given their low wages (Wang Mengkui, 1987). Thus, the possibility of pooling idle funds is limited to the idle cash that is not deposited in the banks and is not committed to specific uses; this amount is necessarily small. For ease of macro control, it is better to attract these funds through banks than by issuing stocks (Fan Maofa, Xun Dazhi, and Liu Xiaoping, 1986: 21–2). The purchase of stocks may even shift funds out of banks. Finally, opponents of the stock-financing system do not like to see shares of state-owned enterprises purchased either by the general public or by collectively owned enterprises because this weakens the dominance of state ownership and transforms the enterprises into jointly owned ones.

The issue of workers' attitudes concerns the possibility of enhancing state employees' sense of being the masters of the workplace. Virtually all supporters of shareholding, but particularly Jiang Yiwei (1987b), a former director of the Institute of Industrial Economics, Chinese Academy of Social Sciences, and Li Yining (1986a,c), a professor of economics at Beijing University, stress its beneficial effects on workers who become part owners of the enterprises through shareholding. According to this view, workers are interested not only in the results of their labor but also in the management and financial situation of the enterprise. This helps eliminate the shortsightedness of enterprise behavior. In addition, through collective management in which representatives of worker–shareholders participate in the board of directors, workers become the real masters of their enterprises. All these perceived benefits, both financial and attitudinal, led advocates of shareholding to embrace it as an institutional breakthrough to reinvigorate China's sagging economic reform in the late 1980s.

Critics argued that it is unlikely that owing a small number of shares will strengthen the workers' sense of being the masters. Nor can numerous small stockholders influence the decisions of the board of directors and the enterprise's behavior, just as workers' shareholding in capitalist economies ("democratization of capital") has not made capitalist corporations and societies more democratic. Besides, there are better ways than stock ownership to mobilize workers' incentives under socialism. Furthermore, if share ownership among workers is uneven, "contradictions" are created between shareholders and nonholders and between large and small holders (Wang Mengkui, 1987; Wu Shuqing, 1987). Finally, if outsiders are permitted to own shares, this would weaken the workers' sense of being the masters and increase their sense of being "hired labor" (Wu Shuqing, 1987). The sense of social inequality due to the resultant unequal distribution of income and the speculative psychology inherent in stock trading are considered to be harmful to workers and society.

In response, supporters of stock ownership make the following rebuttal. First, on the possibility of increased income inequality, Li Yining points out that everyone would be enriched under the system and no one would be poorer, even though some may become richer than others (*WSJ*, Feb. 2, 1987: 27). Others point out that individual owner's dividend income can always be limited by a progressive income tax to prevent excessive inequality if society so desires. On the role of small shareholders, it is argued that although individually they may not directly influence enterprise policies, collectively they influence stock prices, which will be watched carefully by the board and the management. In this way, the interests of shareholders and of the manager will be closely integrated (Zhang Weiying, 1987). As to the speculative mentality associated with stock ownership, Xu Jing'an (1987) argues that speculation as an attempt to predict the market correctly is inherent in a commodity economy and should be viewed more positively; the production and exchange of commodities for the market, like investment in enterprise stocks, is an act of speculation because the outcome depends on the correctness of the prediction.

In a broader framework, Huang Franzhang (1989) regards shareholding ownership as the best form of socialist ownership because it effectively prevents the state from interfering in enterprise management while at the same time permitting citizens to truly exercise their ownership right. He would set up a "state assets management committee" to invest in and control public enterprises; the state would own shares of enterprises through the committee. In addition, he advocates the development of various financial investment institutions and public funds that accept deposits and share ownership by citizens in a way similar to the "citizens' funds" advocated by Swedish economist A. Lindbeck (Huang Fanzhang, 1989; 1987: 198–202). These institutions and funds would invest in the stock market and hold shares of enterprises. The citizens, through their holding of shares in the funds, would indirectly influence enterprises. In this way, the means of production would be jointly owned by the state and the people, and the people would simultaneously enjoy producer sovereignty, investor sovereignty, and consumer sovereignty.

It is clear that this proposed system is a long-term ideal rather than an immediate solution to the socialist ownership problem, for it requires the existence of a well-developed capital market, which ordinarily exists only in developed market economies and not in the less developed economies. Huang Fanzhang concurs with the author on this point (author's interview, May 21, 1989). In addition, this author is not convinced that the establishment of a state assets management committee will end the government's interference in enterprise affairs. In a bureaucratic party-state such as China, enterprises still have to deal with numerous representatives of the state – tax officials, financial officials, party committee secretaries, planning committees, banks, and so on, as Guo Jia (1987) has pointed out – no matter which state organ manages the state assets.

Nevertheless, Huang's idea is interesting because it suggests a new conception of socialism – financial or fund socialism – for China. It also implies the convergence of socialism and capitalism in terms of ownership, whereas most Chinese economists envisage convergence only in terms of the adjustment mechanisms of the economy (see Chapter 2).

In this manner and with countless variations on these themes, the debate unfolded in 1985–8 and extended through the first half of 1989. It is interesting to note that many authors based their arguments on their perceptions of the Western experiences because neither China after 1949 nor any other socialist country has had any experience with shareholding ownership. The discussions of its ideological correctness and of its economic pros and cons provide a rich menu of theoretical justifications of alternative policies for policymakers to choose from. In late 1987, the Thirteenth Party Congress ruled that the stockholding system is an acceptable way to organize the property of the socialist enterprise, thereby settling for the time being the ideological question about its compatibility with socialism in China.

However, many practical issues continued to be debated throughout 1988 and into early 1989. A major question concerned the proper scope of share ownership: Should the system be extended to all state enterprises, or should it be limited to a small number of enterprises on an experimental basis? Should banks be involved in stock ownership, as is already the case in Beijing (*JJXWZ*, No. 6, 1987: 5)? Should enterprise stocks be sold to the general public or should they be owned primarily by the state, the enterprise itself, and its workers (*GMR*, Nov. 3, 1988: 2)? In this regard and on the basis of Western experience, some economists question the wisdom of enterprises owning their own stocks because this might conflict with the interests of other stockholders (*GMRB*, Nov. 19, 1988: 3; Nov. 26, 1988: 3; *JJRB*, Oct. 25, 1988: 3). Another practical question concerns the proper way to assess the assets of the enterprise as the basis for the state's shares (*JJXWZ*, No. 6, 1987: 4). There is no consensus on that issue or on the way the shares of workers are to be determined; some economists support the dubious idea of basing them on the "values" of workers' labor power and skills (*GMRB*, Oct. 27, 1988: 3). It is impossible to do this objectively in the absence of a competitive labor market.

The need for ownership reform coupled with serious inflation in 1988 prompted Hua Sheng, Zhang Xuejun, and Luo Xiaopeng of the Academy of Social Sciences to propose an ingenious idea – to transform state ownership and at the same time to reduce the inflationary pressure in the economy through induced share ownership. The central government would issue "asset certificates" as part of its budgetary allocations to provincial and local governments and state institutions such as research institutes and universities. This would reduce the central government's deficit and money supply. These certificates would be good only for buying the shares of state enterprises that the central government would auction off. Local governments could acquire no more than 15 percent of the shares of enterprises under their jurisdiction and no more than 20 percent of enterprises elsewhere (*EC*, Feb. 11, 1989: 36). In this way, state ownership would be transformed into diffuse institutional share ownership while the influence of local authorities on local enterprises would be restricted, which is an important objective in enterprise reform (see the next section).

One problem with this proposal is that, with the asset certificates replacing part of their budget allocations, local governments and state institutions might have to borrow more money from local banks to meet their operational needs. If so, the inflationary pressure in the economy would not be reduced. In this regard, Xiao Zhuoji (1988) of Beijing University argues that sales of enterprise stocks to the public would absorb idle funds for public investment, which would reduce the government's deficit and hence the money supply and the inflationary pressure. However, in early 1989, following the decision in late 1988 to postpone price reform for two years in order to fight inflation, the Chinese leadership decided to put a two-year freeze on the sale of shares of state-owned enterprises. Obviously, Chinese leaders do not consider any share-ownership scheme to be anti-inflationary. Because the temporary suspension of stock issues is due to economic rather than ideological factors, it can be expected that the discussion will continue.

Should enterprises, local governments, state institutions, and workers be permitted to sell the shares they own to private individuals, thereby indirectly privatizing state enterprises? If the answer is "yes," the consequences would be profound. In practice, however, few individuals except those related to top officials can afford to buy a large number of shares. For this reason, many economists fear that large-scale privatization under current conditions would lead to "bureaucratic capitalism" in China. In any case, it is safe to predict that individuals will not be permitted to hold the lion's share of stock in state-owned enterprises in order to preserve the leading role of public ownership in the economy. Similarly, to prevent class exploitation, shares would not be concentrated in the hands of a few people, as Liu Guoguang (1986a: 22) and many other economists have argued.

One final clarification is in order. We have discussed the pros and cons of different forms of ownership as seen by their supporters and critics in China. This does not mean that they are all in favor of a single form of ownership and that other forms cannot coexist with it. On the contrary, most economists have in mind a system in which different forms of ownership coexist. For example, private ownership of small businesses and collective ownership of small to medium-sized rural enterprises as they existed in 1988 are accepted by most economists. Similarly, few economists would challenge state ownership of natural resources, public utilities, defense industries, and the infrastructure of the economy in which market competition is difficult and state control is considered important. The debate, therefore, concerns the other industries that do not fit into these categories. In other words, most economists agree on the desirability of a mixed ownership system; it is the nature of the mix that is under debate. In this regard, an important version of socialist mixed ownership is discussed by Dong Fureng (1987). Dong previously advocated workers' ownership but by 1987 had changed his view because of Yugoslavia's disappointing experience with workers' self-management. He now defines socialism as a mixed economy with the dominance of public ownership. However, dominance in his view does not mean dominance in quantity; it means being in a position to regulate and influence the economy. He supports share ownership because it is consistent with the dominance of state ownership while coexisting with share ownership by enterprise workers and individuals (author's interviews, Aug. 9–10, 1988).[4]

In this version of a socialist mixed economy, it is not public ownership per se but the state's ability to regulate and influence the economy through public ownership that is the essence of socialism. Because public ownership is only one of the means – and not necessarily the best one, as the experiences of many countries have shown – to attain the goal of state regulation and influence, it can be expected that the importance of public ownership in the Chinese conception of socialist mixed ownership will continue to evolve once the Chinese realize that public ownership may not be essential to regulation and control.

The socialist enterprise

The enterprise in China's microeconomics

Given public ownership of the means of production, it follows that the socialist economy is a planned economy, according to the socialist conventional wisdom of China. This is because production is no longer carried out for private profit according to the whims of the market, but is undertaken for social purposes according to rational planning.

One can distinguish between two major aspects, micro and macro, of the planned socialist economy. The micro aspect is that the socialist enterprise, that is, the state-owned enterprise, as the basic production unit under socialism, has a prescribed role to play in the economy. Its task is to fulfill the production quotas and attain other economic goals handed down by the state planners. In other words, its functions and its relationship with the state are defined by the plan. The macro aspect is that, in theory, the economy has balanced and proportionate development without the anarchy of the market. In this section, the micro aspect is discussed; the macro one is discussed in the next section.

In Western microeconomics the "firm" occupies the center, and much microeconomic analysis is derived from the presumed "rational behavior" of the firm. Thus the "theory of the firm" is the jewel of Western microeconomics and a staple of all studies of economics. Intuitively, one would

---

[4] However, because of the underdevelopment of the capital market in China, Dong Fureng feels that China lacks the precondition for large-scale issuing of stocks because their values cannot be accurately determined (author's interview, Aug. 9, 1988).

expect the same to be true of the socialist enterprise in China's economics because one would expect the enterprise to be the showpiece of whatever superiority there is in socialism. After all, the socialist enterprise is a microcosm of the socialist political economy where virtually all facets of socialism converge – ownership and distribution, planning, workers and work enthusiasm, workplace and organization, education and political consciousness, and so forth. Yet in the Chinese economics literature both before and after the late 1970s, the enterprise has not attained the exalted place of its counterpart in Western economics. In fact, until recently, there was no such concept as the "theory of socialist enterprise behavior." Whatever microeconomics existed can be characterized as the theory of enterprise *control* rather than the theory of enterprise *behavior*. Furthermore, until around 1986, the Chinese almost never used the term "rational" to describe or evaluate the behavior of their enterprises; "rationality" was used exclusively to characterize socialist planning and policies at the macro level. Enterprises are either "model" ones, being exemplary in production, inventiveness, socialist fervor, and so forth, or in need of more "socialist education," "comradely assistance" from fellow enterprises, and a heart-to-heart talk with the party committee secretary because of below-par performance. Naturally in a tautological way, the rationality of the socialist enterprise was taken for granted. The enterprise was socialist in nature, in terms of ownership, organization, and purpose of production, and was therefore rational by definition as long as it fulfilled the targets assigned by the state. However, there was no analysis of the rationality of enterprise "behavior" as such. The question is: Why?

The answer must be sought in the methodological framework that has guided Chinese theoretical analysis and that, in turn, is shaped by the nature of the Chinese political economy. Until the mid-1980s, Chinese theorists invariably viewed their state-owned enterprises in the larger picture of a hierarchical planned relationship between the all-powerful party-state and the enterprise; the former sets the norms of economic activities to be followed by the latter. In such a command relationship, there is no room for an enterprise to behave according to its own objectives and decisions. Rationality in enterprise behavior presumes freedom and the ability of enterprise to choose among alternatives in accordance with its own objectives and calculations; the traditional state enterprise had no such freedom of choice. Under such circumstances, it is impossible to have a meaningful theory of socialist enterprise behavior.

In the following section, we explain how the traditional relationship between the state and the enterprise was theoretically or ideologically justified in the past, how in 1979–88 economists came to question that justification and proposed ways to change that relationship, and how, since the mid-1980s, they started new discussions of rational enterprise behavior.

Traditional views

Until the late 1970s, socialist planning was synonymous to the Chinese with "mandatory planning" (*zhiling jihua*), which is also referred to as planning and management by "administrative methods." This conception of planning was born of the orthodox Soviet model of planning, which the Chinese copied during the First Five-Year Plan (1953–7), although in its successive Chinese applications it became, out of necessity and of choice, less comprehensive and more decentralized. The essential characteristics of China's mandatory planning include the following: (1) State plans are made on the basis of political leaders' preferences. Plan objectives are disaggregated into mandatory production quotas for state-owned enterprises after some negotiations with the enterprises themselves as to their production capability and requirements. (2) Market relations play no role in the production and allocation of producer goods and play only a limited role in the distribution of consumer goods (state–household exchanges). Prices, set by the state, perform merely an accounting function in the former and a limited allocative function in the latter. (3) The state procures the major agricultural products from the agricultural collectives, with procurement quotas and a limited price incentive. (4) Plan implementation is supervised by both government officials and party cadres at various levels.

In this model of planning, the enterprise's task is to fulfill the mandatory output quotas and other economic indicators assigned by the state. Even when planning authority was decentralized – that is, delegated to lower-level government, as it was periodically in China – decentralization did not bring about greater enterprise autonomy. Nor did it give workers room for initiatives in spite of the socialist ideology that workers are the masters of the means of production under socialism. Consequently, there existed a rigid administrative–command relationship between the planners and the enterprise, with little incentive for the latter to improve productivity.

This lopsided planning relationship between the state and the enterprise was previously rationalized by Chinese theorists in terms of a number of propositions and beliefs that the Chinese refer to as the principle of "socialist material interests." This principle prescribes or seeks to justify various "proper" relationships between the whole and the parts under socialism. The whole can be the nation, the whole people, the state, the Communist Party, or the national plan representing the state or national interests, or the collective production unit in relation to its members. The parts can be the regions, local governments, local plans, enterprises, or individual workers and peasants.

The basic proposition underpinning these vertical relationships is that, because public ownership of the means of production under socialism has eliminated the private-profit motive and class exploitation, the long-term interests of both the whole and the parts are basically congruent under socialism, and this is claimed to be an important aspect of the superiority of socialism over capitalism. There are two reasons for this harmony of socialist interests. First, workers are no longer separated from the means of production. Hence they work conscientiously for the overall interests of all working people, as well as for their individual interests. Second, under the leadership of the political party of the proletariat, state policies simultaneously take into account the interests of the state, of the collective units, and of the individuals, but with priority given to the interests of the state or of the whole. Hence the harmony of interests under socialism.

It is recognized, however, that in specific instances there can be conflicts of interest between the whole and the parts, especially in the short run. The conflicts arise because, more often than not, the localities, the enterprises, or the individuals, because of their narrow perspectives or ignorance, pursue their narrow short-term interests to the detriment of the larger national interest. For example, localities might divert funds or materials from state projects to local ones when they would have been more productive in the former; or enterprises might produce inferior products or disregard pollution in fulfilling their plan targets. In these cases, the basic principle for conflict resolution is that "the interests of the parts should obey those of the whole, short-term interests should obey long-term interests, and individual interests should obey collective interests" (GMRB, May 31, 1980: 4).[5] The theoretical justification for this principle is that the interests of the whole, of the long term, and of the collectives are the precondition for the realization of the interests of the parts, of the short term, and of the individuals, just as "small rivers will be full if the main river is full" and "small rivers will be dry if the main river is dry" (cited in RMRB, May 19, 1983: 1; Mar. 29, 1984: 1–2).[6] In the same vein, another analogy, "the nation as a chess-

---

[5] It is interesting to note that the reasoning is similar to the Western "externality" justification for government intervention in the case of environmental pollution. There is a crucial difference, however. In the Western case, externality justifies the exception to the rule of government nonintervention, whereas in the Chinese case, the principle justifies the rule of general government guidance and leadership. The Chinese had not introduced the concept of externalities until the mid-1980s, when a number of Western analytical concepts were introduced.

[6] As can be seen from this and other examples given later, the Chinese have a traditional predilection for analogies (and sometimes false analogies) in their exposition. Analogies are imperfect substitutes for analytical concepts, however.

board," is commonly invoked to prescribe the proper relationship between the state and its subordinate units, in which each and every move made by the latter must follow the state's overall game plan. In short, in its infinite wisdom and paternalism, the state knows best and is all-caring.

Accordingly, in a proper relationship between the state and the enterprise, the distribution of decision-making power regarding the latter's economic activities is necessarily weighted in favor of the state in order to safeguard the unity of socialist interests. As part of the mandatory plan, state-owned enterprises are given mandatory quotas and other indicators to fulfill. Enterprise budgets and the means of production are allocated to them in the plan. Profits are remitted to the state, and losses are made up by the state. Enterprises cannot change the mix of product varieties in accordance with changes in market demand, cannot sell above-quota output to unauthorized buyers, and cannot purchase material inputs from unauthorized sources or fire redundant or inefficient workers. Under such circumstances, Chinese microeconomics in the 1950s and early 1960s naturally concentrated on ways to make enterprises fulfill their targets better, on the perfection of enterprise economic indicators, and not on the rationality and behavior of the enterprise.

This type of socialist planning and control is the model of bureaucratic socialism par excellence. It has resulted in various problems – bureaucratic rigidity; lack of enterprise economic incentives and accountability; the divorce of production from demand, which results in a surplus of unsalable products in the midst of a general shortage; general allocative inefficiency, and so on – problems that have also plagued other planned socialist economies. To deal with these problems, reformist economist Sun Yefang suggested as early as 1961 that state enterprises should be given more autonomy for their production and sales decisions, but his suggestions were ignored (Wu Renjian and Li Xiuzhen, 1985: 577). Instead, Chinese authorities relied, without success, on periodic decentralization in planning – that is, on the delegation of greater planning authority by the central government to the lower-level governments – as the adjustment mechanism to instill planning flexibility.

Because the general problems of socialist planning are well known, we shall explain only one particular type of incentive problem that is frequently reported in the Chinese press and yet has not received attention in the Western literature; it is also relevant to the discussion later in the chapter. The problem is referred to by the Chinese as "whipping the fast ox" (*bianda kuainiu*), that is, punishing the more efficient production units and individuals. This problem stems from the fact that in this type of socialist planning system, government bureaucrats, as the agents of the state, have enormous power over their subordinate enterprises. This power is often abused to promote the bureaucrats' own interests, which are disguised as state interests. For example, in implementing the plan, many officials at the provincial and county or municipal levels are responsible for meeting the plan's targets for their respective areas and for making local plans. They disaggregate the former into specific production quotas and other economic indicators for enterprises under their jurisdiction. To help fulfill or over-fulfill their aggregate targets, which are indicators of their own leadership performance, these officials tend to assign higher and higher quotas every year to enterprises that have recently surpassed their output quotas, even though this practice dampens the latter's incentives. Until the 1985 agricultural procurement reform, this practice was also common in the assignment of agricultural procurement quotas. This tendency to whip the fast ox has prompted enterprises to adopt various defensive measures, including the widespread "year-end syndrome": Once their quotas have been fulfilled or surpassed and their bonuses received, they tend to slow down for fear of being given higher quotas for the next year; surplus materials at year's end are concealed to avoid higher quotas or cutbacks in material allocation for the next year.[7] Ironically, enterprise responses such as these are seen by true believers of state mandatory planning as proof that narrow, short-term perspectives can cause enterprises to deviate from the larger national interest; hence the need for strict state planning and control to ensure the unity of socialist interests.

Reforming the state–enterprise relationship

Starting in the late 1970s, when the problems of China's past planning and management practices and the excesses of the Cultural Revolution were openly discussed, the traditional rationale for the state's planning and control of the enterprise began to be questioned. This, coupled with the release of pent-up energy in the aftermath of political change, led to much theoretical blooming and contending in various directions. Between 1979 and the mid-1980s, there emerged at least three schools of thought that suggested new ways to reform the traditional relationship between the state and the socialist enterprise.[8] After the mid-1980s, there emerged a fourth school of

[7] The problem of whipping the fast ox and the responses to it have been frequently mentioned in the Chinese press and the economics literature, particularly in the early 1980s. See, for example, GMRB, Apr. 26, 1980: 4; JJRB, Dec. 19, 1983: 1; RMRB, Dec. 7, 1979: 1; Dec. 18, 1980: 3; Oct. 29, 1984: 5; ZGCMB, Sept. 18, 1982: 3; Dec. 21, 1982: 2.

[8] A minority view, too limited in influence (at least in publications) to constitute a school of thought, questions the dominance of the whole and of the state over the parts, the enterprises, and individuals, as illustrated in the "main river–small river" analogy. It espouses Adam Smith's thesis, hitherto unthinkable in China, that the wealth of the people (*min fu*) is the prerequisite for the wealth of the nation (*guo fu*), just as "the main river will be full if the small rivers are full" (*RMRB*, Feb. 1, 1983: 5). It thus implies that enterprises and individuals should be permitted to pursue whatever they regard as best for themselves with-

thought that looked at the socialist enterprise from an entirely different perspective. The first three schools of thought are summarized in this section; the fourth is discussed in the next section.

The first school of thought is concerned with the role of workers in the enterprise and may be characterized as the "workers' self-management" or industrial democracy school of thought. As mentioned earlier, the traditional conception of socialist planning gives workers no opportunity to participate in managerial decision making in spite of their presumed new status as the masters of the means of production. As a reaction against this situation, several prominent authors have proposed ways to translate the theoretical promise into reality. For example, Dong Fureng (1979: 24) argues that workers should "directly manage the publicly owned means of production and the production, exchange and distribution activities of the enterprise." In this way, workers will be concerned with the result of using these means of production, thus unifying the interests of the society with those of both the enterprise and the workers. Similarly, Jiang Yiwei (1980a) argues in his "enterprise-based theory" for greater enterprise autonomy and workers' collective management. More recently, Jiang Yiwei (1987b), Li Yining (1986a,c), and other authors have supported shareholding as a new form of ownership in order to have workers participate in management through their shareholders' representatives on the board of directors, as discussed earlier in this chapter.

Thus the proposed workers' self-management entails enterprise operational autonomy in relation to the state. In addition, its proponents invariably support alternative forms of public ownership to replace or modify state ownership. Aside from the widespread support for shareholding, many of these proponents also support either workers' ownership or versions of enterprise ownership in which all the workers, the society, or the enterprise own the means of production; enterprise profits either go back to the society or are to be used by the enterprise, as explained earlier in the chapter. Thus, Chinese economists' models of workers' self-management differ from the Yugoslav model in various ways, depending on specific authors, although the influence of the Yugoslav experience is obvious.

This school of thought has neither become part of post-Mao China's mainstream economics nor has had a major influence on China's enterprise reform for two major reasons. First, the majority of economists feel that average industrial workers are not competent enough to manage complex modern industries. Second, they believe that workers' self-management

out undue state restrictions. This view has proved to be too "bourgeois" for the Chinese authorities and has not been published in official publications since the campaign against "spiritual pollution" in late 1983. From conversations with Chinese economists, however, it is clear that many younger people subscribe to this view.

would jeopardize necessary macro planning and control, and that what the workers might do at the enterprise level ("What if they decide to eat it up?") or collectively at the national level would conflict with the larger interests of the state and the nation. For their part, advocates of workers' self-management have not convincingly refuted these criticisms.

The wide gulf between the advocates and opponents of workers' self-management reflects a duality and an inherent contradiction in the traditional Chinese conceptions of socialism. As mentioned in Chapter 1, socialism as a system of ideals and of anticapitalist critiques has two related but distinct tenets that appeal to different people – the anti–market-anarchy tenet that promises state planning and control of the economy, to the delight of political leaders and state bureaucrats, and the anti–capitalist-exploiters tenet that promises industrial democracy or workers' self-management. Both of these are based on public ownership of the means of production and are presumed to be compatible, given various ideal assumptions. In reality, however, they have been and are likely to remain incompatible and irreconcilable. The reason is that, once in power, socialist political leaders and planning authorities, with few exceptions, abhor anything unplannable or uncontrollable, whether it is the anarchy of the market or that of workers (and students). This was the case in China before 1979; it was still the case after 1979, although to a lesser extent.[9] In addition, as Lippit (1987: 215, 223) points out, the reform emphases in the 1980s on the professionalization of management and on the "manager responsibility system" for the sake of productivity also run counter to greater workers' participation.

Consequently, it is difficult for this workers' self-management school of thought to become part of China's mainstream economics and to influence China's enterprise reform.

The second school of thought seeks to replace the traditional mandatory planning with "guidance planning" (zhidao jihua) and is thus labeled here

---

[9] It is true that, ever since the early 1950s, Chinese workers have enjoyed an important socialist benefit: job security (the "iron rice bowl"). Enterprises cannot fire redundant or inefficient workers, to the detriment of incentives and productivity. However, aside from its political importance, job security does not interfere with the state's planning and control. On the contrary, it simplifies them because the uncertainty of the labor market is eliminated. The party-state's basic distrust of workers can be seen in the fact that both before and after 1979, each enterprise has a party committee secretary who was (and is) responsible for workers' "socialist education." This education takes various forms (e.g., participation in group discussions) that, according to Walder (1983) and Lippit (1987: 147), have the effect of increasing workers' subordination to the party-state rather than their participation in management. During the Cultural Revolution, labor unions were dissolved. After 1979, the unions were re-established and workers were given some power in electing enterprise managers through the congress of workers and staff. Workers' job security is to be modified ("porcelain rice bowl") to promote productivity.

as the guidance planning school of thought. As discussed in Chapter 2, guidance planning is a relatively flexible type of planning in which enterprises are given suggested targets rather than compulsory quotas, and the state uses economic levers (prices, interest rates, taxes, exchange rates, credit allocation, etc.) rather than administrative controls to induce enterprises to comply with the plan so that aggregate plan targets and other macro objectives can be attained. In this way, enterprises have greater autonomy and incentives, and the state has the indirect means to ensure macro balances and the harmony of socialist interests. Thus, guidance planning is similar to Western "indicative planning" in its suggestive nature and its reliance on indirect economic incentives for implementation. However, it differs from the latter in two important ways: The indicative plan is not broken down into targets for individual enterprises, and the state plays a much larger role in guidance planning in price setting, enterprise personnel, and so on, because the enterprises are state-owned (Hsu, 1986: 383).

The validity of the theory of guidance planning rests on the effectiveness of the economic levers with which China has had little experience. Nevertheless, its goal of "micro flexibility and macro control" appeals to the majority of Chinese economists. Furthermore, the theory seems to contain a simple and painless formula for curing the ills of mandatory planning without abandoning the planned nature of the socialist economy. Consequently, by the mid-1980s, this school of thought had become one of the most influential economic doctrines in China's mainstream economics in the post-1979 period, and the majority of economists as well as the government embraced it as a major means of planning reform. The debate on guidance planning centered, therefore, not on its desirability but on its proper scope in the economy so that the state would still retain the necessary level of control over the major industries.[10]

---

[10] The debate on the proper scope of guidance planning concerns how the planned economy should be divided into the mandatory-plan sector and the guidance-plan sector. In the early 1980s, the Chinese debated the pros and cons of the following criteria for the division: (a) division on the basis of ownership: mandatory planning for state-owned enterprises and guidance planning for collectively owned enterprises; (b) division according to the size of the enterprise: mandatory planning for the larger key enterprises and guidance planning for the smaller ones; (c) division according to the importance of the product: mandatory planning for important products and guidance planning for less important ones; (d) division according to the supply condition of the product: mandatory planning for products in short supply and guidance planning for others; (e) division along the macro–micro line: mandatory planning for general macro targets and guidance planning for micro activities. In 1984–5, the government adopted a compromise policy that combines most of these criteria. Basic industries that produce important industrial products and defense industries are to be subject to mandatory planning, whereas consumer goods industries are to be subject to guidance planning.

The third school of thought may be characterized as the "financial accountability" school. It advocates operational autonomy for the enterprise on the grounds that this is the best way for the enterprise to accomplish its tasks efficiently. An essential part of this autonomy is the financial accountability that makes the enterprise responsible for its own profits and losses. This serves as an incentive, as well as a form of financial discipline for the enterprise to use society's property efficiently, in a manner that is consistent with its own interests and those of the society. Thus this school of thought continues and expands the ideas pioneered by Sun Yefang in 1961. Although discussions continued from 1979 to the mid-1980s, the major theoretical viewpoints favoring and opposing it had been laid down by the end of 1980. Kuang Ri'an and Xiao Liang (1979) argue that the state-owned enterprise has a dual role to play in the economy. On the one hand, it is an integral part of the state ownership system, since its means of production are owned by the state. On the other hand, in its operation and management it is (read: should be) an independent production unit because it is entrusted by society to use and manage the means of production efficiently. The implication of being an independent production unit is that it must be able to pay for its expenses with its own revenues, that is, it should have independent financial responsibility, which will also spur greater productivity. In order to have this financial accountability, it must also be given commensurate management autonomy, including the power to use various funds (e.g., fixed capital, circulating capital, depreciation funds) and to engage in equal exchanges with other enterprises. The same line of reasoning is pushed further by other proponents of enterprise autonomy to argue for the elimination of administrative interference by superior bureaucrats so that the enterprise will have autonomy in finance, use of materials, employment, sales, and income distribution. Ma Hong (1979), China's eminent industrial economist, supports enterprise financial independence for a more pragmatic reason: It makes the workers more concerned with the enterprise's performance, as shown in the case of collectively owned enterprises.

Although most economists agree that state enterprises should be given more decision-making power and financial incentives, some economists, at least in 1979–80, did not want to go as far as giving them independent financial accountability. Their reservations, as expressed by Guan Mengchue and Jiang Xuemo, two leading conservative economists in China, were based primarily on equity and ideological grounds: (1) As long as prices are not rationally based on value, enterprise profits and losses do not necessarily reflect enterprise efficiency or performance. Therefore, enterprises should not be financially rewarded or punished accordingly. (2) Enterprises have different equipment, technology, and labor productivity, which affect their income levels. With enterprise financial accountability, this would adversely affect the material interests and initiatives of many workers. (3) Unlike collective enterprises, state enterprises are established with state funds. It is theoretically unjustifiable that their profits should be used by the enterprises rather than being returned to the state. Such financial independence also obliterates the difference between collective and state enterprises. (4) With financial independence, income taxes would replace profit remittance to the state in the financial relationship between the state and the enterprise. Some critics do not like the equity implications of the income tax. They would rather give enterprises profit retention to stimulate their incentives (Wu Renjian and Li Xiuzhen, 1985: 580–1). By the mid-1980s, however, the opposition had waned as the government moved to give enterprises greater autonomy (see later). The discussion campaign had reached its final phase and a consensus had seemingly emerged.

Although these three schools of thought differ in focus concerning enterprise reform, they are not necessarily mutually exclusive; on the contrary, they are compatible and mutually supportive in various ways. Both the guidance-planning and enterprise-autonomy schools want to change the planned relationship between the state and the enterprise by giving the latter more power, either by reforming the planning system or by reforming the industrial financial system, which is also part of the broader planning system. To make the use of the economic levers of guidance planning more effective, the enterprise should be given complete or a large degree of financial autonomy so that it will be concerned about the financial consequences of the economic levers. Consequently, these two schools of thought have been close allies in the mainstream of China's post-1979 economics, and many reformist economists belong to both of them.

The workers' self-management school of thought concentrates on the internal aspect of enterprise management and labor organization. The demand of the other two schools for greater enterprise autonomy in relation to the state is consistent with the demand of this school of thought for greater workers' control and is implicitly taken for granted by its advocates. However, the reverse is not true. Advocates of guidance planning and enterprise autonomy usually do not want to give much more power to enterprise workers at the expense of the enterprise manager.

By the mid-1980s, both the guidance-planning and enterprise-autonomy schools of thought had been widely accepted by economists and increasingly implemented in actual policies. They became the new orthodoxy of the 1980s. A growing number of industrial products were put under guidance planning since 1979. Changes in the machinery industry typify this trend. In 1979, mandatory plans covered about 86 percent of the gross value of that industry's output. In 1980, the figure had declined to 54 percent and to 20 percent in 1981 (*JJGL*, No. 4, 1984: 8). The rest of the industry's output was produced under guidance plans. By 1984, most of the manufactured consumer goods in the economy were produced under guidance plans. Starting in 1985, the number of manufactured products subject to mandatory planning by the State Planning Commission was reduced from 123 to about 60 (*RMRB*, April 13, 1985: 2). This constituted about 20 percent of the value of all manufactured products. China's material supply is also subject to similar dual-track planning. In 1984, about 800 producer goods, including materials, were subject to mandatory planning (Wang Shaoqing and Xu Jingyi, 1984: 18). These included specialized materials planned by specific industrial ministries, general materials planned by the material supply departments, and those planned by local governments. The number of materials subject to mandatory planning by the State Planning Commission and the State Bureau of Materials and Equipment was reduced from 256 in 1984 to 65 in 1985 and to 26 by the end of 1987 (*RMRB*, Apr. 13, 1985: 2; Nov. 9, 1987: 1).

In terms of giving enterprises greater financial accountability, the reform similarly progressed in stages through trial and error. Starting in 1978, enterprises were permitted to retain part of their profits. This system of profit retention produced excessive fiscal deficits for the state. Thus it was incompatible with the "fiscal balance" of macro planning, and the "profit contract system" was introduced in 1981–2. In this system, enterprises were permitted to retain a certain percentage of the profits over and above a certain base figure, which was negotiated with the local government. However, as Naughton (1985: 226–44) notes, this system gave local governments too much financial authority over local enterprises; in addition, there was no penalty to the enterprise for failing to reach the base profit. Consequently, it was replaced by the "tax for profit" system, which was introduced in stages since 1982. The system includes sales tax, income tax, capital charges, and so forth to increase enterprise autonomy from arbitrary government interference and to make enterprises more accountable for both profits and losses. This also makes it more effective to use taxes as an economic lever in guidance planning. In 1986 the Bankruptcy Law was enacted; it was the culmination of years of discussion on the issue, as noted in Chapter 2. This is potentially the single most important measure to make enterprises accountable for their losses, although the actual number of bankruptcies to date has been very small. Finally, in 1986–8, there was much experimentation with the enterprise management responsibility system and enterprise leasing, in which enterprise employees or private individuals sign a management contract or a lease with the authorities to run a state enterprise for profit, with a specified amount of payment to the state. Touted as the "separation of the two rights'' (ownership right and management right), this management arrangement is merely the latest institutional attempt to minimize the state's role in the enterprise in order to ensure the latter's autonomy.

Theories of enterprise behavior

In 1986–8, both the guidance-planning and the financial accountability schools of thought remained the dominant doctrines in China's mainstream economics. Guidance planning is no longer discussed because it is largely implemented and taken for granted, but the issue of enterprise financial accountability remains an important topic in enterprise reforms, as we shall see. At the same time, as new problems of state-owned enterprises have emerged in spite of the successive reforms mentioned earlier, economists have increasingly focused their attention on the behavior of the enterprise.

The problems that prompted this development relate to the irrational or shortsighted behavior of many reformed enterprises, behavior that is contrary to the expectations of enterprise-reform advocates. Many enterprises in recent years have been criticized for pursuing short-term interests and for taking advantage of loopholes in the system without regard to their social consequences. Instead of striving to raise productivity and lower costs in order to increase profits, many resort to raising prices, lowering the quality of products, and engaging in speculative trading, black market activities, and even fraudulent practices. Many enterprises also fail to fulfill their sales contracts with the state in order to sell more in the free market and the black market at higher prices. In addition, although the economy suffers from overinvestment, inflation, and shortages of critical materials, many local enterprises continue to expand their unplanned investment and to compete with planned state projects for materials in short supply. On the other hand, as Walder (1987: 33–6) observes, some enterprises distribute all their profits indiscriminately as bonuses to the workers, thereby fueling "bonus inflation" while disregarding the need for accumulation and reserve funds.

In light of these problems, it is clear that Chinese economists need to go beyond their traditional concern with the relationship between the state and the enterprise and examine enterprise behavior in a broader context. As a result, starting in 1986, a growing number of economists have been asking new questions about how a rational socialist enterprise should behave and about the type of environment it requires, and have been suggesting ways to foster such an enterprise. This line of inquiry is the most significant development in China's microeconomics because it places the enterprise at the center of a new and broader analytical framework; it views the enterprise as the main actor, the "micro foundation" of the macro economy, in the words of Wei Jie (1986; also author's interview, May 30, 1989), rather than as an appendage of the state administration. In the following, some major elements of the discussions are outlined.

An important concept of the discussions is that of "constraint." Kornai's (1980a,c) concept of the "soft budget constraint" of the Hungarian socialist enterprise has played a very important role in its development. In fact, Kornai's contribution has been twofold. First, his distinction between "soft" and "hard" budget constraints became popular because, aside from the Chinese cultural propensity to use neat, contrasting categories, it struck a responsive cord among Chinese economists. It expressed and reinforced their concern that socialist enterprises have to be responsible for both profits and losses, a theme discussed earlier. In addition, it helped to popularize and legitimize the concept of constraint as an analytical tool. Previously, the Chinese had never used this term to characterize the relationship between the state and the enterprise. As explained before, that relationship was theoretically justified in terms of the congruence or harmony of "socialist material interests." The various directives given by the state to the enterprise were presumed to be consistent with the latter's own long-term interest, and thus they fitted into the socialist order of things; it was totally inappropriate to view them as constraints as such.

With the popularization of the budget constraint, other constraints on enterprise behavior soon followed: the employment constraint under which enterprises cannot fire redundant or inefficient workers; the price constraint under which the prices of some essential products are controlled by the government at low levels; the "mothers-in-law" constraint under which each enterprise has to obey *several* mothers-in-law (government officials and party cadres); the market constraint under which there are administrative barriers against competition or the marketing of products from other areas; and so forth.

Soon other related concepts logically followed. Because the constraints are imposed on the enterprise and cannot be changed in the short run, the enterprise operates in a given restrictive or imperfect *environment,* including the imperfect socialist market. It interacts with various forces, making calculated responses to changes in the environment. The relationship between the state and the enterprise is merely one element, although an important one, of the environment, but it is no longer the total environment.

The enterprise responds to the environment in a certain manner in accordance with its own "motive-force structures," that is, workers' motivations and enterprise *objectives.* The Western concepts of "objective function" and "utility function" have even been used by a few economists for this purpose. Many economists agree with Wei Xinghua et al. (1986) that enterprises should be permitted to have their own "relatively independent objectives" and to strive for the attainment of these objectives, but they have not been able to agree on the precise objectives of the rational socialist enterprise. Fang Gongwen (1985) considers the pursuit of profits to be the legitimate "direct objective" of the socialist enterprise, whereas the "ultimate objective" is to serve the society's interests. Most authors consider some combination of enterprise profits and workers' material and nonmaterial incomes to be the primary factors in the objectives, although these are modified by various other factors.

Given the objectives of the enterprise and the motivations of the workers, an enterprise's behavior in response to an external event or constraint can be viewed in a very different light. For example, the presumed irrational behavior of an enterprise's year-end slowdown for fear of receiving higher future quotas, as discussed earlier, is considered by Zhou Zhenhua, Liu Zhibiao, and Zhang Erzhen (1986: 70) as a rational response to the irrational government practice of whipping the fast ox. Similarly, they contend that speculative activities for quick gains may be a rational response to an imperfect market environment in which fair competition does not exist. And seemingly irrational investment and expansion may be necessary and rational for enterprises that have to create jobs for redundant workers they cannot get rid of. It is the government that is irrational because it shifts the burden of unemployment relief from itself to the enterprises and then criticizes them for the consequences.

It should be pointed out that not all economists would agree with these views because their criteria of rational enterprise behavior may be different. As surveyed by Hu Yongming (1988: 142–4), there are at least four criteria of rationality in recent discussions: (1) the maximization of profits through "equal competition" and improved management; (2) the use of resources in such a way that the interests of the enterprise and of the society are unified, that is, the minimum use of inputs and the maximization of society's wealth; (3) the efficient response to signals from the market and the government in order to maximize enterprise income; and (4) the proper handling of the enterprise's external and internal "relationships of economic interests," such as those between taxes and enterprise profits and between bonus distribution and enterprise accumulation.

In short, most Chinese economists regard the consistency between, and the efficiency in attaining, both micro and macro objectives as the criteria for rational behavior. These stringent requirements certainly make it difficult for any market-oriented enterprise to behave rationally. Nevertheless, there is a growing realization that enterprises are not entirely to blame for their irrational behavior. The views of Zhou Zhenhua et al. (1986) cited earlier are an example; others are given in the following paragraph.

In general, Chinese economists attribute irrational enterprise behavior to external and/or internal causes. External causes arise in the enterprise's external environment, which in recent years has been considered by virtually all Chinese economists to be irrational, irregular, and full of uncertainty because of the transitional nature of the Chinese economy under the reform. Specifically, the following external causes of irrational enterprise behavior have been emphasized by various Chinese economists: (1) irrational prices, which often have little relationship to costs of production and market demand, causing unfair income differences among enterprises; (2) the imperfect tax system and the problem of whipping the fast ox, prompting enterprises to bargain with the government; and (3) frequent changes in government policies, making it difficult for enterprises to form rational expectations about the future (Fan Maofa, Xun Dazhi, and Liu Xiaoping, 1986; Hu Yongming, 1988: 147; Zhou Zhenhua et al., 1986). Zhou Shulian, director of the Institute of Industrial Economics, the Chinese Academy of Social Sciences, regards the "paternalism" of government officials toward their subordinate enterprises as the cause of the latter's "soft budget constraint" (author's interview, July 8, 1988). According to him, the paternalism stems from the officials' desire to "beautify" their own leadership record by rescuing failing subordinate enterprises. In a similar vein, Tang Zongkun of the Institute of Economics, the Chinese Academy of Social Sciences, attributes some of the shortsighted enterprise behavior to "shortsighted government behavior" (author's interview, July 14, 1988). From a different perspective and utilizing a Western concept, Wu Jinglian (1988), an eminent economist, views the activities of enterprises as "rent seeking" made possible by government regulations and the irrational price system.

"Internal causes" refer to defective mechanisms or characteristics within enterprises. Within this broad category, different authors have emphasized different factors: (1) the lack of a mechanism to handle properly the relationship between profits and wages, and between accumulation and consumption, which leads enterprises to overemphasize workers' earnings and ignore the need for enterprise accumulation (Huang Taiyan, 1986; Ma Jiantang, 1986); (2) the lack of a "hard budget constraint" to make enterprises accountable for both profits and losses, as well as to respond to market and macro signals in a responsible manner (Hua Sheng et al., 1986); and (3) incompatible multiple objectives (maximum profits, output values, and income per worker) of the enterprises during the transitional period, leading to inconsistent and shortsighted behavior (Hu Yongming, 1988: 147–9; Hu Yongming and Lu Hongwei, 1986).

The varied nature of these external and internal factors reflects the complexity of China's economic problems in the late 1980s. All economists imply that these problems are transitory because the economy is in the process of shifting from the traditional planning system to a market-oriented one. Thus, the proposed remedies to eliminate irrational enterprise behavior are also the ways to speed up the building of the new system. They correspond to the external and internal causes of the problems.

To improve the external environment of the enterprise, two major solutions have been proposed: (1) Some economists have stressed the perfection of the market system or mechanism, including price reforms to make prices rational (see Chapter 5). However, as mentioned in Chapter 2, the Chinese conception of the perfect market system differs from that held in the West; it includes a certain level of government regulation and macro control. (2) Others have stressed the role of the state in complementing the market system. This includes the arbitration of disputes and the provision of economic information, price stabilization, investment policy, fiscal and monetary policies, and so forth (Hu Yongming, 1988: 153–4).

Internal measures are aimed at restructuring the enterprise itself. The "hardening" of the enterprise budget constraint is widely prescribed. In addition, two different types of measures have been proposed by different authors. The first type of measure stresses the building of a distributive and incentive mechanism to separate the economic interests of the enterprise from those of the workers or to make them compatible while at the same time safeguarding the interests of the state. Opponents argue that a well-functioning market system is the best mechanism to accomplish this objective. The second type of measure concentrates on the property relationship of state-owned enterprises. Some authors would implement an "assets management responsibility system," linking the rewards of managers and workers to increases in the value of enterprise assets. Others would transform state-owned enterprises into joint-stock companies, permitting enterprise workers to own some stocks. In this way, it is argued, the enterprise's autonomy and incentives would be increased and state interference would be minimized (Hu Yongming, 1988: 151–2; Li Yining, 1986a). Skeptics such as Sun Minghua (1987) argue, however, that unless the state's right to control through the board of directors is also taken away, the enterprise cannot be truly autonomous in its management.

There is a final concept in the discussions that personifies the rational enterprise, namely, the "socialist entrepreneur." Traditionally, entrepreneurs were considered to be unique to capitalism; with perfect planning and the workers' unbounded socialist enthusiasm, there would be no need for them. Now it is conceded that socialist entrepreneurs, with their knowledge of the "socialist market" and their enterprising and organizational abilities, are just as important to the socialist enterprise (Chen Suzhi, 1987; Zhou Shulian, 1986: 9), and many economists regard the training of socialist entrepreneurs as part of the rationalization of enterprise behavior. However, it is not clear how they can be trained, for they are generally expected to have the "correct political orientation" and "self-sacrificing spirit," on the one hand, and enterprising and innovative abilities, on the other hand (Chen Suzhi, 1987: 6). In addition, in their euphoric embrace of socialist entrepreneurs, some economists envisage them to possess "the thought of philosophers, the brain of economists, the expansiveness of statesmen, the versatility of diplomats, the decisiveness of militarists, and the vision of strategists" (*JJRB*, July 18, 1987: 2). It seems that the gifted socialist entrepreneur has replaced the elusive selfless socialist man of the past as the model for the Chinese; and he or she may prove to be just as elusive.

In conclusion, as of mid-1989, Chinese economists' ideas of rational enterprise behavior and their proposed ways to attain it were wide-ranging, but also idealistic and difficult to implement. However, compared with the Western ideal of the "perfectly competitive firm," the Chinese ideal is no more unreal and perhaps more desirable, at least in China's context. What is most significant is that many conceptual changes and analytical advances have been made in the decade from 1979 to 1988. From being a mere appendage of the state administration in the late 1970s, the socialist enterprise was, by 1988, conceived at its best to be an autonomous organism in the economy, potentially full of vitality, initiative, and social conscience. The "enterprise culture" is glorified in the press as the "growth point of China's new culture" (*JJRB*, Aug. 10, 1988). This change reflects to a large extent the rapid changes in the Chinese economy itself, as economic theory evolved in tandem with the practice of economic reform to justify it, to assess its pros and cons, and to suggest ways to cope with new problems.

But the extent and significance of the changes in the conceptions of the socialist enterprise go far beyond the interplay between theory and practice. China's prereform socialist microeconomics, if it could be called that, was based on doctrinaire interpretations of socialism and its presumed superiority, and was severely constricted by the policies and power politics of the party-state. By 1988, Chinese economists had rid themselves of the traditional dogmatic interpretations of socialism and were developing a new type of microeconomics that was increasingly based on objective, logical analysis in terms of *cause and effect, ends and means,* and *motivation and behavior.* This embryonic microeconomics places the enterprise at the center, rather than at the periphery, of the theoretical construct. In addition, it is becoming a relatively autonomous area of inquiry, with its own objective standards and analytical tools, that is capable of critical analysis of not only enterprise behavior but also its environment, including government policies. The implications of this development for China's economics and economic policies in the future are likely to be profound and far-reaching.

Planning and macro balances

The macro aspect of planning deals with economywide implications of socialist planning. This is the aspect that received most of the emphasis in the economics literature in the 1950s and early 1960s. The traditional approach was based on the proposition that socialist planning enables the economy to have balanced and proportionate growth. On the basis of this conclusion, two analytical approaches were developed. The first approach focused on various optimum ratios or proportions in the economy and on various planning balances, although, following the imbalances of the Great Leap Forward movement (1958–60), many economists also discussed the advantages of imbalance as a planning strategy. In the second approach, some economists constructed growth models to expand on some Marxian concepts, such as the reproduction scheme, or to show the implications of socialist growth. Most outstanding among these economists are Liu Guoguang (1962) and Dong Fureng (1963). Liu's model shows the relationship among a number of variables: the rate of growth of national income, the rate of accumulation, the capital-output ratio, the ratio of investment between the producer-goods sector and the consumer-goods sector, and so forth. Dong's model is even more elaborate and sophisticated, and permits a type of dynamic general equilibrium analysis. These two models have been summarized by Lin (1981: 27–34).

In the post-Mao period, from the late 1970s to the early 1980s, Chinese economists continued to devote considerable attention to macro planning balances and, to a lesser extent, to growth models. They also criticized some past planning practices that resulted in imbalances and economic difficulties. After the early 1980s, interest in the issues of planning balances gradually waned as economists became increasingly preoccupied with issues of reforms and development. In the following, the Chinese concept of planning balances and their policy implications are explained. We concentrate on the post-1979 period, particularly the early 1980s, when the discussions on planning balances were at their peak, with brief references to the period before the late 1970s.

The concept of "balance" (*pingheng*) pervaded China's planning discussions in both periods. The term is used in connection with a variety of "relationships" (*guanxi*) in the economy, such as the relationship between sectors of the economy (agriculture and industry), between different uses of national income (consumption and accumulation), or between different aspects of government operations (revenues and expenditures). Consequently, it has two different meanings for two different types of relationships.

The first type of balance means an optimum proportion or ratio that is most appropriate for a particular objective. For example, the balance between agriculture and industry, and between consumption and accumulation, belongs to this category. The second type of balance means overall equality, such as the balance between supply and demand or between government revenues and expenditures. In this regard, the Chinese use the term "overall balance" (*zonghe pingheng*) in the economy to include fiscal balance, credit (between deposits and loans), material balance, labor balance, market balance, and foreign exchange balance. These are also called the "six great balances," or the "five great balances" if market balance is excluded. The first type of balance reflects planning priorities and is, therefore, based on major policy decisions. The second type entails detailed calculations by economists after decisions on planning priorities and targets are made.

Optimum balances or proportions

In both periods, Chinese economists discussed the optimum balances or proper proportions between consumption and accumulation of the national income, between the production of capital goods and that of consumer goods, between "productive" and "nonproductive" investment,[11] and between heavy industry on the one hand and agriculture and light industry on the other hand. Of these, the balance between accumulation and consumption has received the most attention in theoretical discussions. In all of these relationships, post-1979 views differed profoundly from those prevailing before. Previously, accumulation, capital-goods production, productive investment, and heavy industry were regarded as key to socialist development. As a result, consumption and the standard of living largely stagnated except during the First Five-Year Plan period (1953–7). In 1979–82, consumption, consumer goods, agriculture, and light industry were stressed, if only to correct the imbalances in the economy due to the previous one-sided emphasis.[12]

To pave the way for this dramatic turnabout, Chinese scholars had to begin with a basic question: What is the purpose of socialist production? A nationwide discussion campaign was conducted in 1979–81, in which prominent authors participated, on the purpose of socialist production. The discussions came to the expected conclusion that the purpose of socialist production is to satisfy the growing material and cultural needs of the laboring masses, a theme originally advanced by Stalin (1952). Although the conclusion seems elementary, hardly worthy of extended discussions by the nation's top social scientists, it was a necessary exercise in China's diagnostic economics, serving as an "ideological clearance" for parallel changes in China's functional economics on planning balances, as outlined later.

---

[11] The Chinese terms for these are "productive construction" and "nonproductive construction." The former refers to capital investment that will increase the production of material goods. The latter refers to investment in the construction of hospitals, schools, and the like.

[12] However, in 1983, as inflationary pressures increased due to rapid increases in wages and consumption, Chinese economists began to stress that the growth rate of the nation's consumption has to be compatible with the growth rate of national income, and that wages and bonuses have to be compatible with increases in labor productivity.

With the legitimacy of consumption in socialist production established, it was easy for Chinese economists to evaluate past accumulation ratios. During the First Five-Year Plan period, accumulation was 24.5 percent of national income, and the standard of living as well as the national output steadily increased. With the exception of 1963–5 (22.7 percent), the other plan periods had higher accumulation ratios (26.3–33.6 percent) and poorer economic results.[13] Hence the figure of 25 percent of national income was suggested by virtually all authors in the early 1980s as approximately the optimum rate of accumulation in China. It may be higher (25–30 percent) or lower (20–25 percent), depending on whether the standard of living has been increasing or decreasing. Thus a range for the optimum ratio is sometimes given. The maximum rate is the one above which the level of consumption for the growing population will be lowered. The minimum rate is the one that is necessary to support a certain growth of consumer-goods production. It is contended that it is preferable to set the rate closer to the minimum than to the maximum under China's conditions (Liu Guoguang and Wang Xiangming, 1980: 31).

A more rigorous approach to this optimum accumulation ratio is to derive it on the basis of a planning objective in a macro model. In one such study, it was found that if the objective is to maximize the annual growth rate of national income, 25.57 percent is the optimum. If the objective is to maximize consumption, the optimum rate is 24.2 percent in a forty-year planning horizon and 22 percent in a twenty-year planning horizon (GMRB, Apr. 17, 1982: 3).

Various authors have also stressed that the growth of national income is not a simple matter of accumulation. The efficiency of accumulation, as measured by the increase in national income per unit of accumulation fund, is also important. When the accumulation rate becomes too high, its efficiency will decline for three reasons: (1) the neglect of consumption will adversely affect the masses' incentive to produce; (2) the resultant excessive scale of investment will create shortages of materials; and (3) it will adversely affect the development of agriculture and light industry, which in turn will affect the production of consumer goods (Liu Guoguang and Wang Xiangming, 1980; Liu Guoguang and Zhao Renwei, 1979). These are all sensible arguments, in this author's view, similar to some points expressed in Western development economics.

The bulk of the accumulation fund is used for fixed capital investment (or "basic construction"), which consists of both productive and nonproductive

---

[13] Xue Muqiao (1981: 173–4) makes the good point that the actual accumulation levels were higher than these figures because in agricultural investment projects, which are highly labor-intensive, payments to the peasant laborers are typically included in the consumption fund when in fact they should be included in the accumulation fund.

investment (schools, hospitals, etc.).[14] The proper ratio between productive and nonproductive investment is likened by the Chinese to that between "bones and flesh." On the basis of what prevailed during the First Five-Year Plan period, the Chinese have suggested a ratio of 6:4 as the optimum. The other plan periods had the ratio ranging from 7.5:2.25 to 8.7:1.3, all considered too high for the purpose of improving the people's standard of living (*GMRB*, June 6, 1981: 4).

The proper balance between accumulation and consumption is related to that between heavy industry, on the one hand, and agriculture and light industry, on the other. There are two reasons for this: (1) agriculture is a major source of accumulation for the state through agricultural taxation and the procurement of agricultural products at state-determined prices; (2) agriculture produces food for direct consumption and materials for light industry producing consumer goods. All Chinese economists in the post-1979 period have been critical of China's development strategy adopted since the late 1950s, which favored heavy industry at the expense of agriculture and light industry. As a result of that strategy, a heavy burden was placed on agriculture as a source of accumulation, primarily in the form of low state procurement prices for agricultural products. In the distribution of the accumulation funds, agriculture and light industry also received a disproportionately low share. All of these factors adversely affected the balance between accumulation and consumption. In terms of policy recommendations, the consensus is that agriculture, as the foundation of the economy, should receive the first priority in development, followed by light industry and heavy industry.

Finally, all the optimum balances discussed earlier are related to and partially overlap with the balance between the production of capital goods (Department I) and that of consumer goods (Department II), an issue discussed by Marx in *Capital* (Vol. 3). Chinese economists have touched on whether or not it is an "objective law" for the production of capital goods to grow faster than that of consumer goods and have reached no consensus. Some economists contend that it is an objective law as long as new machines and better technology are being introduced and the organic composition of capital is being raised (Liu Guoguang and Wang Xiangming, 1980: 36; Ouyang Sheng, 1979: 14; Ren Zhongyi, 1980: 5).[15] Others argue that empirically it is not an objective law because, in the industrialized capitalist countries be-

---

[14] The rest of the accumulation fund is used for working capital and reserves.

[15] The organic composition of capital is defined by Marx as the ratio between constant capital and total capital, the latter being the sum of constant and variable capital. In Marx's labor theory of value, "constant capital" refers to the value of past labor embodied in materials and in the depreciation of the plant and equipment used in production. "Variable capital" refers to wage payments to workers for their living labor expended on production.

tween the 1950s and the 1970s, the production of consumer goods grew faster than that of capital goods (*GMRB*, Nov. 28, 1981: 3). All economists agree, however, that the proper balance between the two should be based on the concrete conditions of the economy and that there has long been an imbalance between the two in China in favor of the production of capital goods. Even those who favor faster growth of capital goods as an objective law agree that this should be based on the premise that the standard of living of the population is being continuously raised.

Some economists in the early 1980s also discussed growth models that incorporate some of these optimum ratios or proportions. Because these models are rather complex, they will not be examined here.

Overall balance

All these optimum balances or proportions are closely related to the second type of balance, the overall balance and its components. This concept was first introduced in China in 1951 by Lo Zhongyuan and theoretically elaborated on in 1956 by Ma Yingchu, an eminent economist and former president of Beijing University (Tian Jianghai and Zhong Hua, 1985: 623). During the First Five-Year Plan, veteran planner Chen Yun incorporated some semblance of overall balance in actual planning, which consisted then of the "three great balances" (credit, fiscal, and material balances). In the late 1950s and early 1960s, a lively debate arose in the literature on various related issues such as "active balance versus passive balance" or "short-line planning versus long-line planning," balance versus imbalance, and the relationship between growth rate and balance. Between 1979 and the early 1980s, Chinese economists resumed active discussions of all these issues. In addition, new issues such as the relationship between overall balance and the economic structure and the economic system were introduced. Thus, there is a vast literature on the subject of overall balance, and only some selective issues that reflect major post-Mao changes will be highlighted.

The debate on "active balance" (*jiji pingheng*) versus "passive balance" (*xiaoji pingheng*) started in early 1958 during the Great Leap Forward when an editorial in *Renmin Ribao* [the *People's Daily*] criticized the orientation of the First Five-Year Plan as passive balance and advocated instead active balance (*RMRB*, Feb. 28, 1958). The idea of active balance is to set out with a high target, the highest possible one that can be attained in the priority sector of the economy with a sufficient supply, or "long line" (*changxian*), of materials. Production quotas based on that high target will be assigned to other sectors, including those that have a deficient supply, or "short line" (*duanxian*), of materials. The latter sectors will have to strive to fulfill the quotas, "accomplishing 100 percent of the task with 80 percent of the materials." The strategy is to plan with deliberate "gaps to provide momentum," rather than to plan with "leeway," as was the case during the First Five-Year Plan. Against the background of the Great Leap Forward, the active-balance school of thought rapidly became the mainstream in the literature. Some economists subsequently attacked Ma Yinchu's idea of overall balance and advocated instead imbalance in the economy. Similarly, during the Cultural Revolution, overall balance was criticized as short-line balance, and planning with leeway was criticized as "low target planning" (Tian Jianghai and Zhong Hua, 1985: 638).

Since late 1978, the dominant view among economists has swung back in favor of overall balance. Various economists have criticized the active-balance school of thought as putting a high growth rate above efficiency and sustainable growth, and have criticized planning with gaps for creating imbalances, waste, inefficiency, low growth rates, and even anarchy (Zhou Shulian, 1981). It has been emphasized that overall-balance planning should not contain gaps; on the contrary, allowing for some leeway is desirable (Liu Guoguang, 1979: 42–3; Liu Guoguang and Wang Xiangming, 1980: 41; Tian Jianghai and Liang Wensen, 1978).

The debate on "speed versus balance" has also been resumed. Dong Fureng argues that balance is the prerequisite for a high growth rate. Liu Guoguang advances the idea of "optimum speed," the growth rate that is consistent with overall balance. However, he does not want the planned growth-rate target to be given to the enterprises as a mandatory indicator, but only as a suggested guidance-plan target, to be used by enterprises as a reference figure, subject to revisions so that it will be compatible with micro activities (Tian Jianghai and Zhong Hua, 1985: 640–1). Liu Guoguang's idea of viewing enterprise activities as the "micro foundation of macro balance" is innovative in China, and is consistent with his advocacy of guidance planning and of the planned market, as discussed in Chapter 2.

Finally, in terms of the practical methods of constructing overall balance and relating it to various optimum ratios discussed earlier, post-1979 economists have discussed five methods. Overall balance can be worked out on the basis of any of the following: (1) the core investment projects; (2) the desired accumulation-consumption ratio of the projected national income; (3) sectoral priority; (4) planned output of certain heavy industrial products such as steel; and (5) the consumption needs of the people. The first four methods have been adopted for different plans in the past. The fifth one was proposed by Liang Wensen and Tian Jianghai (1980) at a time of new national emphasis on consumption. On the basis of past experience, Chinese economists generally favor the second method, initially adopted in the Second Five-Year Plan (1958–62), and reject the fourth method, adopted in the late 1950s and from the Third Five-Year Plan (1966–70) through the Fifth

Five-Year Plan (1976–80), as having been a failure (Tian Jianghai and Li Guang'an, 1981: 8–9). Theoretically, however, these methods are not necessarily inconsistent with one another if all the optimum balances discussed earlier are made consistent with one another.

Thus there is continuity as well as basic differences between the post-1979 period and the earlier period – continuity in the framing of issues and the posing of questions and differences in the proposed solutions. The debate is reminiscent of the debate on balanced growth versus unbalanced growth that took place in the 1950s and 1960s in Western development economics, although neither side was aware of the other's existence. Naturally, the Chinese concepts of balance, imbalance, optimum growth rates, and so forth are less precise and rigorous than their Western counterparts because the Chinese did not utilize various useful concepts such as "input-output coefficients," "supply and demand elasticities," and the like until after the mid-1980s. Interestingly, both Chinese advocates of imbalance and Hirschman (1958), the leading advocate of unbalanced growth in the West, linked imbalance with higher growth rates, and did so in a similar fashion – through the "momentum of gaps" (socialist X-efficiency?) in the Chinese case and through the "stimulus of surpluses and shortages" in Hirschman's case. As to their empirical relevance or validity, China's imbalance or active-balance theory was the theoretical rationalization for the planless (or planned?) imbalances and chaos of the Great Leap Forward and the Cultural Revolution. In the West, empirical tests of the unbalanced-growth hypothesis did not support its claim of promoting higher growth rates (Yotopoulos and Lau, 1970). To that extent, proponents of planning balances in the post-Mao period are on solid ground. On the other hand, some of them have gone too far in attributing the higher growth rates of the post-Mao period to the reintroduction of overall balance in planning because structural and systemic changes should have also contributed to the higher growth rates, and because the government in fact failed in several years to attain some of the macro balances, particularly the fiscal balance and the foreign exchange balance.

Some problems

There are problems with China's theory of planning balances and with its implementation. One practical problem with the overall balance is that, to be effective as the major equilibrating mechanism in a centrally planned economy, the plan has to be accurate and comprehensive, containing the general equilibrium solutions to the economy, and faithfully implemented. But in a large, underdeveloped country, the central government cannot possibly plan for everything and control its implementation. Nor has the decentralization of planning authority, as China has periodically undertaken in the past, been effective in bringing about planned balances because of the problems of regionalism and lack of coordination. In other words, mandatory planning in China, whether centralized or decentralized, has not ensured the attainment of overall balance.

Futhermore, in the post-1979 period, the gradual replacement of mandatory planning with guidance planning, coupled with greater enterprise autonomy, as discussed earlier, has created new problems for attaining macro balances. For example, for several years in the 1980s, China's central government attempted to scale down the nation's investment program as part of its effort to correct past excesses and imbalances and to fight inflationary pressures. It was not very successful because of the huge unplanned investment made by local enterprises and local governments that were financed outside the state budget, either by the enterprises and governments themselves or with unplanned credit from local banks. These local investment projects competed with planned state projects for materials, thus upsetting the material balance as well as the fiscal and credit balances. The enterprises and local governments had the incentives and the means to make the extrabudgetary investment because of increased enterprise autonomy to profit from high market prices and because of the "fiscal contract responsibility system" (*caizhen baogan zhidu*) under which local governments were entitled to share excess tax revenues over and above a given amount to be delivered to the central government. Although the central government used various economic levers to increase coordination and macro control, it was not successful for various reasons. For example, attempts to tighten the money supply could not be effective when important local officials were in a position to "certify" the importance of their favored projects in support of requests for loans and when local bankers felt obliged to honor the requests lest they incur official displeasure. In this way, "officials' notes become bank notes" (*tiaozi bian piaozi*).[16] It is not surprising, therefore, that macro balances continued to elude the economy.

Thus we have to conclude that fundamental problems exist with China's planning system and its planning theories. Planned balances in the abstract are attractive features of an idealized socialist economy, but as the actual systemic characteristic of a functioning socialist economy, especially when the economy is also large, bureaucratic, and underdeveloped, they are as difficult, if not more difficult, to attain, as in an unplanned market economy. Socialist planning theories such as those discussed by Chinese economists are potentially useful as guides to or ideals for socialist economic

[16] I am indebted to Huang Fanzhang for this interesting point.

planning, but the gap between planning theory and practice has been wide and difficult to bridge in China's experience. Furthermore, the problem is not primarily due to the lack of planning experience, as many Chinese have claimed. The Chinese economy performed best during the First Five-Year Plan period in terms of growth and macro balances when the Chinese had no prior planning experience. Its performance deteriorated in the subsequent planning periods as the Chinese gained more planning experience, culminating in the anarchy of the Cultural Revolution.

The cause of the disparity between planning theory and reality is essentially political in nature. Between the late 1950s and the late 1970s, the implementation of economic plans was often obstructed by both party leaders (such as the shelving of the Second Five-Year Plan by Mao) and lower-level officials and party cadres. This should not be surprising; the traditional Chinese conception of socialism as a planned and controlled system helps to legitimize and perpetuate the enormous political and administrative power at various levels of government and the Communist Party – power that is often arbitrary, unaccountable, and abused because, in the final analysis, it grows out of "the barrel of a gun," as Mao was fond of saying. Whereas economists are concerned with planning balances, party leaders, bureaucrats, and party cadres who implement the plan have other, more "important" concerns. Thus, unless this power problem can be solved, it is difficult to see how the socialist economy can attain macro balances more readily than the capitalist market economy.

Since the mid-1980s, Chinese economists have adopted a two-pronged approach to macro balances. On the one hand, they have started to learn the theories and techniques of Western monetary and fiscal policies as part of the "Western learning for Chinese use." The objective is no longer to achieve the ambitious overall balance but merely to promote the "basic balance" between aggregate demand and aggregate supply in order to fight inflation. On the other hand, they have increasingly stressed the importance of eliminating political and administrative interference in the operation of the economy, especially at the enterprise level. In other words, political reform is needed for both genuine enterprise autonomy and effective macro policy implementation.

It remains to be seen whether or not party cadres and government bureaucrats can eventually be persuaded to give up some of their power for the sake of China's reforms and modernization. However, the Tiananmen Square massacre of June 1989 does suggest that, under China's current political system, party leaders who derived their power from the barrel of a gun will not hesitate to use the gun again to protect their power and resist meaningful political changes. Thus Chinese reformers face a formidable challenge: how to induce the political power holders to accept a reform that will weaken their own power. Unfortunately but understandably, few Chinese economists have discussed this issue (discussed further in Chapter 6).

At a different level, there are other limitations associated with China's planning theories, as some Chinese economists have pointed out in recent years. First, in their exclusive emphasis on balances and proportions or the lack of them, Chinese planning theorists have ignored the fact that many important economic problems cannot be expressed or solved in terms of balances and proportions. For example, as Yu Guangyuan (1987a: 2), a prominent economist, has pointed out, the location and development of urban areas is not primarily a matter of proportions and balances but one of productivity and locational economics. According to Yu, because of Chinese economists' exclusive concern with planning balances in the past, China has never had an urban development plan. In this author's view, Yu's point is also true with respect to China's numerous development problems, which often cannot be expressed in terms of proportions and balances. Nor are they necessarily macro in nature, which is the traditional emphasis of China's planning theories. As Yu Guangyuan (1984: 201) notes, many of China's development problems are intermediate between macro and micro in scope, or "meso-economic," as he calls them. Since 1984, Yu has repeatedly urged Chinese economists to pay more attention to the meso-economic problems of development. A growing number of economists have come to agree with him, and since the mid-1980s have increasingly focused their attention on development problems as well as the continuing problems of economic reforms. Their discussions of development strategies are examined in Chapter 4.

Another related point is that proponents of overall balance have traditionally failed to pay attention to the composition of aggregate supply and demand. Theoretically, in a developing economy, a good match between the changing composition of supply and demand is as important as, or is indeed a prerequisite for, the attainment of overall balance between aggregate supply and demand. Some of the economic imbalances before 1979 stemmed precisely from the mismatch in composition between industrial production and investment, on the one hand, and consumption and interindustry demand, on the other hand. Since 1979, the composition of both aggregate supply and aggregate demand in China has changed substantially because of reforms and structural changes, yet these have been ignored by economists who have concentrated on the overall balance. It was only in late 1987 after Zhao Ziyang, then the new party secretary general, stressed the strategic importance of reforming the industrial structure that an increasing number of economists began to discuss the improvement of the composition of production and investment.

Last but not least, new theories of "socialist economic cycles" developed in 1984–8 directly contradict the traditional presumption of socialist planned balance. The existence of economic fluctuations in China and their relationship to investment cycles were first explored by Hua Sheng (1984). In 1986–8, many articles on the topic were published. As surveyed by Wang Bifeng (1988), these studies attribute periodic economic fluctuations in China mostly to fluctuations in fixed capital investment. The latter, in turn, are attributed to various causes by different authors – to demand factors such as the "investment hunger" and "consumption thirst" and to supply factors such as low economic efficiency. Others stress the tendency for investment projects to bunch together, thereby causing the cycle to peak, whereas the low efficiency of investment impairs further investment and causes the inevitable downturn (Wang Bifeng, 1988: 77). At least one author, Gong Zhuming (1986), concludes that there is no empirical evidence to suggest that planned economies are more successful than market economies or mixed economies in eliminating economic fluctuations.

A recent cycle theory that is very comprehensive and takes into account the greater autonomy and market orientation of China's reformed enterprises was developed by Li Yining (1987b), a prominent professor of economics at Beijing University. Li contends that it is normal for a socialist economy to experience socialist economic cycles in production and income. The immediate causes of the cycles are changes in enterprise investment in accordance with changes in inventory, market conditions, and profit prospects. Subsequent changes in total output, coupled with changes in the supply of funds and the rate of return on investment, cause enterprises to make further changes in investment and other factors incessantly and cyclically. In the longer run, changes in demand, resource supply, and technology also cause longer cycles. According to Li, the state can use financial tools to dampen the cycles but not to eliminate them.

A different type of cycle theory, developed by Du Hui (1988), is based on the concept of "resource constraints," which are caused by shortages in various factors of production. "Normal resource constraints" are the regular shortages of the socialist economy, which can be alleviated through queuing, rationing, and other short-term measures. "Contradictory resource constraints" are more critical shortages such as those in energy and raw materials. The cause of these constraints is structural – the slower growth of the energy and raw material sectors compared with that of total investment in the economy. Over several years (on average, five years in China), the discrepancy can be eliminated, but it will reappear due to investment expansion, which is inherent in socialist countries' overemphasis on heavy industries.

Although China's theories of economic fluctuations are still rudimentary – for example, it has not been rigorously demonstrated that the fluctuations are necessarily cyclical – and although it is still too early to predict their eventual influence, they do have much intuitive appeal and empirical relevance in light of China's experience. If the theories become widely accepted, as they probably will, then the last theoretical or ideological basis of the presumed socialist superiority – that socialist economies, unlike capitalist ones, are immune to cyclical fluctuations – will have disappeared even in the minds of Chinese economists themselves. The next logical question to ask, therefore, is: What is left of socialism in China? We return to this question in Chapter 6.

Conclusion

On all important aspects of the socialist economy – ownership of the means of production, distribution of income, enterprise management, and macro planning and balances – Chinese economists since 1979 have revised considerably their traditional views. The change first took place in the early 1980s in the areas of macro planning and enterprise management, and only since the mid-1980s in the area of ownership, because the former involve primarily changes in planning techniques and management practices, whereas the latter entails more fundmental changes in the economic system and in basic beliefs, which the Chinese are more reluctant to undertake.

Interestingly, young radical economists in China such as Hua Sheng, Zhang Xuejun, and Luo Xiaopeng (1988b: 30) consider all these presumed aspects of socialism discussed earlier as "elements of fantasy" in Marx's speculation about socialism, and they contend that it is the "distorted and prolonged development of these fantasies," while forsaking the essence of Marxism, that are the economic and political causes of the challenge to socialism in the last half-century. The majority of China's leading economists, however, are more circumspect and only say that what Marx and Engels said about socialism is more appropriate for the mature stage of socialism.

Chinese economists have gone to great lengths to justify their new views as being consistent with socialism, given China's current conditions; the theory of the primary stage of socialism is the major product of this effort. But what is important to this author is that, whatever the ideological label, Chinese economists' new views are more consistent with the requirements of economic incentives and efficiency. Although the new theories have limitations of their own, in due course they will undergo revisions – the political environment permitting – as their limitations become apparent. This is the way analytical advances are made, in China as elsewhere. It is heartening that Chinese reformist economists have taken the first step, the most important and difficult step, in getting rid of the dogmatism of the past interpretations of socialism. And in so doing, Chinese economics has entered a new age.

CHAPTER 4

Strategies of economic development

As Chinese economists became more development conscious in the 1980s, development economics became a main element of China's functional economics. China's post-1979 development economics differs greatly from the previous socialist development literature in many ways. It is much less ideological and more concerned with productivity and technology. It shares with Western development economics the objectives of increasing per capita income, GNP growth rate, and factor productivity. It also accepts and utilizes many concepts, theories, and methods of Western development economics, which were first introduced into China in the late 1970s. The term "strategy" in relation to economic development is one of the concepts introduced; in recent years, it has been widely used by Chinese economists. In a broader sense, because institutional change is part of economic development, many of the Chinese theories of economic reform can be viewed as part of China's new development economics as broadly defined.

In this chapter, we first examine the overall development strategy of China and its implications for income distribution. Then we examine in more detail Chinese economists' views concerning the development of agriculture, industry, foreign trade, capital, and technology.

Efficiency and equality

How should one characterize China's overall development strategy in the 1979–1988 period? Lippit (1987: 212) stresses the central role of economic reforms and states that the reform "implies a strategy of development that maximizes the autonomy of producing units and individuals and uses their initiative to replace centrally directed physical capital formation as the prime motive force of development." This characterization focuses on the level of decision making and the nature of incentives as the central aspect of the new development strategy.

Many Chinese economists would disagree with this characterization. Although China's reforms are far from complete, the reforms that have been introduced to date are not designed to give enterprises and individuals *maximum* autonomy and initiatives as the strategy of development. Most

106

economists still want the state to play an important role in China's economic development. In fact, some economists, such as Yu Zuyao (1988) of the Institute of Economics, the Chinese Academy of Social Sciences, see various contradictions between the reforms introduced to date and economic development, and have recommended additional reforms to *reduce* enterprise and individual autonomy in order to facilitate development. For example, household farming contradicts economies of scale in farming, and a larger scale of farming is recommended; full financial autonomy of enterprises reduces state fiscal revenue for investment, and some reduction in the former is therefore recommended (Yu Zuyao, 1988).

From a different perspective, Dong Fureng (1986a: 67) states that a country's development strategy is necessarily multidimensional, and he criticizes Western development economists' tendency to stress one particular aspect of development strategy, such as the outward-looking development strategy and the inward-looking or import-substitution development strategy. Thus, one would expect him to object to Lippit's emphasis on microautonomy as being too narrow. Instead, he characterizes China's development strategy as follows: (1) its primary objective is to satisfy the people's needs; (2) it is balanced and coordinated; (3) it focuses on increasing economic benefits and promoting intensive growth; and (4) it adopts an open-economy policy toward the rest of the world (Dong Fureng, 1986a: 60–3; 1988a: 62–81).

Alternatively, Liu Guoguang (1987a: 154) opts for simplicity and argues that the essence of the new development strategy lies in the shift from the traditional "speed-centered development" to "efficiency and benefits-centered development," with its attendant emphasis on higher-quality products, lower costs of production, a rational economic structure, and so forth. This characterization is commonly accepted by Chinese economists. As a description of the *ideal* of reforms and the direction of change it is no doubt accurate, but it is not a description of the reality of China's development. Liu's characterization is nevertheless useful, for it captures the spirit of reform and at the same time reflects the new emphasis on economic benefits and efficiency. And although Dong Fureng's (1986a) multidimensional approach is also useful, it is often desirable or necessary to concentrate on the most important characteristic of a country's development strategy for comparison or analysis. Consequently, in this chapter we use Liu Guoguang's (1987a) emphasis on efficiency as Chinese economists' characterization of China's development strategy, and examine the manner in which and the extent to which Chinese economists have advocated policy measures that are consistent with that professed strategy.

Since the early 1980s, a growing number of Chinese economists have followed the Western practice of using the term "economic efficiency" to mean both *technical efficiency* in terms of the best input–output relationship and *allocative efficiency* in terms of the optimum allocation of resources. The optimum allocation of resources is generally and vaguely defined by the Chinese to mean the use of resources that is consistent with natural conditions, is responsive to society's needs, and is capable of bringing about the best economic benefits. However, the full implications of such an efficient allocation of resources are not always appreciated or emphasized by Chinese economists. For example, although prices play a crucial role in allocative efficiency, it was only after the mid-1980s that the need for rational prices – that is, prices that reflect both supply and demand – was widely accepted (see Chapter 5). In the early 1980s, some economists even argued that changes in prices would change income distribution but would not increase society's total income or wealth (Lu Wen, 1982: 8; Yang Fangxun, 1982: 27–8). Their concept of efficiency, then, was primarily that of technical efficiency. The dramatic increases in agricultural output in the early 1980s following the increases in government agricultural procurement prices and other rural reforms have demonstrated the importance of prices in economic efficiency.

Given the new emphasis on efficiency in the development strategy, what are the implications for equality, an important socialist ideal? Are efficiency and equality compatible, or are there trade-offs between the two? These are important questions in both diagnostic and functional economics.

These questions became important in the early 1980s when it became increasingly clear that reforms in the rural areas had made a small number of peasants exceptionally wealthy by China's standards. As early as 1983, the rural nouveau riche were defended by some economists as conducive to "common socialist prosperity" because they set an example for others to follow (*RMRB*, Aug. 15, 1983: 5). The official position on this issue was given in a speech in 1985 by Du Runsheng, a high official involved in rural policy making. Du reiterated the party's goal of common prosperity for all but argued that in the process of reaching that goal, it is desirable to let some people become rich before others, thereby creating the examples and the wealth to help make the others wealthy. Otherwise, equality will simply mean equal poverty for all. Furthermore, public ownership of the means of production will ensure that the "temporary" inequality will not become excessive or permanent. Thus, unlike the situation under capitalism, there will be no insoluble conflict between efficiency and equality under socialism (*RMRB*, Jan. 27, 1986: 3). In this manner, Du's speech officially sanctioned the "temporary" trade-off between efficiency and equality under socialism.

Du's policy statement is based on intuitive reasoning that, except for its implied time horizon, is consistent with Kuznets's (1955) thesis of an inverted U curve in income distribution – inequality first rises and then falls as a country develops; it is also consistent with the findings of a cross-sectional study of many countries made by Chenery, Ahluwalia, Bell, Duloy, and Jolly (1972). However, this is not the first time such an idea was advanced in China. As early as 1962, Wang Yang hypothesized that income distribution in China might first become more unequal as productivity developed before becoming more equal at an advanced stage of socialism (Zhao Renwei, 1985b: 12). However, both Kuznets's thesis and Wang's hypothesis relate to very-long-term trends, whereas Du's policy statement implies that the eventual decline in inequality will occur within a relatively short period of time. Yet if one applies the official primary-stage theory of socialism to this issue – the belief that China will remain at the primary stage for a long time – one infers that the Chinese leadership is prepared to see the increasing inequality continue for a long time before expecting it to decline.

The new official position is generally supported by reformist economists on the grounds that it is conducive to efficiency and is consistent with the socialist principle of "distribution according to labor" (discussed further in Chapter 5). In addition, some have justified it by reinterpreting equality, as discussed later in this chapter. Zhao Renwei (1985b) and others support it on the basis of Kuznets's findings and on the grounds that various empirical studies have shown China's Gini coefficient – a commonly used measure of income inequality in Western economics – in the early 1980s to be much lower than that of capitalist countries to begin with. However, a few economists are uncertain whether it is appropriate to use the Gini coefficient to measure income distribution under socialism (Zhao Renwei, 1985b: 12–14). Still others have suggested measures that will limit the extent of inequality while pursuing efficiency. Taken together, these discussions have covered the ideological and functional aspects of the issue.

At the ideological level, one popular revisionist interpretation of equality is made by Zhou Weimin and Ru Zhongyuan (1986). They contend that the Marxist concept of equality really means equality of opportunity, not equality of the end result or of wealth. Since equality of opportunity does not discriminate on the basis of race, sex, age, and so forth, and permits all to compete, it is fair and consistent with efficiency and is conducive to the creation of wealth to the benefit of all. In other words, to Zhou and Ru, fairness is no longer equated with egalitarianism, as shown in the past practice of everyone eating out of the same big pot.

This new conception of equality is a reaction against the excessive egalitarian ideology and policy of the past, which is still distorting China's post-Mao wage structure (see Chapter 5). As such, it risks "throwing the baby away with the bath water" by glossing over a legitimate socialist concern over the distribution of income. Nevertheless, the argument is sensible and realistic in China's context; it is also consistent with the reformist emphasis on efficiency. Consequently, it is widely supported by other economists (*GMRB*, Dec. 14, 1987: 3; Feb. 11, 1988: 3; Aug. 6, 1988: 1; Oct. 24, 1988: 3; *JJRB*, Dec. 20, 1988: 3; *JJYJ*, 1986, No. 7: 78–81).

If it is desirable to permit some people to become rich before others, who should these people be and what should be the extent of income differentials? There is a consensus among economists that those who contribute most to the creation of society's wealth, thereby setting a good example for others, deserve to become rich first. Here is the embryo of a marginal-social-product theory of income distribution. Entrepreneurs are invariably considered to be among these people. Others are scientists, including social scientists, and outstanding laborers (*GMRB* interview with Xiao Zhuoji, Dec. 24, 1987: 2). He Wei (1987a,b) of the People's University considers managers of large and medium-sized enterprises to be the primary creaters of society's wealth. He suggests that these managers deserve high incomes because their incomes consist of two components: labor income based on "distribution according to labor" and risk income as compensation for the risks they bear. The former may be three to five times the average wages of factory workers; the latter should be in proportion to management performance and the amount of risk borne, and should have no upper limits.

He's concept of risk income echoes the new official position, as expressed by then new party leader Zhao Ziyang in his report to the Thirteenth Party Congress in October 1987, that "enterprise managers' incomes should include, in part, compensation for risks" (*RMRB*, Nov. 4, 1987: 3). It is reminiscent of Frank Knight's (1921) conception of capitalist profit as the reward for taking risks and of the general Western concept of risk premium, that is, the additional return to capital that is necessary to entice investors to invest in risky businesses. The similarity, however, is more apparent than real. Unlike risk-taking capitalists, Chinese managers of large and medium-sized enterprises do not have personal funds invested in their enterprises; they are merely state employees. Entrepreneurs who run state-owned enterprises under the new management contract responsibility system may run greater risks because they may use personal property or funds as collateral to guarantee the fulfillment of contract targets. However, if the contractor loses money and cannot fulfill the contract for reasons beyond his control, such as inflation, he is usually not held accountable. It is not clear, therefore, what extraordinary risks managers bear compared with those of other state employees to justify a risk income that does not require an upper limit in He Wei's view. In addition, even if managers do bear more risks than ordinary workers, operationally in the absence of a competitive labor market, it is not clear how their risks are to be measured in order to determine their risk income. Finally, because Chinese prices are still irrational (see Chapter 5), enterprise profits do not accurately reflect management performance and the amount of risk borne. For these reasons, the theory is still analytically crude, and one can expect Chinese economists' views on efficiency and equality to continue to evolve.

In personal conversations, He Wei qualifies his view by introducing the concept of two-step income distribution, that is, income distribution before and after income taxes. The view discussed earlier relates to the pretax distribution. Pretax incomes should be based on contribution or efficiency alone, without upper limits. These income levels determine the level of social status and prestige. The second-step or posttax income distribution determines the level of consumption; hence the differentials should not be excessive (author's interview, May 30, 1989). He Wei's idea, though not novel to Westerners, is relatively new in China because traditionally income tax was nonexistent there and the government minimized consumption differentials by minimizing income differentials, thereby inadvertently reducing incentives and efficiency. The question remains, however, whether the Chinese would be motivated by larger pretax income differentials and social prestige, as He Wei claims, or whether they are more concerned with posttax incomes and consumption, as seems to be the case in other countries.

Another group of people who have received relatively high incomes and hence much media attention are the self-employed "individual business operators" (geti jingyingzhe or getihu). This group first came into existence in 1978 when the government decided to permit private individuals to engage in petty trades and services – areas where the state sector has performed poorly – in order to help solve a growing unemployment problem. Starting with a very small number, by 1988 they numbered about 15 million (RMRB, July 11, 1988: 1). Because they provide much needed services and are flexible in terms of business hours and locations, they have prospered in general and tend to earn more, sometimes many times more, than state employees. This has caused much unease and resentment, leading to such popular lines as "surgeons make less than barbers" and "missile experts make less than shoe repairmen."

This perception of unfair income differentials is demoralizing to the populace and injurious to the cause of reforms (see also Chapter 5 on wage reform). Many economists have tried to solve the problem by placing the issue in a broader context, suggesting that the differentials are not generally excessive once other relevant factors are taken into account. For example, Zhang Xianyang (1988) and many other authors have pointed out that the earnings of individual business operators include not only wage income but also property income, risk income, and transfer income. On the other hand, state employees receive much more than wages; they get transfer income in the forms of subsidized housing, medical care, pensions, and so forth, which the individual operators are not entitled to. In addition, the latter pay taxes to the government and provide employment opportunities to other people without the need for state investment. Finally, they have to work longer hours, often with their families' help, under more difficult working conditions, and their profits are by no means guaranteed. The general conclusion tends to be that as long as there is equality of opportunity and as long as no laws are violated, the income differentials are no cause for concern (*GMRB*, July 2, 1988: 3; Aug. 6, 1988: 1; *RMRB*, July 11, 1988: 1).

The concept of risk income is widely accepted by Chinese economists. Most authors no longer touch on the tissue of capitalist exploitation, but there are a few exceptions. Li Xuai (1988: 50-1) of Xiamen University cautions that risk income is an element of capitalism and should not be "purified" theoretically into something noncapitalist or even socialist. His reasoning is that risk taking does not create value; only labor can create value from the Marxist perspective. Risk taking is only a reason for appropriating value, and it does not change the "fact" that other people's labor is appropriated "without compensation." Nevertheless, he concedes that this is acceptable in China now because, from a Marxist viewpoint, remnants of capitalism, including exploitation, are inevitable and even necessary at the primary stage of socialism. The new society in its infancy needs to use remnants of the old society to build itself, as was the case with capitalism in its early stage.

In short, in the trade-off between efficiency and equality, equality has been reinterpreted flexibly – or "historically," as many Chinese would say – in support of reform and efficiency. In the following, we examine how the Chinese apply the efficiency-oriented development strategy to different sectors of the economy.

Agricultural development

Regional comparative advantage and allocative efficiency

Between the founding of the People's Republic of China in 1949 and 1979, efforts to develop agriculture took place mainly in two areas: institutional changes and technological changes. The former were aimed at changing the "production relations" in agriculture and included the land reform (1950-2), agricultural collectivization (1953-7), communalization (1958-60), and subsequent internal organizational changes within the communes. In Western economic terms, these institutional changes were aimed at increasing the X-efficiency of the peasants, although the actual result was often X-inefficiency. Collectivization of agriculture also had the intended effects of siphoning off economic surplus for collective investment and increasing the economics of scale in farm operations, thus increasing the technical efficiency of production. Efforts to introduce technological changes were aimed at raising the productivity of land and labor through mechanization, electrification, irrigation, and fertilization. Labor-intensive capital projects were also constructed to improve the quality of farmland. All of these projects were pursued with various degrees of success.

However, allocative efficiency in agriculture was lacking. This was the result of government control of the prices and distribution of major agricultural products, and of the disregard of regional comparative advantage in different crops in government agricultural planning. As discussed in Chapter 3, the traditional rationale for central planning was based on the principle of the proper relationship between the whole and the parts under socialism. An important application of that principle to agriculture concerns the issue of regional specialization in accordance with regional or local comparative advantage or superior conditions (*difang youshi*).[1] The dominant view before 1978 was that the nature of a region's true comparative advantage cannot be determined in the narrow context of regional costs and benefits; it can only be determined in the larger context of national costs and benefits. Thus regions may be discouraged from growing lucrative economic crops because food grains are considered to be the nation's priority crops. This emphasis on the vertical relationship in determining regional comparative advantage differs completely from the Western approach, which compares a region's costs and prices with those of other regions in a horizontal market relationship.

The practical consequence of this Chinese principle was to justify the authority of the central government over the regions in production decisions concerning important agricultural products, because theoretically the state has already taken into account both national and regional costs and benefits, whereas the regions are not in a position to undertake such calculations. Thus, for the regions, to follow the national plan is to pursue their true comparative advantage.

Early post-Mao authors agreed that regional comparative advantage has to be determined in the national context in accordance with national needs and priorities. However, many also pointed out that national priorities can be set unscientifically or undemocratically by the leaders, resulting in irrational patterns of cropping in the regions. For example, during much of the 1960s and 1970s, party leaders made it a national priority to make all regions self-sufficient in food grain. This led to indiscriminate deforestation and

---

[1] The Chinese commonly use the term *youshi* to refer to the superior or favorable conditions of a region or locality. It can mean absolute and/or comparative advantage, depending on the context.

reclamation of land in order to increase farmland, resulting in severe environmental problems. Regions best suited to economic crops such as sugar cane, tea, and tobacco had to divert part or much of their land to grain crops. As a result, their grain yield was low. Furthermore, China had to pay much more to import sugar than it would have paid to import more grain. As late as 1978, then party chairman Hua Guofeng still urged the grain-deficient provinces to become self-sufficient in grain within a few years, citing the experience of European countries comparable to China's provinces in area and population as proof that the goal could be attained (*HQ*, No. 8, 1978: 30).

The allocative inefficiency that resulted from this grain-centered policy was so flagrant that in the early 1980s there was a chorus of criticism by a large number of Chinese economists; the obsession with regional self-sufficiency in grain was criticized as irrational, and a diversified agriculture was advocated. The new consensus was that "it is only when the advantages of the regions are fully utilized that the greatest economic benefit for the nation can be achieved" (*GMRB*, May 10, 1980: 4; June 14, 1980: 4). This is certainly a valid application of the theory of comparable advantage to agricultural production in regions of a country.

Nevertheless, grain procurement was an important part of state planning in the early 1980s, and the government was alarmed that many peasants had switched production from grains to other, more lucrative crops and sideline activities because state grain procurement prices remained relatively low despite successive increases. This created a dilemma for economists. On the one hand, they realized that low procurement prices provided little incentive for peasants to grow and sell grains to the state. On the other hand, they hesitated to recommend large, rapid increases in procurement prices for fear of large government deficits. Also, the majority of them did not want to raise grain retail prices in the cities to pay for higher procurement prices because this would be inflationary. For these reasons, some economists argued that changes in relative prices would not increase real national income and wealth; they would only result in redistribution of income (Lu Wen, 1982: 8; Yang Fangxun, 1982: 27–8).

Following the same logic, some economists argued that regional comparative advantage and specialization should be based on the level of physical productivity, as determined by natural and technical conditions, rather than on price and profit considerations, and that specialization on the basis of the latter would not increase real national wealth because the output of higher-priced crops would be increased at the expense of that of lower-priced crops (*JJRB*, Feb. 4, 1983: 3; Lu Wen, 1982; 7–8). Consequently, peasants should ignore the profit differentials of different crops and resist the temptation to grow crops with relatively higher prices. In addition, regional specialization in a product is beneficial to the nation only to the extent that it follows the proper proportions and national needs, as specified in the plan. Otherwise, there will be "blind production," resulting in imbalances in the economy such as overproduction in the regions (*GMRB*, June 14, 1980: 4; Lu Wen, 1982: 8; Qin Ming, 1980: 60–1). It follows, therefore, that the comparative advantage of a region has to be determined in the context of the whole nation because the consequences of a region's production cannot be seen in isolation from the rest of the nation and because the "overall proportions and needs" of the country have to be taken into account (*GMRB*, June 14, 1980: 4; Lu Wen, 1982: 8; *ZGCMB*, Feb. 27, 1982: 1). Furthermore, because the state is in a better position than the regions to know the overall proportions and needs, the regions should follow the state's plan and the grain procurement contract (*GMRB*, June 14, 1980: 4; Li Zhe, 1981: 49–50; Lu Wen, 1982: 8–9).

In short, Chinese economists' understanding and exposition of allocative efficiency and regional comparative advantage as applied to agriculture had a difficult birth and a confused infancy in the early 1980s, partly because of conflicting policy objectives. On the one hand, Chinese economists criticized past crop priorities as inefficient and advocated allocative efficiency in accordance with regional advantages. On the other hand, many of them acquiesced in the face of irrational prices that are not consistent with allocative efficiency. In addition, they concluded, using circular reasoning, that the state knows best the true advantages of the regions and should plan accordingly. The regions therefore should follow the state's guidance.

To do justice to Chinese economists, it should be pointed out that theoretically, planning and comparative advantage can be compatible if the planners are competent and undertake a careful cost–benefit analysis using prices that reflect the true resource cost of production. And where externalities in production exist, competent planners are certainly in a better position to take them into account than local producers. Chinese economists' emphasis on overall situations and priorities are consistent with this belief. In the Western development literature, Chenery (1955) and some other economists have long shown that it is possible to integrate planning with comparative advantage through the use of input–output data and shadow prices if prices are not scarcity prices.

In her critique of Chinese agricultural policies in the early 1980s, Hartford (1985: 57) referred to the "*inherent* contradiction between comparative advantage and planning" as a basis of her analysis (italics mine). Her assumption of this general inherent contradiction is not justified, for reasons given earlier. However, Chinese economists in the early 1980s characteristically based their arguments on ideal assumptions that are not valid in China. Chinese planners have not been theoretically and technically competent and are not in a position to make a national agricultural plan that will scientifically determine and incorporate the true comparative advantages of the regions. Nor are they in a position to incorporate the externalities of crop production in various localities; in the past, it was the national crop priorities, rather than the production decision of the localities, that caused such negative externalities as environmental degradation. Such unwarranted confidence in the competence of the planners also ran counter to the spirit of market-oriented reforms in the post-Mao period. Consequently, Chinese economists' muddled theories of comparative advantage in the early 1980s gave undue support to the lingering state control in agriculture and may have helped delay the introduction of necessary changes to make Chinese agriculture more efficient.

Starting in 1985, a dual-track agricultural price system was introduced under which peasants can sell their surplus grains over and above the contract sales to the government at higher market prices. The intent of the dual-track price system is to combine market forces with planning in the production of important products (see Chapters 2 and 5). Thus the problem of allocative inefficiency in agriculture due to artificially low prices was partially eased, at least initially. However, state grain purchase prices have remained low relative to the prices of cash crops and to those of industrial and consumer goods sold to the peasants. As a result, peasants' incentives to grow grains have been low under the dual-track price system (see Chapter 5).

Finally, if the principles of comparative advantage and allocative efficiency are pushed to their logical conclusions, shouldn't China give up self-sufficiency in food grains and concentrate on the production and export of labor-intensive manufactured goods, in which it has a comparative advantage, and import land-intensive grains as well as technology-intensive capital goods? As we see later in the chapter, China has become more export oriented, and some economists have advocated an outward-looking trade and development strategy. However, all advocates of the export-oriented strategy want to use export earnings to import technology and capital goods, not food. Yet in terms of factor proportions, China has more than 20 percent of the world's population and only 7 percent of the world's arable land. In addition, in terms of transportation costs, it may be cheaper for China's coastal areas to purchase grains from abroad than from China's inland provinces. Calculations made by Yang and Tyers (1989) show that a food self-sufficiency policy in China in the early 1990s would entail high economic costs – more than 2 percent of GNP annually – because of trade distortions. Thus, strictly from a narrow cost–benefit viewpoint, it would be sensible for China's heavily populated coastal areas to export simple manufactured goods in exchange for imports of grains. In fact, socialist ideology notwithstanding, China has not been averse to making a socialist profit in a capitalist market in the past. For many years, China has been exporting small amounts of rice in exchange for imports of wheat to take advantage of the price differentials in the world market. Yet not a single Chinese economist has ever entertained the idea of large food imports, so far as this author knows. Why?

When asked this question, Qin Qiming, a senior researcher at the Institute of Rural Development, the Chinese Academy of Social Sciences, gave two reasons: (1) the quality of China's manufactured goods is not high enough to finance large imports of food, and (2) the transportation cost to the interior is such that it would be cheaper for inland areas to produce food themselves. He admitted that it is conceivable that in the distant future, the coastal areas may depend on food imports and concentrate on the export of manufactured goods.

Yet one suspects that more fundamental reasons are involved in the Chinese reticence about the possibility of large food imports. There is an age-old Chinese saying that "China as a nation is based on agriculture" (*yi nong li guo*). Although not always efficient, China's agriculture has sustained its population for thousands of years, and the idea that it may cease to do so is simply unthinkable. Furthermore, food imports can be interrupted during international hostilities, and China's memory of the American embargo must still be fresh. Finally, as discussed later, the Chinese firmly believe that with modernization, their agricultural output can still be greatly expanded to feed the population, comparative advantage or no comparative advantage. Thus one can expect the Chinese discussions of comparative advantage and allocative efficiency in agriculture to remain limited to within China's borders. In the context of China, this is understandable.

Agricultural modernization and mechanization

The modernization of agriculture entails raising the productivity of the factors of production used in agriculture. There have been extensive discussions of agricultural modernization in China, especially in the late 1970s and early 1980s, and divergent views have been expressed.

One elementary question debated concerns whether the primary objective of agricultural modernization is to raise the unit yield of land or to raise the productivity of farm labor. A third view would use the three indices of land productivity, labor productivity, and capital utilization to measure the change in total productivity and regards all of them as important (Zhang Lin, 1985: 11). The discussions were not sophisticated because the critical concept of marginal product of the factors of production was not utilized. However, they are relevant for the related discussions on farm mechanization, as we shall see.

Policy debate on the role of mechanization in agricultural modernization has a long history in China. Partly because of the early Soviet influence, Mao Zedong and other leaders had long associated modern agriculture with mechanized agriculture. Thus Mao declared in 1959 that "the fundamental way out for agriculture lies in mechanization." However, state economic planner Bo Yibo contended in the mid-1950s that in labor-surplus China, mechanization was not practical and that measures to increase crop yields per unit of land were more appropriate. Bo's analysis was supported by the results of surveys conducted in 1956 on the potential effect of agricultural mechanization. As a result, the farm mechanization policy formulated in 1956 emphasized the transitional step of improving traditional farm implements. However, the program was not successful because its linchpin – the double-wheel, double-share plow – proved to be unworkable in the south. In the early 1960s, the emphasis was shifted to small hand tractors and other light machines for paddy fields. The same emphasis was continued throughout the mid-1970s, but the program was continuously plagued by shortages of steel, electric power, coal, and gasoline and by organizational and management problems (Hsu, 1982: 69–73; Riskin, 1987: 174–197).

In the post-Mao period, government policy on mechanization also changed over time. In 1977–9, with the new drive toward the Four Modernizations under the leadership of Deng Xiaoping, agricultural mechanization was given high priority as the basis of agricultural modernization. An ambitious agricultural mechanization program was adopted in 1978, which aimed at 70 percent mechanization by 1980 and 85 percent mechanization by 1985 of the "main work" in agriculture. In 1979, however, Chinese leaders readjusted their development priorities and scaled down their ambitious modernization programs because of growing economic imbalances and financial difficulties. As part of the readjustment, the objective of basic mechanization of agriculture by 1980 was abandoned. Since then, Chinese leaders have become more aware of the limitations of mechanization as the major means to agricultural modernization. The policy emphasis in agriculture has also shifted to institutional reforms.

Concurrent with these policy changes, there were debates in the late 1970s and early 1980s on agricultural mechanization. Proponents of mechanization started from the premise that high labor productivity characterizes modern agriculture and that mechanization is the only means to achieve high labor productivity (RMRB, Dec. 8, 1978: 3; Zhang Lin, 1985: 12). In addition, Zhu Daohua (1979) argues that mechanization is an important means of raising the unit yield of land beyond what labor and draft animals can ever accomplish, and that the introduction of improved techniques and inputs such as better seeds, irrigation, chemical fertilizers, and pesticides requires the use of mechanized tools. The same points were made by him in 1963 (*GMRB*, Sept. 16, 1963: 1).

Opponents do not deny the usefulness of mechanization, but they do not think that it should be the central focus of agricultural modernization. They argue that modern biological and chemical techniques have played an increasingly important role in modern agriculture. In addition, mechanization primarily raises labor productivity; this is more appropriate in countries such as the United States and the Soviet Union, where land is abundant and labor relatively scarce. Modern biological and chemical techniques are more effective in raising land yield and are more appropriate in countries such as Japan and China, where land is scarce and labor abundant (Zhang Lin, 1985: 13–14).

According to Qin Qiming, a senior researcher at the Institute of Rural Development, the Chinese Academy of Social Sciences, the majority of Chinese agricultural economists currently regard mechanization as important in China's agricultural development, although not necessarily more important than better seeds and chemical fertilizers. According to him, labor power, even when assisted by draft animals, is not a good substitute for farm machines in some farming activities. For example, draft animals cannot plow as deeply as tractors. However, machine plowing and harvesting are not always economical on small parcels of land cultivated by individual households, as was the case after the introduction of rural reforms. Thus, in recent years, there have been discussions of increasing the scale of farming through farm consolidation in order to facilitate mechanization (author's interview, Aug. 5, 1988).

The pros and cons of mechanization in China, compared with those of alternative methods of raising agricultural output, cannot be determined without careful cost–benefit studies in various farming regions. In this regard, the Chinese discussions have been handicapped by the lack of two useful concepts: agricultural production function and the marginal products of factors of production. Neither supporters nor opponents of mechanization in the early 1980s provided or cited empirical estimates of the marginal product of farm machines and other inputs to support their arguments. This reflects the lack of integration between technical economics and other branches of economics, as mentioned in Chapter 1.

Starting in 1981, because of the agricultural responsibility system, which permitted individual households to become the basic units of farming and which permitted peasants to engage in nonfarming activities, many prosperous rural households had the means as well as the need to purchase small farm machines (*BR*, Nov. 19, 1984: 20–2; *JJRB*, Apr. 11, 1986: 2; July 9,

1988: 3; *RMRB*, May 9, 1983: 5; Nov. 30, 1985: 2). However, the fragmentation of farms under household cultivation limits mechanization to small machines such as hand-held tractors. In addition, peasants often purchase these small tractors for the purpose of transporting agricultural products and materials because they are cheaper than trucks and easier to drive (Qin Qiming, author's interview, Aug. 5, 1988).[2] The acreage plowed and harvested by farm machines has actually declined in recent years.[3] Thus the current status of agricultural mechanization is multifaceted, reflecting the influence of a host of economic factors that affect both the benefits and the costs of mechanization.

The prospects for China's agricultural modernization and the role of mechanization in it are not clear. In terms of potential, the Chinese rightly believe that there is room for further increases in agricultural output. Only one-third of China's farmland produces a high yield. Another one-third produces medium yield and another one-third a low yield. Thus, in spite of an unfavorable population–land ratio, total agricultural output can be expanded with the application of modern science and technology, including mechanization.

The actual pace of agricultural development and the role of mechanization in it, however, will depend on many factors, including the development of the industrial sector and the scale of China's farming units in the future. For both agricultural modernization and mechanization to continue, industries need to produce more and better modern inputs for agriculture and to absorb rural surplus labor. State investment in agriculture needs to be increased. Grain prices need to be raised to provide peasants with more incentives to produce, as well as the means to purchase modern inputs. All of these factors will affect peasants' demand for farm machines. In addition, the scope of mechanization depends on the size of farming units. As mentioned earlier, China's agricultural responsibility system has decentralized farming decision making to the household level. However, with the rapid development of village-township enterprises in the eastern coastal region since the early 1980s (see the next section), many rural households in the region are devoting most of their labor to higher-paying nonagricultural activities. At the same time, they want to hang on to the land allocated to them for their use

---

[2] Xu Hua (1988: 5) has argued that the peasants' primary reason for purchasing hand-held tractors is for transportation, not for agricultural production. As a result, this investment has not benefited agriculture as much as other forms of investment, such as irrigation, production of chemical fertilizer, and so on. This conclusion is not completely valid because transportation is essential if the increased output is to be marketed. It can be argued, however, that a more efficient method of transportation can be organized.

[3] For example, the area plowed by farm machines was 42.4 million hectares in 1979 and 41.0 million hectares in 1980. It declined to 34.4 million hectares in 1985, rising to 36.4 million hectares in 1986 and 38.4 million hectares in 1987. See State Statistical Bureau (1988).

so that they can return readily to farming should their nonagricultural business fail.

The diversion of farm labor to nonagricultural activities has adversely affected agricultural production, particularly grain production. Between 1986 and 1988, grain production in China failed to reach plan targets. In 1988, as grain production declined further from the 1987 level, a new concern was expressed about the need to recentralize farming operations and to increase the scale of farming units (*CD*, July 13, 1988: 4; *GMRB*, Jan. 16, 1988: 3; May 28, 1988: 3; July 9, 1988: 3). One ingenious proposal, made by Li Yining (1988: 10), is to establish "farming and harvesting corporations" and "land deposit banks" or cooperatives. The former would sign contracts with inactive farmers to do their farming and harvesting for a fee. The latter would accept farmers' "deposit" of land or "land use right" and pay "interest" on it; the longer the term of the deposit, the higher the interest rate. In this way, the size of the operating farm could be increased, with benefits to society and farmers alike. If this proposal is adopted, the need for mechanization will be increased.

In short, the future of China's agricultural modernization and mechanization will depend heavily on the organization of land use. China's rural economy has gone through many organizational changes since 1949, and more can be expected in the future.

Labor accumulation

One aspect of agricultural development that has worked relatively well in the past is "labor accumulation" (*laodong jilei*), that is, the mobilization of rural surplus labor, primarily in wintertime, to construct rural capital projects. In Western economics, a similar idea was proposed by Nurkse (1953: 36–47) for the less developed countries. The Chinese have discussed labor accumulation extensively, and these discussions are useful in throwing light on the prerequisites for, and the limitations of, the mobilization of rural surplus labor. In addition, the concept itself is innovative and of analytical interest; Nickum (1974: 165) regards it as Chinese academics' "only major theoretical contribution to Marxist economics."

When the concept of labor accumulation was first discussed in China 1965, it referred to the use of rural labor in the creation of farmland and water conservancy projects, which result in "direct congealment of living labor in agricultural land" (*JJYJ*, No. 9, 1965). Subsequently, however, many authors have used it to refer to a wide range of labor-intensive agricultural basic construction projects such as road construction, housing, forestry, biogas generation, and so forth.

As defined by the Chinese, labor accumulation differs from regular capital accumulation in that the former uses predominantly living labor, does not increase the output of consumer goods in the short run, and can be practiced only by rural organizations by mobilizing their members (Zhang Yinggao, 1983). Given the shortage of capital and farmland and the abundance of labor in rural China, it was appropriate for the government to promote labor accumulation throughout the 1960s and 1970s to develop agriculture. As one facet of the collective life of the rural economy, labor accumulation in China before the late 1970s had the following unique characteristics, which are no longer present in the 1980s: First, the agricultural collectives were responsible for the employment of their members, who were prohibited by the government from migrating to the cities. Thus the collectives were in a unique position to mobilize their members for capital projects. Second, peasant participation in labor accumulation was sometimes compulsory, without pay (corvee labor), and sometimes compensated in the form of work points. The system of income distribution on the basis of work points was effective in providing incentives to the participants; increased work points earned through labor accumulation entitled peasants to a greater share of the collective's income at the time of income distribution. Third, because income distribution according to work points was a type of deferred wage payment, labor accumulation was a non-inflationary method of saving and investment in kind, and peasant consumption might not be increased until real output was increased. Under these conditions, the agricultural collectives practiced, through labor accumulation, what the *Economist* (Dec. 31, 1977: 15–16) aptly called "village Keynesianism," converting surplus labor to capital projects at little opportunity cost.

In the early 1980s, the new leadership continued to promote labor accumulation, as shown in a speech given by then party secretary general Hu Yaobang to the Twelfth Party Congress in 1982. Consequently, a number of articles were published on it in 1982–3. Most of them stressed the importance of expanding labor accumulation to develop agriculture. There was also a consensus that there were many cases of excessive and poorly planned labor accumulation in 1958, the 1960s, and the early 1970s, thereby adversely affecting agricultural production and peasants' incentives (Liang Wensen and Tian Jianghai, 1983; Zhang Yingguo, 1983: 51). Greater efficiency in future labor accumulation was stressed.

There was no consensus, however, on the prospects for labor accumulation under the agricultural responsibility system and with the subsequent breakup of the rural communes. There were two opposing groups – the pessimists and the optimists – concerning the prospects. The pessimists argued that (1) because of the long gestation period involved, peasants would hesitate to invest labor and funds in basic construction projects; (2) with households as the basic unit of operation, it would be more difficult to mobilize the necessary labor and funds; and (3) given the existing low level of consumption, peasant households would be more interested in raising their consumption than in investing (Liu Dong, 1983: 15–16; Zhang Yingguo, 1983: 51).

On the other hand, the optimists contended that labor accumulation could easily be expanded for three reasons: (1) The rural population was growing, whereas the size of farmland had declined. Nonfarm activities and urban employment could not absorb all the new population; hence there would be more surplus labor for labor accumulation. (2) The increased prosperity of many peasant households provided the material conditions for expanded labor accumulation. (3) The peasants needed improved rural infrastructure in order to improve their productivity, and China's rural areas provided a wide range of opportunities for infrastructure improvement (Liu Dong, 1983: 16–17).

The pessimists seemed to rely more on the motivations of the peasants, whereas the optimists relied more on the objective material conditions for their arguments. Overall, the pessimists have been closer to the mark; basic agricultural infrastructure has been neglected in recent years following the dissolution of communes and production brigades. The new village governments are government units and do not want to get involved in labor accumulation projects because now the government is supposed to refrain from interfering in economic activities. However, there are exceptions. Fragmentary evidence suggests that where the local leadership is effective and flexible, labor accumulation need not be adversely affected by the reforms. In some localities, for example, "specialized teams" or "companies" are organized for irrigation and other projects. Peasants engaged in higher-paying nonfarm activities can pay others to do their share of labor accumulation (Putterman, 1985: 72; *RMRB* May 3, 1987: 2). These arrangements facilitate greater division of labor and the winter employment of surplus labor and are, therefore, conducive to greater allocative efficiency. The organization of these types of activities is beyond China's rudimentary and imperfect market mechanism and should, therefore, be the responsibility of village governments. In their reform separating the government from economic activities, some localities seem to have thrown away the "baby" with the bath water in the case of labor accumulation.

Aside from these institutional factors that are specific to China, Chinese economists' discussions have provided the following insights, which should be useful to other developing countries as well:

1. In Western development economics, there is disagreement on whether or not surplus labor with zero marginal labor product is widespread in the less developed countries, so that it can be utilized with no opportunity cost. However, one point that is

often neglected is that even if the surplus labor is truly redundant in the sense that its marginal product in farming is zero, the construction of capital projects with this labor will not be as costless as is often assumed. Some tools and materials are needed because the peasants cannot dig ditches with their bare hands and build dams with dirt alone. Liang Wensen and Tian Jianghai (1983) cite five water conservancy projects in Jiangsu province that are considered typical labor accumulation projects. The value of labor was 48.6 percent of the total costs; the rest consisted of materials and the depreciation of tools, which were jointly financed by the state and local collectives.

2. It is unrealistic to assume that the consumption of project workers will not increase once they are employed on the construction projects, as is often assumed in the Western development literature; it will increase because construction activities are more vigorous than low-productivity farm work and because the peasant workers' incomes will increase. And given the generally long gestation period before these projects actually increase agriculture's output, the inflationary potential of the wage payments cannot be ignored. Thus large-scale, labor-intensive projects may have the additional cost of reducing consumption for the rest of the village community due to inflation before agricultural output can be raised by the projects.

3. It is unrealistic to assume that the use of seasonal surplus labor can be fine-tuned to coincide with slack farming seasons so that the employment will have no opportunity cost. Many construction projects take a long time to complete. And once a project is underway, it cannot be turned on and off easily without incurring great wastes. Chinese authors have cited cases in which winter projects were extended well into the summer season, thereby creating a labor shortage on the farms and adversely affecting agricultural output and peasant incentives (Zhang Yingguo, 1983). Thus, where surplus labor is seasonal, as is often the case, it would be prudent not to assume that the use of such labor will have zero opportunity costs.

In conclusion, the significance of the Chinese concept of labor accumulation goes beyond its contribution to Marxist economics. It enriches the world's economic development literature and enhances economists' understanding of the implications of mobilizing rural surplus labor in the less developed countries.

In addition to investment in the form of labor accumulation, China's agriculture needs continuous state investment in projects that are beyond the capabilities of local communities. However, this was given a low priority by the government in the 1980s because of the latter's preoccupation with reforms, industrial development, and the open-door policy. Similarly, Chinese economists in general have paid much more attention to industrialization and export promotion as the vehicles of economic development, as we shall see.

Industrial development

Industrial development in a developing country involves many dimensions: investment priorities, industrial policy, regional development policy, choice of technology, intersectoral relationship with agriculture, industrial organization, and so forth. Chinese economists have discussed these issues to various extents, making their discussions multifaceted. A complete study of these discussions is beyond the scope of this book. We examine a few selective aspects that best illustrate the application of the new efficiency-oriented strategy of development and the problems encountered.

Allocative efficiency and rural industrialization

As mentioned earlier, Chinese economists' concept of efficiency includes both technical and allocative efficiency. However, in industry as in agriculture, conflicting policy objectives and imperfections in the allocative mechanism have made it difficult for economists to elucidate the concept of efficiency clearly and to propound its logical policy implications.

Prior to the late 1970s, China's radical leaders stressed the Maoist principle of "self-reliance" in national development. With the ascendancy of the extreme leftist ideology during the Cultural Revolution, that principle was indiscriminately applied to industrial development at both enterprise and regional levels. At the enterprise level, that principle was reinforced by the fact that under the traditional planning system, there were administrative barriers to exchanges and division of labor between state-owned enterprises under different ministries or in different administrative areas. In addition, there were no incentives for these enterprises to cut costs by specialization because the planned prices for their products were generally based on the "average-cost-plus" principle, and there was no market competition under the planning system to spur cost-cutting efforts. As a result, enterprises strove to be self-reliant by producing as many parts for their products as possible, regardless of objective conditions.

Local areas and even collectively owned rural enterprises also strove to be self-sufficient. Regions attempted to be self-reliant in some areas of industrial production by setting up trade barriers such as "export" levies on raw materials and by prohibiting the "import" of outside products. In some instances, rural collective enterprises that had signed contracts with enterprises outside local areas for subcontracting or sales were ordered by local party leaders to cancel the contracts (HQ, No. 6, 1975: 23; No. 7, 1975: 35).

As a reaction against this flagrant allocative inefficiency, in the early 1980s Chinese economists started advocating greater division of labor and specialization among enterprises in different industries and regions as the way to achieve greater efficiency. To facilitate this in the absence of a well-functioning market mechanism, Chinese economists often advocated the establishment, through negotiation and contract, of cooperative arrangement – such as subcontracting for parts and intermediate products and sales agreements – between enterprises in different industries and regions (GMRB, Apr. 18, 1981: 4; Huang Rongsheng, 1983; RMRB, Apr. 13, 1984: 5).

In spite of economists' exhortation, throughout the 1980s the actual improvement in allocative efficiency through greater division of labor between enterprises and regions was probably limited; it was impeded by widespread interregional trade barriers set up by local governments (usually at the county level) to discourage or prohibit the import of goods from, and export of materials to, other areas in order to protect local industries. Because local governments' revenues depend on local industrial production, local governments have vested interests in establishing and protecting small local enterprises outside the state plan in competition with large state-owned enterprises. Thus raw-material-producing areas set up their own processing plants and diverted raw materials from state procurement to local uses, leaving large state plants idle for lack of raw materials. In Jiang Yiwei's words, economically and fiscally, China is practically divided at the county level into more than two thousand feudal fiefs, each concerned only with its own production and revenue (author's interview, May 20, 1989).

Virtually all Chinese economists have condemned such local practices as contrary to allocative efficiency and national interests. For example, whenever the unplanned small plants in the cigarette industry compete with the larger state-owned plants, they are invariably criticized as being inefficient and undesirable, as "the small squeezing out the large" and "the inefficient squeezing out the efficient" (JJRB, June 4, 1983: 2; Feb. 26, 1987: 1). Similarly, small wineries, textile plants, sugar factories, and canneries that are set up outside the state plan are criticized as inefficient and "small and complete," as invalid cases of developing local comparative advantage (RMRB, Nov. 14, 1983: 1).

In this author's view, to the extent that these local enterprises are established and fostered under *continuous* local protection, they are indeed inconsistent with comparative advantage and allocative efficiency. On the other hand, to the extent that they enjoy an advantage because they are located near the sources of raw material supplies and/or near rural markets, and to the extent that "learning by doing" is involved, the case against them needs to be modified. More important, they have the social benefit of absorbing rural surplus labor, which helps to reduce urban congestion. All these factors have to be taken into account in assessing the overall social costs and benefits of these "inefficient" enterprises.

Ironically, although most economists regard these local enterprises run by county governments as small and inefficient, many economists, as well as Zhao Ziyang, the former party leader, regard the smaller village-township enterprises as holding promise for China's rural industrialization and even export expansion. Since the early 1980s, these enterprises, either privately or collectively owned, have expanded rapidly. In 1987, their output amounted to one-third of the nation's total industrial output, whereas their fixed assets were only one-eighth of the national total. They also earned some $5 billion from exports (*JJGL,* 1988, No. 11: 57). Their rapid growth is generally attributed by supporters to the following factors: (1) they are responsible for their own profits and losses; (2) they have to be responsive to market conditions; and (3) their management is flexible – the very opposite of state-owned enterprises (*JJGL,* 1988, No. 11: 57–9). However, as we shall see, they have also been criticized by other economists for various reasons.

Two types of village-township enterprises have developed in China; both are the product of the reformed rural economy. Chinese economists have dubbed them the "Wenzhou model" and the "Sunan model." The former, named after the city of Wenzhou in Zhejiang province, is based on private household businesses producing small consumer goods, which are marketed by individual merchants far and wide. The latter is based on cooperative township enterprises promoted by township governments. This model is most successful in southern Jiangsu, hence the term "Sunan (southern Jiangsu) model." Both models are touted as examples of the vitality of the rural commodity economy, a product of China's economic reforms.

Enterprises in the Wenzhou model are owned and run either by individual households or jointly by a number of peasant households. Because they are responsible for their own profit and losses, they have to be very responsive to market conditions and tend to be competitive. As a rule, they are not located near large cities and do not compete with or rely on large urban industries. They use labor-intensive methods of production and thus have great potential for absorbing rural surplus labor. On the other hand, the collective township enterprises of the Sunan model are typically larger than the

Wenzhou enterprises. They are technically more advanced, require more capital to set up and operate, and produce higher-quality products. They tend to be located near large cities and either supply parts to larger urban plants or produce products that these large enterprises do not want to produce. Some of their products are even exported (Dong Fureng, 1988a: 176–87).

In a detailed study of the two models, Dong Fureng (1988a: 189–91, 194) concludes that the Sunan model is more conducive to agricultural modernization because part of the enterprise's profits can be easily invested in agriculture by the village-township government, whereas in the Wenzhou model the "peasant entrepreneurs" lack this incentive. On the other hand, enterprises in the Wenzhou model are more dynamic and market-oriented, and provide more rural employment opportunities, which will help reduce urban overcrowding and other problems. Depending on the actual conditions of specific rural areas, one or the other model will be appropriate as the way to promote rural industrialization and modernization.

Dong Fureng's enthusiasm for these new forms of rural industrialization is shared by several of his colleagues at the Institute of Economics, the Chinese Academy of Social Sciences (*JJYJ*, No. 6, 1986: 3–18). However, some of his fellow economists at the Academy have criticized these enterprises on the grounds that they tend to be socially irresponsible in their operations. They pollute the environment, destroy farmland and other natural resources, resort to illegal activities, divert raw materials from planned use by state-owned enterprises, and make excessive profits because, unlike state-owned enterprises, their prices are not set by the state. In addition, these enterprises have diverted too much labor from farming and have adversely affected agricultural production. Thus, although these critics recognize the need for some village-township enterprises, they feel that their recent growth has been excessive (author's interviews, Zhao Renwei, May 19, 1989; Jiang Yiwei, May 20, 1989). Finally, these enterprises have been criticized for having unfair tax advantages. In their efforts to encourage the establishment of these enterprises, some localities have exempted them from paying various taxes for the first few years. Reportedly, some enterprises have abused this privilege by going out of business after a few years and reincorporating under a different name to enjoy the tax-exempt privilege again.[4]

---

[4] I am indebted to an anonymous reviewer for this point. It is not clear, however, how widespread these tax-exempt privileges and abuses are. It should also be pointed out that there is much evidence that these village-township enterprises have been easy prey to unscrupulous local officials for arbitrary taxes and extortion in many localities. Although reliable statistics are lacking, this author feels that these tax burdens tend to outweigh the tax-exempt privileges.

The relative merits of the Wenzhou and Sunan models have also been debated by various economists. Some have criticized the Wenzhou model for promoting private ownership at the expense of public ownership and socialism, and for paying private entrepreneurs and merchants much more than regular farmers and state employees (*JJYJ*, No. 8, 1986: 59–61, 63). These critics suggest, therefore, that the Wenzhou model should be transformed into the Sunan model (ibid: 58). Other authors favor the Sunan model for its greater ability to raise funds (*GMRB*, Aug. 14, 1987: 3).

However, the Sunan model has critics of its own. Wan Jieqiu (1987) of Suzhou University, in particular, is pessimistic about its prospects for the following reasons: (1) Township enterprises produce simple machines, textiles, and other light industrial products, and construction materials. With the exception of construction materials, the market for their products is saturated or will be once the larger state enterprises increase their production of these products. (2) The enterprises are outside the state plan and, therefore, have to compete with larger enterprises for raw materials by paying higher prices for them (see also *JJGG*, No. 1, 1987: 36). (3) They tend to rely on local governments for assistance in obtaining bank loans and raw materials. This leads to administrative interference in enterprise management. (4) These enterprises do not have the funds or the personnel for upgrading their technology. Wan concludes, therefore, that the Sunan model itself requires adjustment and reform to remain competitive. One measure recommended is greater division of labor and cooperation with state enterprises to increase efficiency.

Thus, there is no consensus among Chinese economists on the best approach to rural industrialization. This is not surprising, given the great diversity of China's local conditions and the complexity of the factors affecting rural industries. Most economists agree, however, on the imperative to develop nonagricultural production in the rural areas in order to employ the growing rural surplus labor, given the shortage of arable land in China. From this perspective, the social benefits of rural enterprises – whether they are owned and operated by private households, village-township governments, or county governments – far exceed the profits that accrue to the producers, and any assessment of their efficiency has to include this externality. Another externality that has to be taken into account is the possible foreign exchange earnings. As discussed later in this chapter, in 1988 the government suggested that China's eastern coastal regions adopt an export-expansion strategy of development and that rural enterprises make labor-intensive products for export. Should this strategy prove successful, the resultant foreign exchange earnings will be very useful. Naturally, the negative externality of pollution should also be considered. Finally, barriers to market competition – such as the exclusion from local markets of products produced in outside areas and the preferential treatment of local producers in terms of taxes, loans, and the supply of raw materials – distort the true picture of the relative efficiency and competitiveness of local enterprises and should therefore be considered.

In conclusion, an objective assessment of the relative efficiency and long-term desirability of rural enterprises has to incorporate a number of factors, which may vary greatly from locality to locality and from industry to industry. Consequently, general a priori arguments against these enterprises because of their small size and presumed inefficiency, or in favor of them because of their market competitiveness, tend to be one-sided and may suggest inappropriate policy implications.

Regional comparative advantage and industrialization

At the regional level, allocative efficiency for state investment requires building on the best – that is, allocation of investment funds to the more efficient regions – until the rate of return on the investment is equal in all regions. However, the results of this efficiency principle may conflict with society's goal of balanced regional development. This conflict between efficiency and equality at the regional level and the attempts to resolve it underlie many of the discussions in China concerning industrial development.

For planning and strategic purposes, Chinese planners in the past classified regions of the country in different ways: into coastal and interior regions during the 1950s; into first-line, second-line, and third-line regions in the early 1960s; and into coastal, interior, and minority regions during the Sixth Five-Year-Plan in 1981–5 (Li Hao, Jiang Yiwei, and Zhou Shulian, 1986: 137). During the Seventh Five-Year-Plan (1986–90), the country was divided into the eastern or coastal region, the middle region, and the western region on the basis of the existing level of economic development. The East is more developed, followed by the middle region; the West is the least developed.

On the basis of this classification, Chinese economists have discussed versions of two alternative strategies of industrial development: the equal development strategy and the unequal development strategy. The former would deliberately locate some major industries in the middle and western regions in order to promote more equal development among the regions. The latter would focus first on the development of the East and later on that of the middle and western regions. This strategy is popularly called the *tidu tuijin* model of industrial development – that is, progressive development on the basis of existing differentials. It is analogous to the new income-distribution strategy of permitting some individuals to get rich before others.

In both cases, it is also implied that the eventual catching up will not take very long.

Starting in the 1950s, Chinese leaders repeatedly stressed the development of industrial bases and mineral resources in the interior, which encompassed the western region and part of the middle region. That regional development strategy has not been particularly successful. Although there are relatively developed areas in the western and middle regions (such as Lanzhou and Kunming) and relatively underdeveloped areas in the East (such as Guangxi, as well as mountainous areas in Zhejiang and Fujian), generally speaking, the East remains the most developed region and the West the least developed.

To promote investment efficiency and increase the growth rate, several economists at the Institute of Industrial Economics, the Chinese Academy of Social Sciences, have recommended a two-step industrial development strategy with a twenty-year time horizon. For the 1980s and the first half of the 1990s (the Seventh and Eighth Five-Year Plans), the focus of industrial development should be on the eastern coastal areas and on selective energy bases in the middle region. This would greatly reduce the major constraints on the development of the whole economy in terms of energy, capital, and technology. In the mid-1990s, the middle region should gradually become the focus of development, concentrating on the energy bases and other industrial cities. These would become the "bridgeheads" for future development assistance to the West. After the beginning of the twenty-first century, the focus of development would turn to the West, and Sichuan, Yunnan, Xinjiang, and Qinghai would become China's important industrial bases (Li Hao, Jiang Yiwei, and Zhou Shulian, 1986: 140). This proposal is an important version of the unequal-development strategy mentioned earlier.

Understandably, many economists and government officials of the interior provinces oppose this strategy on the grounds that it will aggravate existing regional inequality. In addition, it has been argued that lack of development in the West may jeopardize its supply of energy and raw materials to the East, and may even cause political and social problems because China's ethnic minorities are heavily concentrated in the West (*JJRB*, May 3, 1988: 3). All these arguments are consistent with Shirk's (1985: 210–16) observation that ever since the early 1980s, China's inland provinces have not been particularly enthusiastic about industrial reforms because they realize that the coastal provinces will gain from the reforms at their expense.

An interesting version of the equal-development strategy is proposed by Wang Zhiyuan and Zeng Xingqun (1988) of the Beijing Academy of Social Sciences and Qinghua University, respectively. They argue that it is inappropriate to discuss China's industrial location in terms of vast areas such as the eastern, middle and the western regions. Within each region there are modern as well as traditional areas, and the differences between China's regions are less than those between the modern and traditional areas within each region. Therefore, they advocate an industrialization strategy that would focus on the modern areas of all three regions. The theoretical basis of this strategy is Perroux's (1981) thesis that industrialization tends to occur unevenly at specific growth poles or growth points where the essential factors of production, infrastructure, and external economies converge, and not evenly throughout a region. In Wang and Zeng's view, all three regions of China contain areas where these favorable conditions for industrialization exist. It is argued that this strategy will not only lead to rapid economic growth, but will also promote the larger national interests in terms of improving national defense, relations with the minorities, the environment, and so forth. On the other hand, the alternative East-to-West strategy would lead to the emergence within China of the disparate first world, second world, and third world, which is contrary to the socialist principle.

At first glance, this strategy has much intuitive appeal. For indeed, it can be argued that it is not the location of an entire region, but the economic conditions of important areas within it – the availability and costs of factors of production and supportive facilities, market conditions, and so forth – that determine its potential for industrial development. One important empirical question, however, concerns the existence and strength of the presumed growth poles in the inland regions. It must be remembered that some of the industrial areas in the interior were created in China's earlier development plans with large state investments. Many of these industries produce energy and industrial materials whose prices and distribution are still controlled by the state. Perroux's growth-pole theory presumes competitive prices and the existence of an integrated regional or national market network. In their absence, it is difficult to assess the viability of the growth poles in the inland regions. In the future, if China's market-oriented reforms are continued and China's interior regions are better integrated with the East in a competitive market, the actual performance of these presumed growth poles of the inland regions will give a better indication of whether they will be competitive enough vis-à-vis the eastern growth poles to be viable.

Between these two strategies, there are various compromise proposals that attempt to pursue both efficiency and regional equality simultaneously. For example, Liu Wei and Yang Yunyou (1988) of Beijing University support the principle of specialization according to regional comparative advantage, which implies faster development of the East. At the same time, they would pursue development in the other regions on the basis of selective growth points or growth poles in areas that are relatively developed. In addition, they would use fiscal redistribution for development assistance to the less developed regions. He Jianzhang, formerly an economist at the State Economic Commission and currently a senior researcher at the Institute of Sociology, the Chinese Academy of Social Sciences, would raise state purchase prices for raw materials produced in the West, and would provide it with manufactured products at low prices, as well as financial and technical assistance (author's interview, July 15, 1988). Xia Shen (1988: 16) of the University of Foreign Trade also supports higher state prices for materials from the middle and western regions, but contends that these regions can also enter the world market by organizing trade and finance-oriented transnational corporations. It is not clear how this can be accomplished given the low level of development in these regions.

In this author's view, as long as the redistribution of income – through various means, including higher realistic prices for raw materials – and the movement of goods and factors of production are possible, it is sensible to stress efficiency and develop the East first, for two major reasons. First, the East has the necessary infrastructure and skilled labor in relative abundance. If China were to pursue the strategy of equal regional development, heavy state investment would have to be made in infrastructure and in upgrading outdated industrial facilities in the interior regions, and it will take a long time for this investment to produce concrete results. Furthermore, much of the state funding has to come from revenues collected in the East, thus impeding the latter's development efforts. Second, given the new importance of international trade, the eastern coastal region has the locational advantage for access to export markets and for cooperation with foreign investors. It does not make sense for China's interior provinces to export their industrial material to foreign countries when China's own eastern factories are starved for lack of these materials. China can earn much more foreign exchange when final products rather than raw materials are exported. Naturally, a mechanism has to be devised to share the foreign exchange earnings with the areas producing the raw materials.

In addition, this author feels that the two-phase industrial development strategy mapped out by the economists at the Institute of Industrial Economics concerning the western region is overly optimistic. It is difficult to envisage western provinces such as Guizhou, Xinjiang, and Qinghai becoming important industrial bases of the country in the early twenty-first century. In terms of promoting allocative efficiency and increasing the growth rate, it would be better after the mid-1990s for the government to concentrate on improving the transport and communication links between the East and the West in order to facilitate the movement of goods, labor, and capital, and let market forces rather than government planning determine the nature of future industrial activities in the western region. For example, although the West lacks capital to develop its natural resources, it might be able to attract capital inflow from the East by leasing some of its mining rights to resource-using companies in the East, as suggested by Zheng Hongqing and Liu Yenan (1988). This would be possible if the transportation and communication links between the East and the West are improved. The West also suffers from a brain drain as some of its skilled people seek employment in the East. Because the Chinese government no longer makes compulsory assignment of college graduates from the East to the interior, only increased profit opportunities in the West can help reduce the brain drain. This is best brought about not by wasteful government investment in industries, which may run counter to allocative efficiency, but by enlarging and improving the market network for the West. In view of the fact that the Chinese market is still highly fragmented, it is doubly important that the state spare no efforts in integrating the regional markets and in perfecting the market mechanism if its efficiency-oriented development strategy is to succeed. It is also obvious that Xia Shen's (1988) idea of involving the middle and western regions in the world market by organizing Chinese transnational corporations is unwise in view of the problems mentioned earlier.

Open door policy and trade strategy

Before the late 1970s, China pursued basically the Maoist principle of national self-reliance, that is, a trade aversion policy. Also, aside from the Soviet aid in the 1950s, there was no inflow of foreign capital. Consequently, Chinese economists had little theoretical discussion of foreign trade and no discussion at all of the role of foreign capital in socialist development. With the adoption in the late 1970s of the "open-door" policy of pursuing foreign trade and attracting foreign capital and investment, appropriate theoretical changes in China's diagnostic and functional economics had to be made.

The first task in diagnostic economics was to justify trade with the rich capitalist countries because international trade was previously regarded as entailing exploitation of the poor countries by the rich ones. For this purpose, in the early 1980s Chinese economists undertook a reassessment of Ricardo's theory of comparative advantage at the pure theory level. As Shuyun Ma (1986: 293), an economist in Hong Kong, has pointed out, there are two reasons for this reassessment. First, only Ricardo's demonstration of *mutual* benefits of trade on the basis of comparative advantage can "save" China from the delicate issue of exploitation and the difficult choice in trade policy between being exploited by the rich countries and exploiting the poorer ones. Second, Ricardo's theory utilizes the labor theory of value, which makes it more compatible with the Marxist ideology. The main result of the reassessment of Ricardo is the consensus that although the rich countries may exploit the poor ones, the latter can simultaneously gain from trade as well (Shu-yun Ma, 1986: 294).[5] In other words, Chinese economists' perception of international trade has changed from the previous zero-sum-game situation to that of a non–zero-sum game in which both parties can gain.

Of the same genre but in a more rigorous and dynamic framework, Chin Qiwei (1986) uses Marx's labor theory of value to demonstrate mathematically that Ricardo's theory is consistent with the Marxist theory of "equal exchange of labor," labor here being defined as the amount of "international socially necessary labor" that is needed for commodity production under world market conditions (see also *JJRB*, May 21, 1987: 3). The principle of Ricardo's comparative advantage is, therefore, "proved" to be scientifically valid.

Many Chinese authors have also adopted an eclectic or potpourri approach – a combination of ideological, empirical, and historical arguments and evidence – to support the open-door policy. The reasoning usually involves some of the following points: (1) According to Marx, exchanges of commodities make it possible to realize the value of commodities (*MEQJ*, Vol. 44, 118–19); hence new channels of exchange enhance the value of commodities produced (*CMJJ*, 1987, No. 6, 34–5). (2) Socialism is intrinsically an open system because its superiority lies in its ability and willingness to absorb aspects of various advanced civilizations, whether they originated in Europe, the United States, or elsewhere. Lenin so indicated on many occasions. (3) Historically, socialism gained its victories in economically underdeveloped countries. This means that these countries need to catch up economically and adopt an open-door policy to absorb the accomplishments of advanced capitalist countries in order to help develop socialism. The early experience of the Soviet Union under Lenin and Stalin in utilizing foreign capital shows the benefits of foreign capital in assisting socialist development. (4) China's past experience, especially during the Cultural Revolution decade, indicates that a "closed-door" or "semi-closed-door" policy is not conducive to economic development and the full development of socialist superiority. As a result of that policy, China has lagged behind many other countries in technology and economic development. Therefore, China should adopt an open-door policy on the basis of independence, equality, and socialist planning (*RMRB*, May 11, 1987: 5).

The issue of exploitation lingered in the literature in the early 1980s because of past ideological influence, but it became increasingly perfunctory, without its previous tone of moral righteousness. Some authors pointed out that an element of exploitation is always involved in foreign capital and

[5] There are also related discussions on the issue of "unequal trade" in terms of the international law of value. The discussions are inconclusive, but are solely concerned with devising an ideological formula for the same purpose. For details of these discussions, see Ma (1986: 296–302).

investment, because foreign capitalists export their capital for the purpose of making profits. But that is the price that China has to pay for using foreign capital. However, in spite of this exploitation, China can still gain from foreign capital as long as China sees to it that it is utilized properly (*RMRB*, Jan. 6, 1983: 5; Mar. 10, 1984: 5; Xu Dixin 1981: 5). After the mid-1980s, however, the issue of exploitation was rarely mentioned in the literature. The reason is obvious: China has had problems in attracting enough foreign capital, and cannot afford the luxury of complaining about being exploited by foreign capitalists.

Having thus legitimized the open-door policy at the ideological level in their diagnostic economics, Chinese economists proceeded to debate in 1985–8 the policy question of trade strategy, namely, whether China should adopt an import-substitution strategy or an export-promotion strategy. According to calculations made by Huang Fangyi (1985), China's "trade bias" in the early 1980s was about the same as that of India – in favor of import substitution and against export promotion.[6] He criticizes such import-substitution bias on the grounds that it will lead to a foreign exchange shortage and even a debt crisis, and advocates a more balanced trade strategy. He does not support an all-out export-oriented industrialization strategy for fear of imported inflation and devaluation of the currency.

Huang Fangyi (1986) further criticizes import substitution as having resulted in the production of high-cost inferior products, and advocates the export-substitution strategy as the effective way to solve the foreign exchange shortage. In this strategy, the import of machines and materials would replace that of finished consumer goods, and the export of finished manufactured goods would replace that of traditional primary products. However, he points out that China would have to adopt a "Chinese model of

[6] As defined by Krueger (1983: 31), trade bias shows the "direction of the degree to which, on average, domestic incentives diverge from those that would prevail under free trade." It is calculated as follows:

$$B = \frac{P_{dm}/P_{fm}}{P_{dx}/P_{fx}}$$

where

P_{dm} = domestic price of imported product
P_{fm} = international price of imported product
P_{dx} = domestic price of exported product
P_{fx} = international price of exported product

Thus, the ratio shows the relative advantage, at the official exchange rate, of import substitution versus production for export. If $B > 1$, the country's trade strategy is biased toward import substitution. If $B < 1$, the bias is toward exports. For a comparative study of the trade biases of various developing countries, see Krueger (1983: 30–41).

export substitution'' because China is a large country, and is thus different from the smaller countries whose industries are heavily dependent on export markets.

Some economists instead advocate import substitution. Liu Changli (1987), for example, supports import substitution as the long-term strategy for China mainly because China is a large country. He contends that all large countries have inward-looking economies with relatively low per capita exports and low dependence on exports for their industries. In his view, it is inevitable that China will pursue import substitution in the long run for the following reasons: (1) China is a planned socialist economy; an import-substitution strategy is more compatible with the planned management of the domestic economy and the minimization of interference from international economic fluctuations. An export-oriented strategy would require trade and capital liberalization, which would jeopardize China's heavy and chemical industries. (2) China's export products, such as textiles and other light manufactured goods, cannot be the basis of China's industrial modernization. Nor can China's exports be expanded continuously in the face of worldwide protectionism. (3) China's import substitution should be centered on the heavy and chemical industries. The late twentieth century and the early twenty-first century are the opportune time for China to develop these traditional industries because the industrialized countries are shifting from them to high-technology industries. Such import substitution would also attract foreign capital, which can help upgrade industries and pave the way for future exports. Similar views are also expressed by some other economists.

Finally, some economists have adopted an eclectic and neutral position. For example, as early as 1981, Beijing University professor Li Yining supported a strategy that combines import substitution with export substitution on a selective basis. He advocates neither strategy alone because both have their limitations. The former tends to protect and foster inefficient industries, whereas the latter creates dependence on foreign markets, international prices, and foreign policies (Li Yining, 1989: 147–57). In a different vein, Huang Shanhe (1988) argues that import substitution and export expansion are not mutually exclusive but are logically two phases of the same process. For a limited period of time and for certain industries, import substitution may be necessary for the country to break out of the traditional international division of labor. Furthermore, it will save foreign exchange for the country. During the late phase of import substitution, part of the output previously produced for the domestic market can be exported. In addition, the import-substituting industries will be able to produce materials, parts, or machinery needed by the export industries, thus raising the domestic contents of the export products. In these ways, import substitution and export expansion are either different phases of the same process or are complementary in nature. The trade strategy that accomplishes this is characterized by Huang Shanhe (1988: 28) as "neutral."

In this author's view, this proposal to combine the advantages of both import-substitution and export-promotion strategies seems ideal in theory, but is fraught with inconsistencies and great difficulties in practice. As Krueger (1983: 30–54) has shown in a large-scale study of the trade strategies of several developing countries, the policy instruments needed to implement one strategy are invariably incompatible with those required for the other strategy. Import substitution requires high tariffs and other trade barriers to protect domestic industries and is usually accompanied by an overvalued exchange rate. The resultant high prices and poor quality of the domestic products make them unsuitable for export and can hardly enhance the competitiveness of the export industries if they are used as inputs. On the other hand, the export-promotion strategy requires relatively free trade and competitive pricing, which in turn require the removal of the policy instruments adopted for import substitution. Thus it is almost impossible to make import substitution and export promotion complement each other.

Alternatively, if the two strategies are pursued as two phases of the same development process, the transition between them is hazardous because it will be resisted by the protected industries. Hence it is a "passage of great danger for any government," as shown by the experiences of many developing countries (Gillis, Perkins, Roemer, and Snodgrass, 1987: 464). This author believes that this will also be the case with China because of its fragile market mechanism and the weakened control of the economy by the central government. It is true that both Taiwan and South Korea have successfully negotiated the difficult passage, but these countries have been exceptional in their development performances, and there is no evidence that China will be able to duplicate them.

In early 1988, the Chinese leadership decided in favor of an export-expansion strategy. The decision was the culmination of strong advocacy of export promotion by some government economists and the personal inclination of then party leader Zhao Ziyang. Foremost among the government economists in favor of export expansion is Wang Jian, a researcher at the State Planning Commission. He proposed the strategy of a "grand international cycle" (*guoji da xunhaun*), which was submitted to Zhao Ziyang for consideration. According to its published version (Wang Jian, 1988), this strategy would link international trade with China's long-term development in the following manner: First, because China has rural surplus labor but lacks capital for industrial development, the strategy would, in the first phase, transform the surplus labor into capital through the export of labor-intensive products such as textiles and other light manufactured goods produced primarily by rural industries. The foreign exchange earned would provide the needed funds and technology for heavy industries, thus promoting overall development. During the first phase, lasting for five to seven years, export efforts would be concentrated in the coastal areas because they are relatively developed. In the second phase, lasting for another five to seven years, the products of the interior would be exported, further supporting the development of heavy industry. In the third phase, China would be relatively industrialized, and capital- and technology-intensive products would gradually replace labor-intensive ones as China's main exports. Heavy industry would also be in a position to provide assistance to agriculture.

Inspired by Wang Jiang's grand vision, Zhao Ziyang toured the coastal areas in late 1987 and formulated a different version of the export-promotion strategy that would concentrate on the coastal areas (*BR*, Feb. 8–14, 1988: 18–23; *RMRB*, Jan. 23, 1988: 1). It was adopted by the Politburo of the Chinese Communist Party in February 1988 as the official strategy. The essence of this coastal-export strategy is that China's coastal areas would export labor-intensive products and import raw materials for processing. Thus, it is less ambitious than the grand-international-cycle strategy discussed earlier, but there are also similarities, especially in the first phase. The crucial differences between the two strategies are that Zhao Ziyang's strategy stresses the import of raw materials and welcomes foreign capital and investment to help upgrade China's technology and product quality. It is hoped that the import of raw materials from abroad will eliminate the perennial competition between the coastal areas and the interior for raw materials and the resultant conflict of interest between the two. Export earnings will be used to develop labor-intensive processing plants as well as selective technology-intensive industries. In the long run, many support industries as well as import-substituting industries can be developed. The middle and western regions of the country are expected to benefit from all these developments.

A modified version of the grand-international-cycle strategy is given by Xu Hua (1988) of Xiamen University, who is impressed with Wang Jian's grand vision for China's industries but wants to rectify its neglect of agriculture. Citing the experiences of Taiwan and South Korea, Xu argues that such unqualified industry-oriented export strategy would drain agriculture of productive labor and starve it of investment funds. He would modify the strategy by using part of the export earnings for investment in agriculture, and by speeding up the export of capital-intensive products produced by heavy industry and hence the latter's assistance to agriculture. Thus, in terms of the relative growth of industry and agriculture, the original grand-international-cycle strategy would result in unbalanced growth in favor of industry, whereas Xu Hua's version would promote a more balanced growth.

Virtually all economists this author has interviewed, as well as most authors cited in the literature, question the feasibility and desirability of the export-promotion strategies proposed by Wang Jian and Zhao Ziyang. For example, many economists criticize the heavy dependence on trade that these strategies will entail and question China's ability to export so much. They argue that it is unrealistic to designate the entire coastal region as export oriented and undesirable for so many Chinese enterprises to depend on the export market. In their view, most Chinese enterprises simply cannot produce products with the requisite quality and variety for the world market. Huan Xiang, executive director of the International Relations Center of the State Council, criticizes Zhao Ziyang's strategy for failing to take into account the formidable competition from other East Asian economies, as well as the protectionist policies of the United States and Europe. He also feels that the value added from export processing is too low (*GG*, 1988, No. 2: 54–5).

Xia Shen (1988) finds the grand-international-cycle strategy lacking on the following grounds: (1) The model is concerned only with international trade; the contemporary pattern of international division of labor entails international finance and investment, as well as trade. (2) It ignores the fact that China has to compete with the newly industrializing economies of Asia, which have a much better economic environment. (3) It relies on simple, unskilled rural labor to produce manufactured goods, and although China's rural labor is cheap, it is also inefficient. Xia Shen contends that it is the skilled urban industrial labor that China should mobilize for export production; hence it is the modern industries in China's coastal cities that China should promote as export industries. However, export production is not enough. To ensure an adequate supply of raw materials for domestic processing, as well as access to foreign markets, Xia Shen argues that China should establish multinational corporations in production, trade, and finance to invest abroad in selective areas. These multinational corporations with "Chinese characteristics" should become the major actors in China's international economic activities.[7]

In this author's view, most of the critiques of the export strategies are persuasive. Given the size of their domestic market, most of China's industries need not rely on export markets to develop because it is easier to pro-

---

[7] It is interesting to note that China is probably the poorest country in the world to have multinational corporations. In 1988 more than 400 Chinese enterprises were operating abroad (Xia Shen, 1988: 15). A number of economists, such as Ye Gang of Fudan University in Shanghai, also support China's investment abroad in selective industries (author's interview, Aug. 17, 1988).

duce for domestic use. In addition, given the size of the country, China would not be able to follow the examples of the "four little dragons" and become genuinely export oriented without bringing about oversupply and chaos in the world market. The resultant protectionism in the industrialized countries would hurt not only China but also other developing countries. Thus, as a long-term national development strategy, a heavy export-promotion strategy would seem inappropriate. The vision of the grand-international-cycle theory is particularly unrealistic and is justly criticized by many Chinese economists as being based on fantasy. It envisages the whole country becoming successfully export oriented in only ten to fourteen years in two phases and well modernized shortly afterward. This speed of export-led development would be unprecedented in the world, even in the smaller export-oriented East Asian economies without China's numerous bureaucratic and economic problems.

It should also be pointed out that even if China does not become heavily export oriented, it can still reap the benefits of increased allocative efficiency that would result from specialization and exchanges among its provinces if China's interprovincial trade is increased on the basis of market competition and regional comparative advantage. Currently, there is much room for improvement in this regard because of numerous interregional and interprovincial trade barriers. China's domestic market needs to be greatly improved before China's true comparative advantage can be accurately assessed and its export potential fully developed.

This does not mean that China should not expand the exports of products in which it has an actual or potential comparative advantage; it should, if only to finance its needed imports. Since 1979, the Chinese government has adopted an export-expansion strategy for selected areas and enterprises. This includes (1) four special economic zones established in 1979 in southern coastal areas and fourteen coastal cities chosen in 1984; (2) selective export production bases and enterprises producing traditional crafts and special indigenous products; (3) enterprises established solely or partly with foreign capital; and (4) the decision in 1987 to establish Hainan Island as a new province for foreign investment and export.[8] This strategy of developing *selective* export bases with careful preparation and government support makes eminent sense. To designate the whole coastal region as the export-oriented area of the country, however, is not only premature but is certain

---

[8] A team of experts from the Chinese Academy of Social Sciences, headed by Liu Guoguang, a vice president of the academy, was involved in advising the government in making this decision. For a discussion of the development strategy for Hainan Island, see Liu Guoguang (1988c).

to court failure in light of China's modest capabilities and international circumstances.

As to supplying raw materials to the export areas and industries, it would be necessary in the short run to increase the import of materials for processing in the coastal areas if China's interior regions cannot or will not supply enough. However, it does not seem sensible to set up Chinese multinational corporations to invest abroad in raw material production. China has good sources of raw materials in its interior, and the country itself needs foreign investment. China's limited foreign exchange can be better utilized in developing China's own sources of raw materials and infrastructure, as discussed earlier.

Finally, certain economists have argued convincingly that some of China's interior border areas should be developed for increased exports to neighboring countries (the Soviet Union, Central Asia, Southeast Asia) because of geographical proximity, cultural affinity, and the tradition of economic interactions (Dong Fureng, author's interview, Aug. 10, 1988; Ji Chongwei and Yang Mu, 1988; Xia Shen, 1988: 16). This is an area that is relatively neglected in China's policy discussions but holds many potential benefits for China's border regions.

In short, in all aspects and areas of China's economic development – income distribution, agriculture, rural industry, regional development, and international trade – Chinese economists have changed their traditional thinking and have moved in favor of efficiency over equality. With the help of Western analytical concepts and tools, they have shown increasing sophistication in development analysis. However, their expositions and applications of the efficiency principle have not been consistent, in part because their analyses are understandably influenced by prevailing government policies. Nevertheless, great strides have been made, and development economics with Chinese characteristics has become an important part of China's economics.

CHAPTER 5

Prices and wages

In a fundamental sense, meaningful price and wage reforms are the most important economic reform a socialist country like China can undertake because they determine whether the other economic reforms and most economic activities are consistent with the underlying market forces. However, they are also the most difficult reforms to implement because they directly affect the standard of living of all citizens. Consequently, prices and wages are the last areas of the Chinese economy to be considered for reform. As will be discussed, by 1988 China's system of irrational prices was exacting a heavy toll on the economy, and in the first half of 1988, Chinese leaders including Zhao Ziyang, then secretary general of the Chinese Communist Party, repeatedly indicated that China's reform priority would soon be shifted to price and wage reforms. However, in September 1988, the Central Committee of the party met in the midst of serious inflation – China's worst since the 1950s – and decided to postpone price reform for two years in order to avoid aggravating the record inflation that had raged since 1985. As of early 1990, price stability and control were still being emphasized. Thus, after years of effort to reform the economy, the prospects for meaningful price and wage reforms are still uncertain. The ultimate fate of China's economic reforms will depend on whether China can control its inflation and successfully implement its price and wage reforms before the momentum of reform is lost.

This chapter examines Chinese economists' discussions of the theoretical basis for socialist prices and wages, and how China's price and wage systems should be reformed.

Socialist planned prices

Chinese economists have a long history of debate on prices under socialism. However, because the Chinese concepts of prices, costs, profits, and the like differ from their Western counterparts, and because the Chinese themselves do not always agree on the meaning of some terms, their literature can be extremely confusing. In addition, because the Chinese have insisted on basing their price theories on the Marxian labor theory of value, which has long been discredited in the West for its analytical shortcomings, it is difficult for non-Marxists, including this author, to take their price theories seriously. The objective of this section, therefore, is not to give a comprehensive survey, but merely to convey a sense of the nature of the debate.

As surveyed by Xing Junfang (1985), there have been four major periods of price discussions in China since 1949: (1) 1956–7, centering on the prices of production materials and the foundation of socialist prices; (2) 1959–64, focusing on the foundation of socialist prices; (3) 1977–83, discussing the basis of planned prices and issues of price adjustments; and (4) the period since May 1984 on price reform. As will be explained, there is a thread of continuity in the discussions in the first three periods. The discussions in the latest period, which have subsided since June 1989, have broken new ground and are an important part of the reform theories of the middle and late 1980s.

At the level of diagnostic economics, Chinese economists subscribe to the Marxian labor theory of value as an important part of Marxism. This theory posits that the value of a commodity can be created by labor alone, and that it is determined by the amount of the "socially necessary labor" expended in its production. This is the sum of the following: (1) the value of past labor embodied in the raw materials and in the depreciation of machines used in production (constant capital); (2) the value that workers create for themselves, that is, that part of their living labor for which they are paid (variable capital); and (3) the value that workers create for society for which they are not paid; under capitalism, this value is appropriated by the capitalists as surplus value. The labor theory of value further postulates that when there is an equilibrium between the supply of and the demand for a commodity, the price of the commodity corresponds to its value.

The theoretical deficiencies of this theory are well known and need not be repeated here.[1] However, it is useful to reiterate Nove's (1983: 31) point that the theory fails to recognize that "the 'underlying values' are invisible magnitudes, that neither workers nor capitalists can respond to them, for *they* see actual (or expected) *prices,* or wages". In other words, the Marxian "value" is operationally a meaningless concept.

Chinese economists have long admitted that "under current conditions, values cannot be calculated" (Wang Zhenzhi and Qiao Rongzhang, 1988: 27). Nevertheless, up to the mid-1980s, they invariably insisted on using

---

[1] The major problems with the Marxian labor theory of value include the following: It fails to consider competition and demand in the determination of the value of a commodity; it ignores the contribution of capital to labor productivity or assumes the same capital–labor ratio in all branches of the economy. See Nove (1983: 20–7).

value as the theoretical basis for determining planned socialist prices. According to traditional Chinese views, because the socialist economy is a planned economy, the prices of products produced under the plan should also be planned prices, which somehow should correspond to or reflect the values of the products. One presumed advantage of basing prices on value is that all industries and branches of the economy can use the same or a comparable profit rate to calculate their prices.

However, there has been no consensus on how this transformation from values to prices should be done. In 1956–7, Chinese economists were unanimous in regarding the Marxist value as the basis of socialist planned prices and generally ignored the role of supply and demand. However, some favored using the "cost" of production in conjunction with value, cost being defined as including materials and wage costs but excluding capital and land charges. Others wanted prices to be determined by the requirements for the planned and proportionate development of the economy, with value playing a secondary role (Xing Junfang, 1985: 502–3).

The 1959–64 discussions were touched off by Sun Yefang (1959), who proposed using the "production price" as the basis for price determination. As will be explained, this pricing method amounts to levying a capital charge in price calculation, thereby recognizing the role of capital in creating value and contradicting a literal interpretation of the labor theory of value. Consequently, this proposal led to a lively debate among Chinese economists. They all agreed that planned prices should include the cost of production and planned profits, but they could not agree on how planned profits should be determined or how total "social profits" should be distributed among the different branches of the economy through planned prices. In the debate, three different methods were proposed to determine the profits and prices of various commodities:

1. *The labor-cost method.* In this approach, wages are considered to be a reflection of value because they measure the amount of living labor used in production. It is argued that this is the only method that is consistent with the labor theory of value. This method can be expressed as

$$p = c + v + v\left(\frac{s}{V}\right)$$

where p is the planned price of a product; c is the branch average cost of material inputs, including depreciation of equipment per unit of output (i.e., the "constant capital" in the labor theory of value); v is the branch average wage cost per unit of output (i.e., the "variable capital"); S is the total planned "surplus product" or profits in the economy; and V is the total wage bill in the economy. The S/V ratio is the economy's average profit rate on wages. This formula is criticized by most economists for making labor-intensive products more expensive than capital-intensive ones and thus encouraging the substitution of labor for capital and hindering the rise of labor productivity (Nai-Ruenn Chen, 1966: 40–1).

2. *The capital-funds method.* This is the method proposed by Sun Yefang. Algebraically, it can be expressed as

$$p = c + v + k\left(\frac{S}{K}\right)$$

where k is the average amount of fixed and working capital per unit of output, and K is the total amount of such capital funds used in the economy. The resultant prices are called "production prices," as defined by Marx. This method amounts to adopting the capitalist practice of including a capital charge in prices. The rationale is that it will help ensure investment efficiency and economize on the use of scarce capital. In addition, it will help evaluate enterprise performance and select the best investment project. This method is criticized for various reasons: (1) Marx did not intend to apply the concept of production price to socialism; (2) the resultant price does not correspond to value because the capital–labor ratio (i.e., the "organic composition of capital" in the labor theory of value) varies from branch to branch; and (3) this method will encourage enterprises to increase the use of capital to increase profits (Nai-Ruenn Chen, 1966: 42–4).

3. *The cost-of-production method.* This approach criticizes the first method for ignoring past labor and for not being conducive to technical progress, and it criticizes the second method for being divorced from value (Xing Junfang, 1985: 503–5). It proposes to distribute the total surplus product in proportion to the cost of production according to the following pricing formula:

$$p = c + v + (c + v)\left(\frac{S}{C + V}\right)$$

where $c + v$ is the branch average cost of production per unit of output, C is the total cost of material inputs in the economy, and $C + V$ is the total cost of production of the economy. This formula is rejected by proponents of the first method on the grounds that past labor embodied in materials and equipment does not create new value. It is also criticized for encouraging managers to use expensive materials to raise prices (Nai-Ruenn Chen, 1966: 41–2).

With the onset of the Cultural Revolution, Sun Yefang was criticized as a revisionist for his emphasis on capital funds, and the discussion was brought to an end. In the post-1979 period, the point of departure for price discussion continued to be the labor theory of value, and the different pricing methods discussed earlier continued to be the focus of debates throughout the mid-1980s. However, since 1979 there has been substantial and growing support for Sun Yefang's capital-funds method for three reasons: (1) It is argued that it will promote more rational and efficient use of capital. Enterprises and industries that use more capital funds have more equipment, better technology, and higher labor productivity, and hence should earn more profits for the state. (2) The actual profit rate of an enterprise calculated on the basis of capital funds used will accurately reflect the managerial performance of the enterprise irrespective of its capital intensity. (3) Pricing based on labor cost (value) works against modernization because backward enterprises are rewarded and advanced ones punished (He Jianzhang, Kuang Ri'an, and Zhang Zhuoyuan, 1981; Li Dehua, 1979: 70–2; Liu Guoguang, 1980; Wang Yongzhi and Wang Zhenzhi, 1979: 70; Zhang Zhuoyuan, 1987: 82–95).

Some economists criticize this method for giving more profits to capital-intensive industries than to labor-intensive ones. In addition, they point out that different industries have different rates of capital circulation for technical reasons. Thus, even with the same amount of capital funds and the same level of managerial competence, different industries will have different rates of profit on capital funds, making this method inappropriate for evaluating managerial performance (Zhang Chunyin and Zhan Junzhong, 1979: 67).

A small minority maintain that socialist prices should be based on value, and support the labor-cost method as the only one that is consistent with labor value and the principle of distribution according to labor (Wang Zhenzhi, Wang Yongzhi, and Jia Xiuyuan, 1982: 19–20). Most economists, however, reject it as one-sided in emphasizing the contribution of labor in creating value while ignoring that of materials, technology, and equipment. To use it to determine profits and prices, they believe, will give backward, labor-intensive industries more profits and advanced, capital-intensive ones less profits, and is therefore not conducive to the adoption of advanced technology and the raising of labor productivity by the industries (Ji Zhengzhi, 1981: 41).

Supporters of the production-cost method argue that it is easier to administer, and that it will encourage cost reduction by individual enterprises so that their actual profits will rise above the industry's average (Ji Zhengzhi, 1979: 62).

Finally, there is a compromise method called the "comprehensive" or "overall profit-rate method," which uses a weighted average of the profit rate on capital funds and that on wages; for example, a 70 percent profit rate on capital funds and a 30 percent rate on wages have been suggested. Some economists would use different weights for different industries (Ji Zhengzhi, 1981: 38–44; Wang Zhenzhi, Wang Yongzhi, and Jia Xiuyuan, 1982: 20). The rationale for this method is that none of the others is perfect and that it is better to have both combined. The resultant prices are called "dual-channel prices" (*shuangqu jiage*).

The preceding discussion shows that China's price theories incorporate both ideological and functional concerns. Whatever the method of profit and price determination, the resultant prices are not market-clearing prices; they are a type of "cost-plus" prices in which demand does not affect the rates of profit and prices.

One final note on terminology. In the 1980s, some Chinese economists also used the term "theoretical prices" to refer to the theoretical basis for socialist planned prices discussed earlier. However, there is no consensus among the Chinese on the exact meaning of the term. Tian Yuan et al. (1987: 71) define theoretical price broadly as "a conceptual monetary expression of the commodity value. It is a pricing structure calculated according to Marxist theory of price formation and in light of specific conditions. Theoretical prices, which can be used to measure whether actual prices are rational or not, are the approximate value of metamorphized value." However, some economists hold that theoretical prices should be based on value alone, and others contend that supply and demand should be taken into account (Xing Junfang, 1985: 511–13). Zhang Chunyin (1986) and Zhang Zhuoyuan (1987: 80–95) would use "production prices" as theoretical prices. Tian Yuan et al. (1987: 73–4) would calculate theoretical prices by adding the average branch cost of a product, resource use fees, profit on funds, turnover taxes, and "profit on wages" (pensions, bonuses, etc.). According to them, the Price Research Center of the State Council, which was established in 1981, actually calculated alternative theoretical prices for 1981 and 1983 by using variants of their method – omitting resource use fees, using different profit rates and different tax rates, and so forth. The calculations were used for price reform simulations. Wang Zhenzhi and Qiao Rongzhang (1988: 29) report that the Price Research Center has calculated more than 800 theoretical prices for agricultural procurement prices, major industrial product prices, transportation fees, and so on.

The years 1983–4 marked a turning point in China's price discussions. Although in unpublished policy discussion papers equilibrium prices were advocated by a few economists as early as 1982, the papers were heavily criticized and were not allowed to be published (Shi Xiaomin and Liu Jirui, 1989: 18). Obviously, the Chinese were not ready ideologically for market prices in 1982. In 1983–4, articles on supply and demand and equilibrium prices began to appear, especially in *Jingji Yanjiu,* the preeminent theoretical journal (Lou Jiwei and Zhou Xiaochuan, 1984; Wang Yongzhi and Wang Zhenzhi, 1983). The intensity of the value-oriented discussions abated somewhat. A few economists even suggested abandoning altogether the discussion of theoretical prices. However, in 1984–6 the dominant view of the profession was that the adoption of market prices in China should be only a long-term reform goal, and that before the end of the century, most prices should remain value-based, planned prices (Zhang Zhuoyuan, author's interview, May 31, 1989). It was not until 1986–8 that economists generally agreed that China should adopt market prices in its price reform. As a leader in this change and in the profession, Yu Guangyuan (1986a) urged his fellow economists to "put prices at the forefront and value at the rear." He complained that Chinese economists had already spent "too much time and energy on an issue that is not really that difficult" and stated that often "it is not necessary to evoke the concept of value in discussing prices" (ibid: 26, 34).

Yu's observation is perceptive and his admonition to his colleagues courageous in China's context. After 1986, Chinese economists increasingly turned their attention to the issue of price reform. The orientation of their theoretical discussion was also increasingly changed from the labor theory of value to the supply-and-demand mechanism. However, most economists still hold that the two approaches are compatible – that long-run market equilibrium prices should equal Marxist labor values (Zhang Zhuoyuan, author's interview, May 31, 1989). To refute this belief, He Juhuang (1987), using Western microeconomic techniques, has demonstrated mathematically that the two are not the same. Although the proof is probably beyond most of China's leading economists, it is merely another manifestation of a growing trend that culminated in Lin Zili's (1988: 12) declaration that China should abandon the theory of planned prices and adopt the theory of market prices in its price reform.

Price policies, adjustments, and problems

Ever since the founding of the People's Republic in 1949, one of the most important policy objectives of the Communist leadership has been price stability. There is no question that the runaway inflation in China in the late 1940s contributed greatly to the downfall of the Nationalist government; hence the new Communist government sought to avoid inflation at any cost.

In addition, it was believed that socialist prices are planned prices and not free market prices, and that the ability of the government to control prices and protect the citizens' basic standard of living from inflation is a manifestation of the superiority of socialism. All these factors led to the adoption of various measures to control prices, with a profound impact on the economy. In fact, government price control was an integral part of the planned production and allocation of goods and materials in the prereform economy.

The objective of overall price stability has important sectoral implications. For example, energy and raw materials are used in the production of many products. Their prices are, therefore, kept low in order to reduce the costs of production of the latter. Food grains and a few other important agricultural products are essential to the cost of living of the population, especially the urban population. The state procurement prices for these products are, therefore, kept low. Even when the procurement prices were raised, as in 1979 and afterward, the state was usually reluctant to raise its grain retail prices in the cities. Consequently, the state has sustained a heavy burden of subsidy to consumers. For the same reason, vegetable oil, housing, health care, and transportation have been heavily subsidized by the state.

There is also a development objective of price policy. For China's development, modern industries need to be developed, which requires economic surplus for state investment. One way to obtain the surplus is to manipulate the terms of trade or the price ratio between agriculture and state-owned industry in favor of the latter, that is, between agricultural products sold to the state and manufactured goods sold by the state to the peasants. This had led to the "scissors differentials" between agricultural and industrial prices, meaning a double price squeeze on agricultural producers.

All these measures of price control, subsidies, and price manipulation did accomplish their initial economic and political objectives, and their initial benefits probably did outweigh the costs of allocative inefficiency, given the objectives. However, once firmly in place, these measures were politically difficult to remove, and they became impediments to economic flexibility and efficiency, which are increasingly important if growth and development are to proceed. With the adoption of modernization as the primary objective in late 1978 and the subsequent decision to reform the economy, it became logical that flexibility and efficiency should take precedence over price stability as the primary policy objective.

Nevertheless, between 1979 and 1988, the leadership was not able to act boldly and decisively on price reform for reasons touched on before. Before 1984 the role of the market in China's reforms was still under debate, and free market prices were still viewed with suspicion. Thus, only individual price adjustments were made. These adjustments were consistent with the piecemeal trial-and-error strategy of reform, which Chinese leaders consider to be necessary and prudent. Yet from the point of view of price stability as a prerequisite for price reform, the year 1984 is regarded by most economists in retrospect as the best time for price reform. Once that opportunity was missed, it became increasingly difficult to reform the price system because China started to experience unprecedented inflation in 1985–9. This increased the leaders' concern that price reform would aggravate inflation. Consequently, comprehensive price reform was postponed in favor of partial adjustments and reform within the framework of a new two-tier or "dualtrack" (*shuang gui*) price system. Yet partial price adjustments are not sufficient in an economy undergoing other market-oriented reforms and structural changes. In fact, shortly after its introduction in 1984–5, the dualtrack price system itself created or accentuated all sorts of inconsistencies, frictions, and loopholes in the economy, as will be discussed. Inequitable income differentials also increased greatly. All these problems helped to cast doubt on the desirability or fairness of the reform itself.

Thus the Chinese leadership faced a great dilemma, and its inability to resolve it immobilized China's economic reforms at a crucial time in 1988. Price reform became the most difficult part of the reforms. Consequently, it became an important debating issue for Chinese economists in the late 1980s.

Before we examine the policy debate among Chinese economists concerning price reform and the related issue of wage reform, it is useful to review the nature of the gradual price adjustments and the problems they have created because it is under these circumstances that the debates were conducted. The 1979–88 period started out with a price structure that was highly irrational because many prices bore little relationship to the real costs of production, that is, to the opportunity costs or relative scarcity of the resources used in production and to demand conditions. As described earlier, different categories of prices were held at low levels for different purposes. Post-Mao price adjustments first took place in March 1979, when state procurement prices for eighteen agricultural products – including grains, cotton, cooking-oil products, and live pigs – were raised by an average of 24.8 percent. Subsequently, they were raised repeatedly. Using the index of procurement prices in 1978 as 100, it rose to 130.8 in 1980, 153.6 in 1984, and 198.8 in 1987 (Wang Zhenzhi and Qiao Rongzhang, 1988: 76).

The successive raising of agricultural procurement prices, however, did not end the debate on the scissors differentials. Some economists consider them to be basically eliminated. Most feel that they still exist, although they have been reduced. Theoretically, in the absence of the hypothetical equilibrium prices that would have prevailed in a free market, one cannot be sure whether or not and the extent to which agricultural prices are too low.

Most Chinese economists do not have these hypothetical equilibrium prices in mind when they discuss scissors differentials. Instead, they use relative labor earnings or the standard of living as the criterion.

The labor-earning method assumes that agricultural labor should be able to earn a certain fraction (such as one-half or one-third) of what industrial work earns. Then it compares what agricultural labor actually earns, given the procurement prices, with what it should have earned to make the assessment. In addition, some economists have compared the returns to farm labor from growing grains with those from growing other crops whose prices are not controlled by the state. The standard-of-living method assumes that rural and urban households should have comparable rates of increases in their standards of living; it then compares the actual rates of increase to make the assessment. On both counts, the scissors differentials existed throughout the 1980s due to low grain procurement prices (Qin Qiming, author's interview, Aug. 5, 1988). Although these two methods are not rigorous, there is additional evidence to suggest that their conclusion is correct. Starting in 1985, the government permitted peasants to sell at market prices their surplus grains over and above the amount of contract sales to the state (discussed in more detail later). Because market prices have been much higher than state procurement prices, it is clear that the scissors differentials have not been eliminated.

One policy constraint on raising agricultural procurement prices is the urban cost of living. Because the government remains committed to supplying grains and other essential food items to urban residents at low and stable prices, retail prices at government-run food stores remained basically stable. As a result, state procurement prices began to exceed state retail prices in 1979, and the differentials have increased over the years. This has necessitated a large state subsidy of food consumption. In the first half of 1988, the state subsidized 0.34 yuan for every kilogram of grain sold to urban residents; the subsidy for peanut oil was 1.6 yuan per kilogram (Wang Zhenzhi and Qiao Rongzhang, 1988: 18). The price subsidies have created a heavy fiscal burden on the government and have given rise to large government deficits. However, if grain procurement prices had not been raised as rapidly, the profitability of growing grains relative to other crops whose prices were not controlled would have been much lower, and peasants would have shifted more of their land to these crops, thereby adversely affecting the total supply of grains.[2] This outcome would have been politically unacceptable, given the fact that national self-sufficiency in food grains is of paramount importance to the leadership, as discussed in Chapter 4.

[2] The shift has been responsible to a large extent for China's failure in 1985–8 to match the peak grain output of 407.3 million tons in 1984, thereby necessitating large grain imports.

In 1985, the government reformed the grain procurement and distribution system; it eliminated compulsory grain procurement quotas and introduced the contract-procurement system. Under the new system, state commercial departments would negotiate purchase contracts with peasants before the planting season at stipulated prices. Excess grain output could be sold at higher market prices. This constitutes the dual-track price system for grains. Although the new system was only a halfway measure toward agricultural price decontrol, it did increase peasants' incentive to produce because the contractual sales to the state were smaller than the previous compulsory quotas. Consumers also benefited from the availability of better-quality products, albeit at higher prices. In 1988, government retail prices for various foods, such as sugar and meat, were also raised. However, to offset their impact on the urban standard of living, a wage subsidy to state employees of 10 yuan per employee per month was given. It was felt that the combination of higher realistic prices and overt subsidy was preferable to the old system of covert subsidy in the form of subsidized low prices. A wage subsidy also given in the 1960s and in 1979 to offset the impact of higher food prices (Wang Zhenzhi and Qiao Rongzhang, 1988: 63).

However, serious problems with the dual-track price system for grains developed. With increasing commercialization in the rural economy and rising market prices for grains, state contract purchase prices for grains became much lower than market prices. As a result, peasants were circumventing their sales contracts by all possible means. In some localities in 1987–8, 7 to 8 percent of farming households failed to meet their contract obligations; many others delayed their deliveries of grains to the state (*JJRB*, Nov. 23, 1988: 2). In response, cadres in many rural areas resorted to compulsory methods to force peasants to sign and honor the "voluntary" contracts. As a result, some peasants came to regard the new contract system as worse than the traditional quota procurement system (*RMRB*, Dec. 12, 1988: 5). This is an example of what Dong Fureng (1988c) calls the "metamorphosis of reforms," a widespread problem that has subverted the intent of various reforms.

In the industrial sector, floating prices were introduced in August 1979 for some consumer goods. These prices were allowed to fluctuate within limits set by the state and thus were considered to combine the principle of state planning and leadership with the principle of flexibility in accordance with market conditions. In 1983, the output of petroleum products over and above plan quotas was permitted to be sold in the domestic market at international prices (Wang Zhenzhi and Qiao Rongzhang, 1988: 10). In May 1984, the dual-track price system was adopted for many industrial materials and producer goods – low state-set prices (*pingjia*) for output produced within the state quota system and higher negotiated prices (*yijia*) for output produced outside the state plan. The latter can fluctuate within 20 percent of the former. In February 1985, the 20 percent limit was canceled (Wu Jinglian and Zhao Renwei, 1987: 312). Negotiated prices have become free market prices, and they are often a multiple of the government prices for many products.[3]

This dual-track system for industrial prices reflects the dualistic and partially reformed nature of the Chinese economic system itself in the late 1980s – the uneasy coexistence of a declining planned sector and a growing but distorted market sector. Products that remain under government price control include energy (petroleum, coal, and electricity) and several basic raw materials such as steel, pig iron, timber, cement, and chemicals. Here the two-tier system comes into play. For output within mandatory planning targets, the lower planned prices apply; excess output over and above the planned targets can be sold by the producer in the market at market prices. For enterprises that use these products as inputs, the state allocates a certain amount at planned prices to ensure the fulfillment of their plan targets. For additional production, the needed inputs have to be purchased in the market at market prices. In this way, the dual-track system was designed as a transitional system to serve the differing needs of the remaining planned sector and the new market sector.

When floating prices were introduced in 1979, economists responded to them favorably because the changes permitted much needed and long overdue adjustments. Floating prices were considered to reflect changes in commodity values or objective conditions (*CJKX*, No. 4, 1984: 41–3; *JGLLSJ*, 1981, Nos. 1 and 3; *Jingjixue Dongtai* Editorial Department, ed., 1982: 103–4). Partial freeing of the prices of industrial materials in 1985 as part of the dual-price system was viewed even more favorably. A 1985 survey study found that in steel plants that were permitted to sell the excess output over and above planned targets in the market, the growth rate of output was much higher than in plants that were not; and that for users of steel that had to buy part of their input at market prices, the use of steel per unit of output was significantly lower. This study also indicated that most people preferred the dual system to the traditional controlled-price system (*JJYJ*, 1985, No. 11: 4–5; Wu Jinglian and Zhao Renwei, 1987: 313–14). As Wang Zhenzhi (1988: 33) points out, the dual-track price system has stimulated the production of products outside the plan and has made it possible for village-township enterprises to grow rapidly in recent years because, for the first

---

[3] In 1985, the state ex-factory price of No. 6.5 steel wire was 610 yuan per ton, but its market price was 1,500–2,000 yuan per ton; the state coal price was 27 yuan per ton, but its market price was 100 yuan per ton (Wu Jinglian and Zhao Renwei, 1987: 313). In 1988, the state price of copper in Yunnan was about 4,000 yuan per ton, but the market price was close to 20,000 yuan per ton (*RMRB*, Sept. 7, 1988: 2).

time, they have been able to buy the materials in the market. Dai Yuanchen (1986), after examining the pros and cons of the dual system, concludes that it has an "objective necessity" in China's reform process because it eases the difficult transition from the old fixed-price system to the eventual market-based price system. As such, it is a product of reform with Chinese characteristics. For the same reason, other economists regard it as fulfilling an indispensable "historical mission" in China's reform process (*GMRB*, Sept. 24, 1988: 3; *RMRB*, Sept. 7, 1988: 2).

These assessments of Dai and others are no doubt valid, at least for 1985–6, because it would have been politically impossible to free all prices in a short period of time; having been accustomed to low, controlled prices for more than three decades, Chinese citizens and enterprises would not have accepted sudden economywide price changes. However, the dual-track price system was originally intended to be a transitional system; comprehensive price reform was to follow it. Unfortunately, this has not happened. Many people have become accustomed to the dual-track price system and have taken advantage of it, and the transitional system has become increasingly entrenched. Furthermore, in 1986–8 the dual-track price system increasingly compounded the problems of China's reform process, and the inherent incompatibility between the two tiers of prices – and between the two types of allocative mechanisms they represent – became increasingly clear. In particular, it has caused the following new problems:

1. It is exploited by "shortsighted" enterprises in their "irrational" behavior, as discussed in Chapter 3. For example, the possibility of selling part of their output at higher market prices gives enterprises an incentive to circumvent their plan quotas, which in turn makes it difficult for other enterprises using the products as inputs to fulfill their own plan targets for lack of inputs.
2. It is abused by corrupt officials and people related to them because they have privileged access to low-priced inputs and foreign exchanges allocated by the state. A large number of profitable corporations are known to be headed by the sons of top officials. Popular resentment against this type of rent seeking played an important role in the student demonstrations in April–May 1989.
3. The continuing low planned prices of energy and industrial raw materials have discouraged their production and encouraged their wasteful uses relative to other sectors of the economy (Wu Jinglian and Zhao Renwei, 1987: 314–16). Many economists agree that this has contributed greatly to China's chronic "shortage economy."
4. Because the larger enterprises are restricted by planned prices more than the smaller ones, the dual-price system produces the following

anomaly: The higher-quality products produced by the former have lower prices than the lower-quality products produced by the latter (*JJYJ*, No. 4, 1986: 61). Naturally, the higher-quality products are difficult to get and the incentive to produce them is lacking. This produces China's version of "bad money driving out good money."

In short, as Zhao Renwei (1987: 5) aptly puts it, the dual-price system is the "concentrated expression of the dual economic system; it is also the concentrated expression of the latter's contradictions and frictions." Wu Jinglian (1988) uses the Western concept of "rent seeking" to characterize these problems under the dual-track price system. The implications are disturbing, for in a bureaucratic socialist state it is the high officials and the people connected to them who are in the best position to seek rent. This has created a class of powerful vested interests who are bound to resist genuine market-oriented reforms that will erode their interests.

The government is fully aware of these problems. It had planned to initiate in 1987 coordinated reforms of prices, taxation, fiscal policies, and monetary policies, with the price reform of industrial materials as the central focus. However, because of inflation, the plan was aborted (Liu Guoguang, 1988b). In the first half of 1988, government leaders repeatedly indicated that price reform would soon be introduced. Because of escalating inflation, however, little progress was made except for the lifting of some food and consumer goods prices. In September 1988, at the Third Plenum of the Thirteenth Central Committee, the Chinese Communist Party decided to delay price reform for two years in order to "stabilize the economic environment." Price reform was thus sacrificed at the altar of price stability, and the "transitional" dual-track price system took on the air of permanency.

Price reform debate

The oscillations of Chinese leaders on price reform, as described previously, reflect not only differing views of Chinese leaders but also differing policy recommendations made by contending factions of economists. In 1986–8, there was a broad consensus among economists that the dual-track price system should be reformed sooner or later, and that the objective of the reform should be to adopt prices determined by supply and demand in a competitive market, except in the case of natural monopolies such as public utilities, transportation, and communication, where market competition is impractical. Using a rough quantitative estimate, Zhang Zuoyuan, director of the Institute of Finance and Trade Economics, the Chinese Academy of Social Sciences, argues that more than 80 percent of prices should be market determined (author's interview, July 7, 1988).

However, there are many issues on which there is no consensus among economists. How should price reform be implemented in terms of sequence and speed? How should it be related to other reforms, such as enterprise reform? What are the appropriate macropolicies during price reform? In the following, the major disagreements are discussed.

Although there are many different views, it is well known that, between 1984 and 1988, there were two major schools of thought among leading government economic advisers contending for influence. Both schools agree on the eventual objective mentioned earlier but differ in their time horizon for price reform and in their assessments of the benefits and costs of such reform. In addition, among economists at various institutes of the Chinese Academy of Social Sciences, one can discern a third school of thought, which is not as well publicized but may be just as important in China's economics and in policy influence.

The first school of thought contends that enterprise reform or enterprise ownership reform should precede price reform as its prerequisite, and that the costs and benefits of price reform are such that it should be delayed. Li Yining, a professor of economics at Beijing University and an adviser to former party leader Zhao Ziyang, is the leader of this school of thought, which is commonly referred to as the "enterprise (ownership) reform" school. The second school of thought agrees that enterprise reform is important but argues that price reform and macro-reforms should be implemented along with it in a coordinated manner. This is the "integrated reform" school of thought, although it is popularly but misleadingly called the "price reform" school. This school is led by Wu Jinglian, executive director of the State Council's Research Center for Economic, Technological, and Social Development, who has long been associated with the Chinese Academy of Social Sciences.[4]

According to Li Yining (1986a,b), enterprise reform should precede price reform because, unless enterprises become motivated and efficient, they will not respond positively to market signals, including prices, but will merely attempt to cope with the new prices in a premature price reform. Price reform, therefore, would merely provide a new environment, a passive one at best, for the enterprises. Furthermore, given China's imperfect market and the irrational behavior of Chinese enterprises, prices that are market determined cannot be equilibrium prices. Under such circumstances, chaos rather than the optimum allocation of resources would result from premature price reform (see JJRB, Dec. 13, 1988: 3). For the price environment to be

---

[4] Wu Jinglian has been a research fellow at the Institute of Economics, the Chinese Academy of Social Sciences, for a long time. For this reason, in heated debates, this school of thought is occasionally referred to as the "Academy" school, with the connotation of impracticality.

effective, therefore, enterprises have to be reformed first. Li Yining proposes to motivate enterprises by transforming them into joint-stock companies in which enterprise workers would own shares, along with the state and
other enterprises. In a speech given in 1988, Li Yining recommended the
strategy of implementing price–wage reforms only "after the market system
has been perfected step-by-step on the basis of a successful ownership reform" (cited in *JRSB*, Jan. 18, 1988: 3).

In a similar vein, Jiang Yiwei, the advocate of enterprise-based economic
democracy and workers' stock ownership, also argues that enterprises
should be reformed first, before talking about the market and its macro-
regulation. For example, whether the enterprise has the right to set its own
prices will affect the nature of the price system. Metaphorically, unless a
ball (an enterprise) is full of air, it will not bounce in response to an external
market stimulus. And if the market is to be regulated by the government,
one needs to know the nature of the market before one can talk meaningfully about macro-control. The logical sequence of reforms, therefore, is
from enterprise reform to price reform and then to macro-control (author's
interview, July 27, 1988).

Li Yining's view is based in part on his pragmatic assessment of the
probable pros and cons of price reform under China's conditions in the late
1980s. For in addition to the preceding theoretical reasoning, he argues that
price reform entails various risks for which the nation is not ready – for
example, the citizens' adverse response to price increases, local governments' fiscal concerns, and various uncertain and irreversible effects (Li
Yining, 1986b).

The theoretical basis of the integrated reform school of thought is that an
autonomous enterprise that is responsible for its own profits and losses cannot exist without a competitive market, and that "enterprises are not merely
the main actors in the market – they are themselves the sum of market relations" (Wu Jinglian and Zhou Xiaochuan, 1988: 10). Thus, unless and
until a market-oriented price mechanism is established, it is inevitable that
part of the allocative function will be performed by administrators, and enterprises will not be independent of government interference. The lack of a
competitive market coupled with numerous government regulations creates
various opportunities for rent seeking by enterprises as well as government
officials. The problems created under the dual-track price system are examples of such rent-seeking activities. Therefore, price reform, the perfection
of the market, and the elimination of administrative controls of enterprises
are necessary (Wu Jinglian, 1988).

As to the uncertain risks of price reform, this school of thought argues
that they would not be significant when weighed against the "certain" risks
that would arise from delaying the needed price reform – the costs of con-

tinuing the inequitable distribution of income, the inefficient allocation of resources, and so forth (Wu Jinglian and Zhao Renwei, 1987: 315–18; Wu Jinglian and Zhou Xiaochuan, 1988: 86–7). In addition, the price increases due to price reform can be minimized by implementing concurrent macro-reforms, particularly by adopting a tighter monetary policy to control aggregate demand. From this perspective, this school criticizes Li Yining for being inconsistent because Li abhors the risk of inflation due to price reform and yet condones the expansionary monetary policy pursued by the government. Li Yining opposes tight monetary policy because it reduces the growth rate.

In terms of the time horizon for price reform, the enterprise-reform school would allow a relatively long period; in Li Yining's view, the dual-track price system does not have to be abolished before the year 2000 (Ignatius, 1988). On the other hand, the integrated-reform school wants a phased implementation, with about three years for the first phase. Wu Jinglian warns that if China does not start its price reform within three years, it will slide into a deepening economic crisis such as the one the Eastern European countries were experiencing in 1988 (author's interview, July 21, 1988; see also Ignatius in *WSJ*, Oct. 28, 1988: 10).

The position of the third school of thought is somewhere between that of the first two. This school includes various economists of the Chinese Academy of Social Sciences such as Liu Guoguang, a vice president of the academy; Zhao Renwei, director of its Institute of Economics; Zhang Zhuoyuan, director of its Institute of Finance and Trade Economics; and several members of the last-named institute (*CMJJ*, 1988, No. 12: 3–10). Lin Ling (1988), vice president of the Sichuan Academy of Social Sciences, holds similar views. This school also wants a competitive market environment and market-determined prices but differs from the first two schools in other respects. First, it contends that enterprise ownership reform and price reform are equally important and should be coordinated to support each other; therefore, it is not useful, as Li Yining does, to emphasize one over the other in the time sequence. In fact, Liu Guoguang (1988b) contends that enterprise and price reforms are complementary, not mutually exclusive. Zhang Zhuoyuan (1988a: 5) points out that the enterprise's right to set its own prices should be an important part of enterprise reform; hence price reform is essential to China's market-oriented reforms.

On the other hand, this school of thought holds that effective price reform requires some preconditions that China lacked in 1988 because of inflation and lack of market integration. Hence it does not agree with Wu Jinglian's school that China's price reform can or should be implemented in a few years. The first and primary precondition is price stability. However, economists of this school differ among themselves as to what constitutes price stability. According to Zhang Zhuoyuan (1988a: 5–6; also author's interview, July 7, 1988), some economists want the annual price increase to be kept below 1 percent before the necessary price stability for price reform is reached, in their view; others, including Zhang himself, accept a 3 to 5 percent annual price increase as compatible with price stability; still others regard 3 to 5 percent as difficult to attain in China and are willing to settle for 6 percent.

The need for price stability has implications for monetary policy and other government policies. Most economists of this school regard the growth rate of the money supply in China – on average, more than 20 percent annually since 1979 – as excessive. Assuming a GNP growth rate of 8 percent, Zhang Zhuoyuan (1988a: 6) wants to keep the annual growth rate of the money supply within 11 to 15 percent. In conjunction with a tight monetary policy, he would raise the interest rate on deposits in accordance with the rate of inflation, or even the expected rate of inflation, so that the real rate of interest would be 2 to 4 percent (Zhang Zhuoyuan, 1988b). This is part of his scheme for coordinated price–wage–interest rate reforms. Zhao Renwei does not favor a tight monetary policy but would control the growth of investment and consumption and would reduce the fragmentation of the market in order to reduce the inflationary pressure (author's interview, Aug. 1, 1988). Liu Guoguang (1988b) favors the creation of a limited buyers' market to fight inflation.

The diverse views of China's pro-market economists on price reform reflect the great diversity and increased sophistication of China's functional economics. It is clear that Chinese economists have increasingly mastered and applied the tools of Western economics. Naturally, to some extent, the diverse views also reflect different economists' assessment of the political feasibility of price reform. This is an issue on which it would be difficult for outsiders to pass judgment. However, in terms of theoretical soundness and logical consistency, this author feels that the integrated-reform school has the upper hand for the reasons it has given. To put it in terms of Jiang Yiwei's metaphor, it is true that one wants the "enterprise ball" to be full of "air" (vitality) and capable of bouncing in response to the market stimulus. However, one certainly does not want it to bounce aimlessly or in the wrong direction in response to an inappropriate market stimulus, for then the costs of retrieving the stray ball in terms of wasted resources would certainly be greater than those of price increases due to price reform. But most important of all, a competitive market is not possible without market-determined prices. And in a competitive market, the enterprises will have to be responsive to market prices or face the possibility of losses and bankruptcy. This is, after all, the intent of enterprise reform and of the new Bankruptcy Law.

As Zhang Zhuoyuan (1987: 8) points out, Li Yining (1986b, 1987a) is inconsistent in denying the primacy and urgency of price reform while at the same time regarding the market as the primary level of economic adjustment and government regulation as the secondary level of adjustment. Furthermore, Li Yining advocates transforming large state-owned enterprises into joint-stock companies. For the reform to be effective, stock prices have to be determined by supply and demand in a competitive stock market. A competitive stock market cannot develop without the existence of a competitive product market. As China's limited experience to date in enterprise stocks shows, many enterprises have manipulated their stock prices downward for sale to their own workers as disguised bonuses. In other words, without a competitive market framework including realistic prices, any attempt to introduce fragments of the market mechanism on a piecemeal basis is bound to produce distorted and undesirable effects on the economy. The strategy recommended by Li Yining of pursuing price–wage reforms after the market system has been "perfected" through enterprise-ownership reform is illogical and illusory because the market system, by definition, cannot be perfected without free market prices.

Concerning the view of the third school that price stability is a precondition for price reform, although it has much support, the 1 percent and 3 to 5 percent annual rate of price increase given by some economists as necessary for price stability in China seem unrealistically low to this author. The major reason is that in all developing countries, some structural inflation is inevitable if the economy is undergoing structural changes with supply rigidities and market disequilibria. This is certainly the case in China, where rapid structural and institutional changes have taken place in a fragmented market. If price reform cannot be initiated until this level of price stability is attained, it certainly will not be implemented, if ever, for a long time. In that case, the certain risks from delaying the needed price reform would no doubt exceed the uncertain risks of price reform, as the integrated-reform school has argued.

Wage determination and reform

China's wage discussions have traditionally centered on the Marxist dictum of "distribution according to labor." In this author's view, what Yu Guangyuan (1986a) has said about value-centered price discussions is also true of wage discussions, namely that Chinese economists have spent too much time and energy on a proposition that is neither that "difficult" (Yu's word) nor "profound" or "useful" (this author's words) and that does not deserve so much pious attention. In spite of the general decline of the Marxist ideology in China, concern over this principle has not disappeared from China's wage discussions. As late as 1988, following the reformist proposal to create a "labor market," a polemical fire was rekindled over the issue of whether or not labor power is a commodity under socialism (see Chapter 2) and whether or not the principle of distribution according to labor is being carried out in China (*JJLLJJGL*, No. 2, 1988: 20–39).

As surveyed by Zhang Wenmin (1985), China has had four distinct periods of wage discussions since the founding of the People's Republic: 1949–57, 1958–66, 1966–76, and the post-Mao period, all concerned, in one way or another, with the interpretation or application of the principle of distribution according to labor. We shall not attempt to survey all the major issues in these discussions, as many of them are ideological and are analytically shallow, at least from a non-Marxist perspective. We shall only highlight a few main points to illustrate the nature of these discussions and to show how they are related to recent wage reform proposals.

Zhao Renwei, director of the Institute of Economics, the Chinese Academy of Social Sciences, has commented to this author that in post-Mao China throughout the early 1980s, economists were preoccupied with refuting the extreme leftist ideas of the Cultural Revolution period, with the result that many of the "theoretical advances" merely restored China's economics to the orthodoxy of the late 1950s and early 1960s. There is much truth in this observation, as can be seen in China's wage and price discussions. The early post-Mao period saw the continuation of the debate of the 1950s and 1960s on whether "distribution according to labor" is conditional on "from each according to his labor," and whether the principle implies that labor power is "completely privately owned" or "partly privately owned," and whether it is therefore a "commodity" (Zhang Wenmin, 1985 139–40, 145–6). We shall not examine these exercises or indulgences in ideological hair splitting.

Since 1986, economists have gradually departed from this traditional line of diagnostic economics. Some have contended that in China's current stage of socialism, distribution according to labor is not the only method of distribution. In the case of individually or collectively run enterprises, their income is based on performance or results in the market. In the case of joint-stock companies, the distribution of dividends and interest is based on the ownership of capital funds (see Chapter 3). However, some economists interpret this "distribution according to capital" as a special form of distribution according to labor under China's current conditions because the capital funds come originally from labor income. Other economists argue that distribution according to labor is possible only in a non-commodity economy; hence, in China's socialist commodity economy, that principle is not applicable (Xiang Qiyuan, 1987: 6). Still other economists allow for deviations from that principle in China during the primary stage of socialism (*JJLLJJGL,* No. 2, 1988: 28–9). In short, the Marxist principle is no longer sacrosanct, and Chinese economists do not have a consensus on its applicability in China. Nevertheless, it remains the major frame of reference in the discussions of income distribution and wages.

One important issue that is related to both the principle of distribution according to labor and wage reform concerns the low wages of college-educated "intellectuals" or "mental workers" relative to those of manual or "physical workers." China's wage structure in this respect has undergone drastic changes since 1952. In 1952–7, college graduates earned more than production workers, but the differentials were modest, especially when compared with those that existed before 1949. In 1957–75, the differentials were eliminated through successive wage adjustments. In 1976, manual workers started to make more than intellectuals. The basic reason is that although the *basic wages* of the two groups are about the same, production workers receive more supplementary wages in the form of bonuses. According to a survey conducted in Beijing in 1982, the average monthly income of intellectual workers was 79.47 yuan, whereas that of manual workers was 86.36 yuan (He Xiaopei, 1982: 33–5. The official exchange rate was $1 = 1.9 yuan in 1982). A survey conducted in Beijing in January 1988 shows the figures to be 172 and 182 yuan, respectively ($1 = 3.7 yuan in 1988). This same survey shows that among state employees with the same seniority, the average monthly pay of those with high school and college educations was 169 yuan, whereas the pay of those with a junior high school education or below was 194 yuan (*GRMB,* Oct. 6, 1988:1). It is this type of absurd distributional inequity that promoted the *Economist* (Nov. 26, 1988: 36) to remark that "in China, the less you know the more you earn." Teachers' salaries in particular are so low that, of the twelve vocations officially classified in China, education was the third lowest paid in 1988 (*JJRB,* Sept. 9, 1988: 1).

The low wages of college graduates, coupled with the fact that individuals engaged in private businesses are making even more than production workers (see Chapter 4), has adversely affected the entire educational system. Schools at all levels are having problems attracting and retaining students (*GMRB,* Oct. 6, 1988: 1; *RMRB,* Aug. 27, 1988: 3). If the trend continues, its long-term consequences will be disastrous.

China's low wages for intellectuals are the cumulative result of the egalitarian and anti-intellectual bias of the pre-1978 period and of the increased enterprise autonomy in the post-1979 period to increase workers' bonuses. In the diagnostic economics literature, some authors have justified this anti-intellectual bias by accepting the orthodox interpretation of "productive labor" as physical labor that directly produces material goods and surplus products (*GMRB*, Dec. 16, 1963; Lin Chuanshui, 1985: 659). In addition, the Chinese have found ideological support for the low pay of intellectuals in a statement in Engels's *Anti-Dühring* that under socialism the training cost of "complex labor" is borne by the state, and therefore the greater value produced by complex labor should belong to the state (*MEXJ*, Vol. 3: 241; Zhang Wenmin, 1986: 391). Whatever the validity of Engels's point, it suggests no more than wage parity between intellectuals and production workers. China has erred in going beyond it by paying less to the former than to the latter.

In response to this discriminatory anti-intellectual wage policy, post-Mao Chinese economists have criticized its ideological foundation as well as its practical consequences. In the early 1960s, they started debating about the nature of productive labor and about whether intellectual labor is productive labor. After the hiatus of the Cultural Revolution period, the debate was resumed in 1979, reaching its peak in 1982. The major conclusion reached in the post-1979 period is that the mental labor provided by managers, teachers, the premier, and even the Liberation Army that produces "spiritual" or intellectual products is productive labor in a broad sense. The reasons are that it contributes indirectly to the production of material products and that it directly satisfies the growing cultural needs of the socialist society (Lin Chuanshui, 1985: 657–66).[5] A dissenting minority view regards mental labor such as education as important in the *reproduction* of productive labor but does not regard it as productive labor in the Marxist sense, just as rest and recreation contribute to the reproduction of productive labor but are not productive labor per se (Lin Chuanshui, 1985: 666).

Using the Marxist categories of complex labor and simple labor, He Xiaopei (1982: 38–9) argues that complex labor creates much more value than simple labor and should therefore be paid more in accordance with the labor theory of value. As to Engels's statement on the financing of complex labor under socialism, Zhang Wenmin (1986: 392) contends that Engels's point does not justify the lower wages paid to intellectuals in China. Even if

---

[5] One interesting irony that arises from equating mental labor with productive labor concerns the nature of royalties. China has long rewarded authors on the basis of distribution according to labor by estimating the amount of socially necessary labor expended on manuscript writing and multiplying it by the wage rate of the "same type" of physical labor (*GMRB*, Sept. 18, 1988: 1). This practice was increasingly criticized by authors in 1987–8 because it entails a lump-sum payment, which subjects authors to a higher income tax. The critics generally argue that an intellectual product is produced over a long period of time, and therefore should not be taxed as a one-period product. Some authors go further and argue that royalties are not rewards for labor but are payments for the use of an intellectual product; as such, the amount of payment should be based on the commercial profits derived from its use, and the payments can be made as frequently as the intellectual product is used (*GMRB*, Sept. 18, 1988: 1).

society pays the full training cost of complex labor, the amount is necessarily much smaller than the additional value created by complex labor; otherwise, the training will not be worthwhile. Therefore, after paying back the training cost to society, intellectuals are still entitled to receive more in accordance with their labor. Zhang Xianyang (1988), although making the same point, also recognizes that because of fiscal constraints, it is unrealistic for intellectuals to expect higher pay in the near future. Consequently, he urges them to give up secure employment, take risks, and go where market opportunities and higher pay are available. Although this suggestion is consistent with China's need for greater labor mobility, it is a sad commentary on the political reality of China. Chinese leaders seek modernization but are unable or unwilling to reward their educated human resources properly.

This author finds Zhang Wenmin's socialist marginal analysis interesting. From a broader perspective, however, the whole Chinese discussion of productive labor and complex labor constitutes a sad chapter in China's economics. It reflects vividly the *irrationality of policies* and the *sterility of theories* that can result when policies and their legitimizing theories are based on a dogmatic interpretation of an ideology or of a simplistic ideological statement made by Marx, Engels, or anyone else who is not to be contradicted. It is indeed pathetic that Chinese economists have to prove their worth by justifying their labor as productive labor. In its anti-intellectual wage policy, Chinese socialism has sunk to a very low level and in the process has weakened the prospects for its modernization.

Concerning the reform of workers' wages, a relatively innovative post-Mao idea that reflects the reformist spirit of the times was advanced by Jiang Yiwei (1980b). This is the proposal of "two-step distribution according to labor" in order to solve the past problem of egalitarianism between enterprises. Jiang criticizes his colleagues for concentrating on the narrow issue of distribution to individuals within an enterprise while ignoring the larger issue of the need for society to distribute to enterprises according to their contributions to society. Because an individual's labor can become society's labor only through the enterprise, both levels of distribution should be made according to labor or contributions.

Critics do not oppose the idea of linking the laborer's pay to the performance of the enterprise, but they do not consider the state's distribution to the enterprise to be within the purview of distribution according to labor. The reason is that Marx's principle refers to the distribution of consumer goods to individuals, whereas the funds allocated by the state to enterprises are for purposes of both consumption (such as bonuses) and reproduction. Because an enterprise is simultaneously a production unit of the state and a workplace where laborers combine their labor with the means of production to earn their livelihood, an enterprise's economic interest is not related to distribution according to labor and should not be characterized as such (Zhang Wenmin, 1985: 137–8). Another criticism is that the size of an enterprise's profits already reflects or embodies the Marxist principle. Hence it is redundant to have Jiang's first level of distribution according to labor (*JJGL*, 1986, No. 7: 17–20). Similarly, some authors have argued that since the basic unit of distribution in a socialist commodity economy is the enterprise, the two-step distribution scheme is inappropriate (Xiang Qiyuan, 1987: 4–5).

A benefit of Jiang Yiwei's idea is that, whether or not it is consistent with the Marxist principle, it was the first to call attention to the desirability of rewarding enterprises according to their performance. In this sense, it reflected as well as contributed to the reformist spirit of the early 1980s and hence served a useful purpose, although the same purpose could have been served without invoking the Marxist principle. With the subsequent government decision to give enterprises more autonomy in decision making, the proposal became increasingly irrelevant.

Nevertheless, Jiang's central idea that the total wages of an enterprise should somehow be linked to the enterprise's performance was supported by the majority of economists in the late 1980s on both macro and micro grounds (Xiang Qiyuan 1987: 5). From the macro point of view, it is argued that the principle will ensure that the growth rate of wages will not exceed that of national income and labor productivity; this has become an important concern of economists since the mid-1980s because of inflation, including "bonus inflation" (see Chapter 3). On the other hand, it is contended that the principle will ensure that planners will not carry out production for its own sake without paying due regard to workers' consumption, which was a serious problem of the earlier planning system. From the point of view of microeconomics, it is believed that linking total wages to enterprise profits will increase the incentives of enterprises and workers.

In terms of policy implementation, however, disagreement arises among economists on equity grounds because China's enterprise profits are still distorted by vestiges of the old planning system and do not accurately reflect the relative performances of enterprises. Consequently, some economists want to introduce various other changes first before total wages are linked to enterprise profits. For example, prices have to be rationalized; a capital tax and a resource tax have to be introduced so that enterprise profits will only reflect enterprise performance; and a wage tax should be introduced to prevent excessive wage differentials. It is also argued that the state needs to develop a comprehensive and equitable system of indicators and "linkage coefficients." Before these changes are completed, only a "weak linkage" or "half-linkage" is appropriate (Xiang Qiyuan, 1987: 5).

Some economists oppose altogether the idea of linking total wages to enterprise performance by any administrative means on the grounds that it will interfere with the operation of the market mechanism. It will affect not only the autonomy of the enterprise with respect to the use of labor, but also the mobility of workers between enterprises. The best approach to wage reform, according to this line of analysis, is to open up the labor market and let market forces determine the wage levels (Xiang Qiyuan, 1987: 5–6). Before the labor market is liberalized, Zhao Lükuan and Yang Tiren (1988), two advocates of a free labor market, are willing to let the government set the average wage rate of an enterprise by linking it to the enterprise's labor productivity rather than to its profits. It is argued that this interim measure will duly reward workers for their performance while at the same time eliminating workers' pressure on the enterprise to give them competitive wage hikes; this is considered essential in order to keep China's export prices competitive. In addition, the linkage with the average wage rate rather than with total wages will give the enterprise greater autonomy in decision making concerning the use of labor and other inputs, thus paving the way for the liberalization of the labor market. Finally, it is contended that profits are not created by workers alone. If wages are tied to profits rather than to labor productivity, workers may become lazy and seek undesirable ways to increase enterprise profits in order to increase wages.

Song Yangyan and Wang Haidong (1988) want to tie wages to labor productivity by reforming the *composition* of China's wage system. They point out that Chinese workers' wages consist of two components: labor income or a fixed wage, which is part of the costs of production, and nonlabor income such as bonuses and welfare funds, which comes from the enterprises' retained profits. This duality gives rise to a number of problems: (1) It permits workers' income to rise faster than the increase in labor productivity because the former can grow due to increases in enterprise profits, which are not necessarily due to increases in labor productivity. (2) The nonlabor income component reduces the enterprises' ability to invest out of profits and forces them to rely on bank loans for investment, thus increasing the money supply. (3) Bonuses stimulate consumption and lead to price increases. (4) On the other hand, workers' fixed wages are too low to support a family, which forces the state to control the prices of essential products and social services at low levels.

Because of these problems, Song and Wang contend that China's price reform would inevitably lead to price–wage spirals. To overcome this problem, they suggest a reform that would lump the wage fund, bonus fund, and welfare fund together as the "labor contract fund," which would be part of the costs of production. When total costs of production decline, presumably because of higher labor productivity, the labor contract fund would increase, and vice versa. In this way, workers' earnings would be tied to labor productivity rather than to enterprise profits, and the inflationary potential of price reform would be minimized. Song Yangyan and Wang Haidong (1988) have not considered the case where the costs of production increase because of higher material input prices. In this case, it would seem unfair to reduce the labor contract fund.

In general, advocates of linkage between wages and labor productivity implicitly define the latter in physical terms, namely, in terms of the average (not marginal) physical product of labor rather than the average revenue product of labor; there is no discussion of the marginal revenue product of labor, which is the determinant of the competitive wage rate in Western economics. Consequently, when the price of the enterprise's product is increased, the wage rate remains the same. Although this can be justified on the grounds that China's prices are still irrational, problems arise when prices in general are rising. Thus, in recent years, because of inflation, economists have become more concerned with a different type of wage linkage – linking wages to the price level. The policy relevance of this is underscored by the fact that in 1988 the government decided to raise some food prices while at the same time subsidizing wage earners for the increases.[6] In this author's view, the government's decision was justified because it is better to have more realistic prices for allocative efficiency combined at the same time with *overt* wage subsidy for equity purposes than to have *covert* subsidy in the form of controlled low prices at the expense of allocative efficiency. Chinese economists' discussions of wage–price linkage, therefore, presume relatively free prices but administratively determined wages. As mentioned earlier, some economists oppose any administrative control of wages, including this type of wage–price linkage.

Advocates of wage–price linkage have considered two linkage methods, indexing and nonindexing. The former would calculate a wage index on the basis of prices; however, there is no consensus as to how the index should be applied – whether it should be applied to each worker's entire wage ("hard linkage") or a portion of it, to the minimum wage level or the aggregate wage fund, or merely to the limits within which wages can fluctuate. Yang Jingdong (1988) favors "soft linkage" indexing in which the aggregate wage fund is linked to the nation's cost of living index but the distribution of the increase in the fund at the micro level is based on the worker's performance.

The nonindexing method would use bonuses, wage adjustments, or subsidies to compensate for price increases without having a rigid numerical tie to an index; proponents of this method also differ as to whether these wage

[6] The subsidy was given at the rate of 10 yuan per employee per month in 1988.

adjustments should apply to the entire wage level or to some variation of it, as mentioned earlier. Furthermore, there is no consensus as to whether the price–wage linkage system should be uniform for the whole nation or should vary with local conditions (*JJGL*, No. 6, 1988: 33–7). Chen Bingcai (1988), for example, favors a nonindexing wage adjustment system for basic or standard wages; the adjustment is to be set by local governments. He opposes indexing for fear of escalating inflation and because of its fiscal implications for local governments, which have to bear the burden of wage adjustments. Song Yangyan and Wang Haidong (1988) support neither wage indexing nor a general subsidy scheme, as was adopted in 1988. They favor a selective subsidy to be given only to low-income families.

Some supporters of wage indexing recognize the risk of wage–price spirals in indexation and are willing to adopt *partial* wage indexing on the basis of both prices and labor productivity. They maintain, however, that wage indexing is necessary to prevent the decline of real wages and to ensure that the share of consumption in national income will not be eroded by continuous expansion of investment funds (*GMRB*, May 7, 1988: 3).

In conclusion, as of mid-1989, there was no consensus among Chinese economists on price and wage reforms. Because China's price reform has been postponed, so has serious wage reform. However, China's recent price–wage discussion does illustrate its functional economics at work – its attempt to include wide-ranging micro and macro concerns, and its pragmatic pros-and-cons–weighing approach with increasing sophistication. However, most Chinese economists are still not accustomed to using rigorous quantitative methods. For example, they have not utilized rigorous quantitative methods to determine the main causes of inflation or to estimate the possible impact of wage increases on inflation, even though these are essential to the issues under discussion. Thus, China's technical economics has not yet been integrated into its mainstream economics. Ironically, it is left to economists in the West, especially Chinese-American economists such as Chen and Hou (1986) and Chow (1987), to fill the gap. Chow's study is particularly interesting; it shows a very low impact of wage increase on inflation.[7] Although that study is concerned with 1952–83 – a period of mostly controlled prices and low inflation – and therefore may not be applicable to the post-1985 period of high inflation, it does indicate an area in which Chinese economists are weak and a methodology that can be used to improve their discussion of price–wage issues.

[7] Gregory Chow (1987: 331–2) obtains a very low wage elasticity of inflation, 0.043, for the wage variable in his regression of inflation for 1952–83.

CHAPTER 6

Summaries and conclusions

Chapters 2–5 have examined Chinese economists' discussions of various economic reform issues. We have seen that there are broad propositions that are accepted by many leading economists, but that divergent views exist on many specific issues. In this chapter, a summary of some of these shared views and differences is given as a brief review of, or a quick guide to, the broad contours of China's economic theories of the reform decade. In addition, a summary of some economists' political views is given. Although these political views have not been discussed, they are pertinent here because they are related to China's reform problems and because they may throw light on the future of reforms and socialism in China. In the concluding section of the chapter, the author offers some personal reflections on socialism, politics, and economics in China.

Summaries

Before summarizing Chinese economists' discussions, it is important to re-iterate a central point discussed in Chapter 1, namely, the politically constrained nature of academic freedom in China. The limits and tone of academic discussions are invariably set by political leaders, by their ideological leanings, political objectives, and policy preferences. In addition, the limits are invariably much narrower for the ideological foundation of economics (diagnostic economics in this study) than for functional and technical economic analyses. Although the limits of academic freedom during the 1979–88 period were relatively broad and flexible, they did constrain the terms of the debate on economic issues. Thus the consensus and agreements that exist among economists, as discussed in Chapters 2–5 and as summarized here, have to be understood in this context.

1. At the level of ideological beliefs or diagnostic economics, there is a consensus among Chinese economists that the objective of economic reforms is to make socialism more compatible with China's conditions (the primary stage of socialism), not to abandon it; and that China's economic problems arise not because socialism has

170

failed, but because China has failed to interpret and implement socialism properly or flexibly. Thus, although Chinese economic theories of the 1979–88 period amount to a successful reinterpretation of socialism and an effective critique of the traditional centrally planned economic system, they are not seen as the rejection of socialism per se. Socialist reform is believed to be the process of the self-perfection of socialism, just as capitalism has gone through a long evolutionary process of reform and renewal. In addition, it is generally accepted that China should strive to develop socialism with Chinese characteristics because of its unique conditions (Chapters 1 and 3). Parenthetically, whatever the believability of the preceding consensus, this author is convinced, on the basis of many private conversations, that the *ideals* and *potentials* of socialism are still alive and important to many Chinese economists, particularly the older ones who saw the ills of early capitalism in the pre–1949 economy.

2. After a tortuous course of debate, it is generally agreed that the socialist economy is a planned commodity economy. Thus it utilizes both planning and the market as the adjustment mechanisms of the economy, just as a capitalist economy utilizes both of them. Therefore, there is a tendency toward convergence between socialism and capitalism. The market mechanism is necessary for flexibility and efficiency, and market-induced differences in income are necessary as incentives. At the same time, state planning is needed to guide and coordinate micro activities and to achieve macro objectives (Chapter 2).

3. The critical difference between capitalism and socialism lies in the nature of ownership of the means of production, which determines the nature of production relations. At China's primary stage of socialism, a system of socialist mixed ownership is appropriate, with the dominance of public ownership and a minor but useful element of private ownership. However, there is no consensus on the best form of public ownership. Many economists would like to modify or replace state ownership with alternative forms of public ownership such as enterprise ownership, shareholding ownership, and so forth. Nevertheless, many other economists still regard state ownership as the best form of public ownership and claim that its problems can be solved by separating the state's ownership right from the enterprise's management right (Chapter 3).

4. At the level of functional economics, many economists believe that state-owned enterprises should be given much more autonomy and made responsible for their own profits and losses. Many economists

favor the management contract responsibility system to separate the state's ownership right from the enterprise's management right so that state interference in enterprise management can be eliminated. To ensure the compatibility of enterprise autonomy with macro control and balances, the state should rely primarily on guidance planning and use only a minimum amount of mandatory planning to influence enterprise activities. The market environment should also be perfected under proper state guidance in order to rationalize enterprise behavior (Chapter 3).

5. Prices in the economy should be largely market determined, with government-set prices kept to a minimum. The existing dual-track price system is unworkable and inequitable; it also hinders the further development of the market mechanism and should be replaced in a price reform by market equilibrium prices. However, there are sharp disagreements among economists as to whether price reform should precede or follow further enterprise reforms. In addition, there is no agreement as to whether price stability has to be attained first before price reform can be implemented (Chapter 5).

6. Concerning the development of the economy, most economists support the new reformist emphasis on efficiency over the past egalitarian principle. Consequently, they advocate development in agriculture and industry according to regional comparative advantage and support the open-door policy for foreign trade and investment. Rural industrialization is recommended by many economists to employ rural surplus labor. However, critics argue that rural enterprises are inefficient and divert raw materials from state-owned enterprises (Chapter 4).

Economists' political views

Chinese economists' political views are not the focus of this study. Nevertheless, economic and political issues cannot be separated in China, and political matters affect profoundly the outcome of economic reforms. In the relatively open academic environment of 1988 and in the exuberant atmosphere of mass support for the pro-democracy movement in May 1989, some Chinese economists ventured to comment on political issues in informal conversations with this author. Their remarks are enlightening and show a level of political sophistication seldom seen in their economic writings. Although the identity of these economists cannot be revealed, a composite picture of their views can be given. It is impossible to tell whether these economists represent the majority of Chinese economists, but this author believes that their remarks are sincere and genuinely reflect the views of mainstream reformist economists. Consequently, it is pertinent to consider them as one ponders the prospects for China's socialism and reforms. In the following, these remarks are synthesized.

1. The first and most important consensus is that the existing political system or process needs to be reformed and made more pluralistic and responsive if the economy is to develop further and China is to modernize. The basic reason for this is that economic reforms have made the economy pluralistic, which requires a more pluralistic and responsive political system to represent the diverse interests of the economy and society. The first step in that direction is to separate the government from the Communist Party and make the former truly accountable to the representatives of the people rather than to party leaders. It is not clear, however, how this can be done. High party and government officials are generally considered to be corrupt because of the nature of the political system or process.

2. However, as of late May 1989, these economists did not support the overthrow of the Communist Party and the introduction of the Western parliamentary system in the pursuit of political pluralism. There are two major reasons for this. First, there is no other political party in China to replace the Communist Party, and there would be a power vacuum and chaos if it were overthrown. Second, the cultural tradition of the country and the low educational level of the population would make Western-type elections and democracy unworkable under current conditions. A more open government that is truly separated from the Communist Party, coupled with peaceful competition among different factions of the party, as in Japan, is seen as a viable alternative. Reportedly, younger economists and other intellectuals tend to favor Western-style democracy or democratic socialism of the Western European variety.

3. Under China's current conditions, capitalism or the dominance of private ownership will not work. It will lead to exploitive "primitive capitalism" at the level of small employers and "bureaucratic capitalism" at the level of large corporations. Large-scale privatization is not desirable because only families of privileged officials will have the means to purchase public enterprises. Their wealth and their rent-seeking activities will be further enhanced and legitimized.

4. Whatever the personal political fortunes of individual leaders, China should not and will not revert to the pre-reform system of traditional central planning and international isolation. This is not just because the failings of the traditional system are by now all too

clear. It is also because new vested interests have been created. Under the traditional system of central control and the closed-door policy, few personal gains can be made in the cracks of the system. Under the current dual-track price system, coupled with lucrative foreign trade and investment, large loopholes exist for personal enrichment for many well-connected people. Thus many top cadres who ideologically favor central planning would support the status quo; they too have become converted "reformers" in matters of pocketbooks and foreign bank accounts. What China needs, therefore, are deeper market-oriented reforms that would open up opportunities on the basis of competition and ability, not political power.

5. Finally, in spite of China's numerous problems and its dire need for political reform, these economists do not consider socialism in China since 1949 a complete failure. Post-1949 China has had its share of accomplishments, and socialism has a future in China if proper reforms are implemented. China's problems lie mainly in the way party leaders in the past have attempted to introduce socialism, not in socialism itself.

This author agrees completely with these economists on the need for political reform, but not on their assessment of socialism. The reasons are explained in the next section.

Concluding remarks

Engels once wrote:

When, therefore, the French Revolution had realized this rational society and this rational state, it became apparent that the new institution . . . were by no means absolutely rational. The rational state had suffered shipwreck. . . . The antithesis between rich and poor, instead of being resolved in general well-being, had been sharpened. . . . Trade developed more and more into swindling. . . . Corruption took the place of violent oppression, and money replaced the sword as the chief lever of social power. . . . In a word, compared with the flowing promises of the prophets of the Enlightenment, the social and political institutions established by the "victory of reason" proved to be bitterly disillusioning caricatures. (Engels, Anti-Dühring, part III, section 1; MEXJ, Vol. 3: 298, 320, 322)

This passage from Engels's Anti-Dühring is quoted at length by Hua Sheng, Zhang Xuejun, and Luo Xiaopeng (1988b:16) – three young radical reform advocates at the Chinese Academy of Social Sciences – to dramatize and support their bold, wide-ranging critiques of socialism in general and in China in particular. (Their critique of state ownership in China and their advocacy of privatization are discussed in Chapter 3.) And following Engels's statement, they have rendered their own judgment: "Today, more than one hundred years later, when socialist believers contrast the socialist practice of more than half a century with the earlier promises of great socialist pioneers, they cannot but feel that history once again seems to have played a mockery on those who pursue the ideal world.''

In this author's view, any objective observer would agree with their conclusion. For in assessing a political-economic system, it is not its high ideals or theoretical potential, but its actual performance, that is important. As shown by the events of April–June 1989 in China – the student demonstrations for democracy and against corruption, the outpouring of citizens' support for them, and the shocking massacre in Tiananmen Square – Chinese socialism in practice has failed miserably to fulfill the lofty promises that had inspired its early followers. With few changes in words, Engels's critique of the French Revolution could accurately describe the ills that plagued China in the late 1980s. More recent developments in Eastern Europe also suggest that socialism in general has fared very poorly.

It is true that capitalism in its early stages had its share of failures, as many Chinese reformers have repeatedly pointed out. But that does not justify the continuing dictatorship and atrocities of the primary stage of socialism in China or any other country. With modern education and technology in the late twentieth century, no country need experience the follies of early capitalism in order to learn its limitations and the secrets of its success in the post–World War II era. Similarly – and party leaders permitting – no country need endure the persecutions and massacres of primitive socialism in order to pursue the "self-perfection" of socialism and learn the elusiveness of socialist dreams.

It is also true that the problems of corruption, economic mismanagement, and low productivity are not unique to China; many capitalist Third World countries have equally serious or even worse problems. Nor are these problems unique to the post-1949 period of China's modern history; the Nationalist government that preceded the Communist government faced similar problems and also failed to solve them. In fact, the failure of the Nationalist government was responsible to a large extent for the founding of the Chinese Communist Party in 1921 and its triumph in 1949. Thus, unlike Eastern Europe, socialism as a political force in China was not a forced transplant from the Soviet Union at the end of World War II; it had germinated in China's native soil and had developed its roots among a large segment of the populace by the mid-1940s because of the ills of China's early capitalism. In other words, it had a favorable environment for its growth.

Yet forty years after its triumph – a period of time that is long enough for Chinese socialism to have proved itself – China was plagued with so many problems, and its leadership had so few political resources to cope with them, that it resorted to the Tiananmen Square massacre. Ironically, history has returned to haunt the Chinese Communist Party: Many of its early leaders were themselves idealistic student leaders who had demonstrated for democracy. The inescapable conclusion, therefore, is that the nature of the socialist political-economic system itself is the major cause of China's problems. That is why China's political-economic system needs to be reformed. Furthermore, as we have seen throughout this book, without meaningful political reform, economic reform cannot be effective and cannot be the engine of modernization under China's current conditions.

The basic reason for the primacy of political reform in China is what Marx would have said and what the Chinese Marxist leaders should have learned: The outmoded political "superstructure" has become incompatible with the new economic "foundation" and is thus constricting the latter's further development. More specifically, several factors were at work in China during 1979–88 to heighten the need for political change. First, the introduction of the market has instilled in the populace the idea that wealth and power should be based on ability and fair competition rather than on party membership and political connections. Thus, when high officials and top party cadres enjoy unchallenged power and privileges, and are enriching themselves by circumventing equal market competition, citizens cannot be expected to refrain from illegal economic activities and enterprises cannot be expected to change their short-sighted behavior, to the detriment of economic development. Second, economic reforms have given the Chinese people new economic freedom and opportunities. Naturally, most people aspire to political freedom as well, both as an end in itself and as a means to protect their fragile economic freedom. Third, the open-door policy of the reform decade, which was necessary to attract foreign capital and technology, has made the Chinese people painfully aware of the economic-political backwardness of their country, in comparison with not only the United States and Japan but also Taiwan, and hence distrustful of the political system that has periodically plunged the country into turmoil while promising for forty years that socialist prosperity is just around the corner.

It is not surprising, therefore, that the decade of economic reforms culminated in the mass movement for democracy in 1989 in spite of repeated official campaigns against "bourgeois liberalization." And the tragedy of 1989 in China – the fact that idealistic students demonstrating for democracy were hounded down as counterrevolutionaries, and that a few frightened party leaders made the fatal decision to attack them with troops and tanks, in total disregard of due process and human rights – underscores vividly the incompatibility of China's political system with democracy and modernization that the Chinese people are seeking.

This author must conclude, therefore, that the socialist political movement that gave rise to the Communist government in 1949 has run its course, spent its force, and outlived its times; China can be regenerated only in another political movement of a democratic nature. Without fundamental political change, economic reforms cannot progress further and the economy will be trapped in a vicious circle of political abuse, widespread discontent, low productivity, and human degradation.

Whatever the future of economic reforms in China, the economic theories of 1979–88 constitute an invaluable and enduring legacy of the reform decade. Distilled from China's reform experience, rich in diversity and insights, these theories will outlast any political leadership to become part of the permanent intellectual heritage of the period, to be drawn on in the future. As we have seen throughout this book, the progress made by Chinese economists in the short span of ten years is truly impressive for three reasons. First, in spite of their initial lack of knowledge about non-Marxist methodology and theories, by 1988 Chinese economists had learned and applied many analytical concepts and techniques that are primarily Western in origin. Second, they have traveled a great distance in the development of their own economic theories, which, in spite of the foreign origin of some concepts and techniques, are uniquely Chinese in substance and policy relevance. Three, in spite of the heavily ideological and dogmatic nature of their theories in the late 1970s, by the late 1980s Chinese economists had eliminated much of the dogmatism of the past interpretations of socialism and had developed new interpretations of socialism that are much more pragmatic and realistic.

For these reasons, it is appropriate to characterize the 1979–88 period as a new age for Chinese economics. In this regard, proper credit should also be given to the Zhao Ziyang leadership, which, in spite of its numerous failings, did give scholars considerable and unprecedented academic freedom to criticize the traditional socialist system, to point out the shortcomings of various reform measures, and to explore better alternatives.

Although the new economic theories have shortcomings of their own, these theories have been and will continue to be built on to develop better theories – the political environment permitting – as their shortcomings become apparent. This is the way analytical advances are made, in China as in other countries.

As a final personal remark, this author firmly believes that the reform decade of 1979–88 will not be a mere "liberal interlude" in China's economic and political development, and that this book will not become an epitaph for the spirited economic debates of the period. From the perspective of China's long history, the horrors and reverses of 1989 will merely be the birth pains of a more efficient and democratic economic-political system, a system made possible in part by the collective wisdom of the Chinese economists studied in this book.

References

Abbreviations

AER	*American Economic Review*
AS	*Asian Survey*
BR	*Beijing Review*
CD	*China Daily*
CJE	*Cambridge Journal of Economics*
CJKX	*Caijing Kexue [Finance and Economics]*
CMJJ	*Caimao Jingji [Finance and Trade Economics]*
CQ	*China Quarterly*
EC	*The Economist*
GG	*Gaige [Reforms]*
GMRB	*Guangming Ribao [Enlightenment Daily]*
GRRB	*Gongren Ribao [Workers Daily]*
HQ	*Hongqi [Red Flag]*
JAS	*Journal of Asian Studies*
JCE	*Journal of Comparative Economics*
JEL	*Journal of Economics Literature*
JGLLSJ	*Jiage Lilun yu Shijian [Price Theory and Practice]*
JJGG	*Jingji Gaige [Economic Reform]*
JJGL	*Jingji Guanli [Economic Management]*
JJLLJJGL	*Jingji Lilun yu Jingji Guanli [Economic Theory and Economic Management]*
JJRB	*Jingji Ribao [Economic Daily]*
JJXWZ	*Jingjixue Wenzai [Economics Abstract]*
JJYJ	*Jingji Yanjiu [Economic Research]*
JRSB	*Jinrong Shibao [Financial Times]*
MC	*Modern China*
MEQJ	*Makesi Engesi Quanji [Complete Works of Marx and Engels]*
MEXJ	*Makesi Engesi Xuanji [Selected Works of Marx and Engels]*
NYJJWT	*Nongye Jingji Wenti [Problems of Agricultural Economics]*
RMRB	*Renmin Ribao [People's Daily, domestic edition]*
SHKX	*Shehui Kexue [Social Sciences]*
SHKXZX	*Shehui Kexue Zhanxian [Social Sciences Front]*
SJJJDB	*Shijie Jingji Daobao [World Economy Herald]*
SLJJJSJJ	*Shuliang Jingji Jishu Jingji Yanjiu [Quantitative and Technical Economics]*
SSC	*Social Sciences in China*

SYYJ	Shangye Yanjiu [Commerce Research]
WSJ	Wall Street Journal
XSYJ	Xueshu Yanjiu [Academic Research]
XSYK	Xueshu Yuekan [Academic Monthly]
ZGCMB	Zhongguo Caimao Bao [China's Finance and Trade Journal]
ZGJJWT	Zhongguo Jingji Wenti [China's Economic Problems]
ZGSHKX	Zhongguo Shehui Kexue [China's Social Sciences]

Primary sources

Chinese authors' names are given with the family name first, followed by the given name, as is customary in China.

Cao Siyuan. 1984. "A Suggestion Concerning the Drawing up of the Bankruptcy Law," *SHKX*, No. 11, pp. 42–6.

Chen Bingcai. 1988. "On the Linkage Between Wages and Prices," *JJGL*, No. 6, 1988, pp. 33–7.

Chen Qilin and Li Wei. 1987. "Public Ownership and Private Management: A Possible Reform of Publicly Owned Enterprises," *ZGJJWT*, No. 2, pp. 1–7.

Chen Qiwei. 1986. *Guoji Jingzheng Lun [On International Competition]*. Shanghai: Xuelin Press.

Chen Suzhi. 1987. "Strive to Train New Socialist Entrepreneurs," *JJGL*, No. 4, pp. 5–7.

Chen Yun. 1986. *Chen Yun Wen Xuan, 1956–1985 [Selected Works of Chen Yun]*. Beijing: People's Press.

Chen Zhao. 1985. "Socialist Stock System," *JJYJ*, No. 4, pp. 60–3.

Dai Yuanchen. 1986. "Dual Prices in the Transition of the Economic System," *JJYJ*, No. 1, pp. 43–8.

   1987. "Industrial Policy and the Reform of the Economic System," *CMJJ*, No. 10, pp. 1–3.

Ding Changqing. 1984. "The Experience and Problems of Implementing the Three Forms of Planning and Management in the Machinery Industry," *JJGL*, No. 4, pp. 8–10.

Dong Fureng. 1963. "Questions on Studying the Practical Applications of Marx's Reproduction Formulae from the Angle of Unifying the Production and Use of Social Products," *JJYJ*, No. 3, pp. 39–51.

   1979. "Concerning the Forms of China's Socialist Ownership," *JJYJ*, No. 1, pp. 21–8.

   1984. "The Law of Value and the Reform of the Economic Structure," *RMRB*, May 14, p. 5.

   1985a. "More on the Forms of China's Socialist Ownership," *JJYJ*, No. 4, pp. 3–11.

   1985b. "External Environment and Conditions That Strengthen the Vitality of Enterprises," *RMRB*, Nov. 15, p. 5.

   1986a. "China's Strategy of Economic Development and Its Evolution," in *Jingji Yanjiu* Editorial Department (ed.), 1986, pp. 39–72.

1986b. "On the Labor System and Whether Labor Power Is a Commodity," *GMRB*, Oct. 4, p. 3.

1986c. "China's Price Reform," *CJE*, Vol. 10, pp. 291–300.

1987. "The Composition of Multi-form Ownership System with the Dominance of Multi-form Public Ownership," *SJJJDB*, July 13, p. 11.

1988a. *Jingji Fazhan Zhanlue Yanjiu [A Study of the Strategy of Economic Development]*. Beijing: Economics Science Press.

1988b. "Reform of the Economic Operational Mechanism and of the Ownership System," *JJYJ*, No. 7, pp. 27–32.

1988c. "On the Metamorphosis of Reforms," *RMRB*, Dec. 12, p. 5.

Du Hui. 1988. "Resource Constraints and Periodic Contractions," *SLJJJSJJ*, No. 4, pp. 63–9.

Du Runsheng. 1986. "Getting Rich First, Getting Rich Later, and Everyone Getting Rich," *RMRB*, Jan. 27, 1986, pp. 1–2.

Fan Maofa, Xun Dashi, and Liu Xiaoping. 1986. "The System of Stock Financing Is Not the Orientation of State Enterprises," *JJYJ*, No. 1, pp. 17–22.

Fan Maoyou and Zhang Guofu. 1979. "The Relationship Between Planning and the Market in the Socialist Economy," *JJYJ*, No. 3, pp. 61–5.

Fang Gongwen. 1985. "Profits Are the Direct Objective of Socialist Enterprise Production," *GMRB*, Feb. 10, p. 3.

Feng Baoxing, Wan Xin, and Shang Dajian. 1979. "The Socialist Economy Is the Unity of Planned Economy and Commodity Economy," *SHKXZX*, No. 3, pp. 71–7.

Gao Shangquan. 1987. "Carry Out the Internal Unity Between Planning and the Market," *RMRB*, Nov. 16, p. 5.

1988. "Relations Between Planning and Market," *BR*, Vol. 13, No. 15, Apr. 11–17, pp. 23–6.

Gao Zhihua. 1980. "What Is the Best Economic Setup for China?" *SSC*, Vol. 1, No. 1, pp. 7–17.

Ge Hui. 1986. "On Competition Among Export Enterprises," *JJGL*, No. 11, pp. 34–6.

Gong Shiqi. 1988. "Economic Features of Primary Stage of Socialism," *BR*, February 15–28, pp. 18–21.

Gong Zhuming. 1986. "On China's Economic Fluctuations," *SLJJJSJJ*, No. 9, pp. 12–19.

Guo Jia. 1987. "Deepening the Theoretical Principle of the Contract System," *GMRB*, Sept. 5, 1987, p. 3.

Han Zhiguo, Cao Youngrong, and Wang Yong. 1988. "A General Survey of the Discussions of the Stock System in Recent Years," *ZGSHKX*, No. 3, pp. 48–58.

He Jianzhang. 1979. "Problems in the Management of China's Planned Economy Under the System of Ownership by the Whole People and the Direction of Reforms," *JJYJ*, No. 5, pp. 35–45.

1982. "More on Planned Economy and Market Regulation," *SSC*, No. 4, pp. 46–59.

1987. "Stock Issue Is Not the Direction of Reform of State-Owned Enterprises," *GMRB*, Oct. 17, p. 3.

He Jianzhang, Kuang Ri'an, and Zhang Zhuoyuan. 1981. "Reform of the Economic Structure Requires Industrial Pricing Based on Production Price," *SSC*, Vol. 2, No. 1, pp. 120–35.

He Jianzhang, Wang Jiye, and Wu Kaitai. 1980. "Concerning the Coordination Between Planned Adjustment and Market Adjustment," *JJYJ*, No. 5, pp. 19–25.

He Juhuang. 1987. "On Equilibrium Price and the Differences Between It and Labor Value and Production Price," *SLJJJSJJ*, No. 10, pp. 3–13.

He Wei. 1986. "Law of Development of Socialist Public Ownership," *JJYJ*, No. 9, pp. 38–44.

1987a. "Implement the Contract System and Enliven the Large and Medium-Sized Enterprises," *GMRB*, Apr. 11, p. 3.

1987b. "Entrepreneurs Should Also Become Rich," *GMRB*, Nov. 7, p. 3.

1987c. "The Discussion of Labor Power Commodity," *JJXWZ*, No. 12, pp. 4–6.

1988. "On Enterprise Ownership," *GG*, No. 1, pp. 113–21.

He Xiaopei. 1982. "Surveys of Current Remunerations for Mental Labor and Physical Labor," *JJYJ*, No. 8, pp. 33–40.

Hong Yinxing, Zhou Xiaohan, Jin Bei, Hu Yongming, Zhu Zhengming, and Lu Jianren. 1988. *Dangdai Tongou Jingjixue Liupai [Schools of Thought in Contemporary Eastern European Economics]*. Beijing: China Economics Press.

Hu Peizhao. 1988. "On Exploitation," *ZGJJWT*, No. 1, pp. 6–14.

Hu Qiaomu. 1978. "Observe Economic Laws, Speed Up the Four Modernizations," *RMRB*, Oct. 6, pp. 1–3.

Hu Yongming. 1988. "Enterprise Behavior," in *Jingjixue Dontai* Editorial Department (ed.), 1988, pp. 140–55.

Hu Yongming and Lu Hongwei. 1986. "Enterprise Goals and Enterprise Behavior," *JJLLJJGL*, No. 6, pp. 17–22.

Hua Sheng. 1984. "On Solving Investment Expansion," *JJYJ*, No. 3, pp. 23–9.

Hua Sheng, He Jiacheng, Zhang Xuejun, Lo Xiaopeng, and Bian Yongzhuang. 1986. "Rebuilding the Microeconomic Foundation," *JJYJ*, No. 3, pp. 21–8.

Hua Sheng, Zhang Xuejun, and Lo Xiaopeng. 1988a–c. "China's Ten Years of Reforms: Looking Back, Reflection and Prospect," *JJYJ*, No. 9, pp. 13–37; No. 11, pp. 11–30; No. 12, pp. 10–29.

Huang Fangyi. 1985. "Introduction of Foreign Technology and the Restrictive Factors of Foreign Trade," *JJYJ*, No. 12, pp. 22–8.

1986. "On the Choice of China's External Economic Strategy," *JJYJ*, No. 12, pp. 26–30, 13.

Huang Fanzhang. 1979. "On Consumer Sovereignty," *JJGL*, No. 2, pp. 25–7.

1987. *Ruidian: "Fuli Guojia" De Shijian Yu Lilun [Sweden: The Practice and Theories of the Welfare State]*. Shanghai: People's Press.

1989. "Share Ownership Is a Good Form of Socialist Ownership by All the People," *JJYJ*, No. 4, pp. 17–27, 16.

Huang Rongsheng. 1983. "Questions Concerning Cross-Regional Economic Cooperation and Combination," *XSYJ*, No. 1, pp. 54–9.

Huang Shanhe. 1988. "Comprehensive, Pluralistic, Externally Oriented Development Strategy," *ZGJJWT*, No. 5, pp. 26–30.

Huang Taiyan. 1986. "Categories of Behavior of Enterprises Owned by the Whole People and the Counter Measures," *JJYJ*, No. 3, pp. 29–33.

Ji Chongwei and Yang Mu. 1988. "Fully Understand and Implement the Outward-Looking Development Strategy," *RMRB*, July 18, p. 5.

Ji Zhengzhi. 1979. "On the Formation of Socialist Planned Prices," *JJYJ*, No. 4, pp. 58–64.

    1981. "The Amount of Profits in Planned Prices Should Be Fixed According to the Overall Profit Rate," *JJYJ*, No. 2, pp. 38–44.

Jia Lürang and Lin Wenyi. 1981. "Is It Necessary to Create a Buyers' Market?" *GMRB*, July 18, p. 4.

Jiang Rui. 1983. "Considering the Sellers' Market and the Buyers' Market," *CMJJ*, No. 2, pp. 25–7.

Jiang Xuemo. 1979. "The Nature and Forms of China's Socialist Ownership System," *XSYK*, No. 10, pp. 1–9.

    (ed.). 1988a. *Zhengzhi Jingjixue Jiaocai [Political Economy Textbook]*. Shanghai: People's Press, 5th ed.

    1988b. "Commenting on the Thesis of 'Absentee Owners'," *JJYJ*, No. 3, pp. 33–8.

Jiang Yiwei. 1980a. "The Theory of an Enterprise-Based Economy," *SSC*, Vol. 1, No. 1, pp. 48–70.

    1980b. "Some Questions Concerning Distribution According to Labor," *GRRB*, Mar. 21, p. 2.

    1987a. "Models of Socialist Enterprises," *JJGL*, No. 1, pp. 3–10.

    1987b. "Exploring a New Form of Socialist Public Ownership: Collective Shareholding by the Laborers," *RMRB*, Mar. 30, p. 5.

    1987c. "Exploring Problems of the Labor System," *JJGL*, No. 9, pp. 7–11.

    1988. *From Enterprise–Based Economy to Economic Democracy* (in English). Beijing: Beijing Review Press.

Jiang Zuopei and Ding Xianhao. 1986. "Problems of Indirect Macro Control of the Market," *ZGJJWT*, No. 3, pp. 6–10.

Jin Mingjun. 1979. "Competition Is Not Appropriate for the Socialist Economy," *XSYK*, No. 7, pp. 26–7, 31.

Jin Xizai and Liu Chunlin. 1987. "On the Principle of Distribution According to Funds," *JJYJ*, No. 8, pp. 73–7.

Jingjixue Dongtai Editorial Department (ed.). Various years. *Jingji Lilun Dongtai [Movements in Economics]*. Beijing: China Economics Press.

Jingji Yanjiu Editorial Department (ed.). 1985. *Jian Guo Yilai Shehui Zhuyi Jingji Lilun Wenti Zhenming 1949–1984 [Contending Socialist Economic Theories Since the Founding of the PRC 1949–1984]*. 2 volumes. Beijing: China Finance and Economics Press.

    (ed.). 1986. *Zhongguo Shehuizhuyi Jingji Lilun De Huigu Yu Zhanwang [Review and Prospects of China's Socialist Economic Theories]*. Beijing: Economic Daily Press.

Kuang Ri'an. 1986. "Issues Related to Production Prices in Socialist Price Theory," *SSC*, Vol. 7, No. 2, pp. 59–76.

Kuang Ri'an and Xiao Liang. 1979. "On the Law of Value and the Right of Enterprises to Independent Actions," *JJYJ*, No. 5, pp. 68–78.

Li Dehua. 1979. "Determine Prices and Socialize Production on the Basis of Production Prices," *JJYJ*, No. 4, pp. 65–72.

Li Hao, Jiang Yiwei, and Zhou Shulian (eds.). 1986. *Zhongguo Gongye Jingji Fazhan Zhanlue Yanjiu [A Study of China's Industrial Development Strategy]*. Beijing: Economic Management Press.

Li Weisen. 1986. "Preliminary Thoughts on Establishing the Real Ownership System of Laboring Individuals," *JJYJ*, No. 11, pp. 6–12.

Li Xuai. 1988. "Understanding Private Economy and Exploitation," *ZGJJWT*, No. 3, pp. 49–52.

Li Yang. 1986. "On an Export-Oriented Economy," *JJYJ*, No. 12, pp. 22–5.

Li Yining. 1984. "On Coordinating Macroeconomics and Microeconomics in Reforming the Planning System," *JJYJ*, No. 2, pp. 3–9.

1986a. "Thoughts on the Reform of China's Ownership System," *RMRB*, Sept. 26, p. 5.

1986b. "Should Price Reform or Ownership Reform Come First?" *SJJJDB*, Nov. 3, p. 3.

1986c. "Possibilities for China's Ownership Reform," *BR*, No. 52, Dec. 27, pp. 17–19.

1987a. "On the Secondary Adjustment," *CMJJ*, No. 1, pp. 8–15.

1987b. "Hypothesis on Socialist Business Cycles," *JJYJ*, No. 9, pp. 15–22.

1988. "The Overall Design for the Reform of the Economic System," *CMJJ*, No. 7, pp. 3–10.

1989. *Zhongguo Jingji Gaige De Silu [Thoughts on China's Economic Reforms]*. Beijing: Prospect Press.

Li Zhe. 1981. "Questions on Developing the Advantages of Regional Economies," *JJYJ*, No. 2, pp. 49–51.

Liang Wensen and Tian Jianghai. 1980. "Final Products: A New Point of Departure," *SSC*, Vol. 1, No. 4, pp. 61–73.

1983. "On Labor Accumulation," *RMRB*, June 15, p. 5.

Liao Jili. 1984. "Problems in Reforming the Economic System," *JJYJ*, No. 7, pp. 3–5.

Lin Chuanshui. 1985. "Socialist Productive Labor and Nonproductive Labor," in *Jingji Yanjiu Editorial Department* (ed.), 1985, Vol. 1, pp. 657–93.

Lin Ling. 1988. "Price Reform Should Be Implemented Simultaneously with Enterprise Reform," *GMRB*, July 30, 1988, p. 3.

Lin Shuiyuan. 1987. "The Theory of Socialist Public Ownership: Its Change and Development in Practice," *JJYJ*, No. 6, pp. 59–64.

Lin Wenyi. 1987. "Build a Market That Is Proportionally Adjusted Between Supply and Demand," *ZGJJWT*, No. 3, pp. 53–4.

Lin Zili. 1988. "Commercialization of Labor, Socialization of Property and Development of Market Mechanism – On the Theory and Strategy of China's Price Reform," *JJYJ*, No. 9, pp. 3–12.

Liu Changli. 1987. "Import Substitution Is China's Long-Term Strategy for Catching up with or Surpassing the Developed Countries," *JJYJ*, No. 8, pp. 34–44.

Liu Dong. 1983. "Questions on Expanding Labor Accumulation in Agriculture," *NYJJWT*, No. 5, pp. 14–19.

Liu Guoguang. 1962. "A Preliminary Discussion on the Quantitative Relationship Between the Rate and Proportions of Socialist Reproduction," *JJYJ*, No. 11, pp. 16–31.

1979. "Some Questions Concerning the Overall Balance of the National Economy," *JJYJ*, No. 3, pp. 36–44.

1980. "On the Problems of Planned Adjustment and Market Regulation," *JJYJ*, No. 10, pp. 3–11.

1983. "On the Buyers' Market Again," *CMJJ*, No. 9, pp. 7–16.

1986a. "Changes in Ownership Forms: Problems and Possibilities," *BR*, No. 19, May 12, pp. 17–22.

1986b. "The Third Discussion on the Buyers' Market," *RMRB*, Sept. 15, 1986, p. 5.

(ed.). 1987a. *Zhongguo Shehui Zhuyi De Gaige Kaifang He Fazhan Daolu [Ways of Reforms, Opening and Development of China's Socialist Economy]*. Beijing: Economic Management Press.

1987b. "Develop Marxist Economic Theory Through Reform Practice," *RMRB*, July 31, p. 3; Aug. 3, p. 5.

1988a. "Developing Marxist Economic Theory in the Practice of the Reform," *SSC*, Vol. 9, No. 1, pp. 19–39.

1988b. "Theoretical Questions Concerning Choices in Economic System Reforms," *RMRB*, Aug. 19, p. 5.

1988c. "Concerning the Development Strategy of the Hainan Special District," *CMJJ*, No. 9, pp. 3–10.

Liu Guoguang and Wang Xiangming. 1980. "A Study of the Speed and Balance of China's Economic Development," *SSC*, Vol. 1, No. 4, pp. 15–43.

Liu Guoguang and Zhao Renwei. 1979. "The Relationship Between the Plan and the Market under Socialism," *JJYJ*, No. 5, pp. 46–55.

Liu Shibai. 1986. "On Socialist Share Ownership," *JJYJ*, No. 12, pp. 62–6.

Liu Suinian. 1980. "On the Direction of Reform of China's Economic System," *JJYJ*, No. 1, pp. 3–10.

Liu Wei and Yang Yunyou. 1988. "Regional Comparison of China's Industrial Structure and the Principle of Rationalization," *JJYJZL*, No. 1, pp. 42–9.

Lou Jiwei and Zhou Xiaochuan. 1984. "The Direction of Reform of China's Price System," *JJYJ*, No. 10, pp. 13–20.

Lu Wen. 1982. "Regions' Advantages in Agriculture and the Overall Proportions," *JJYJ*, No. 2, pp. 7–9, 15.

Luo Jingfen. 1980. "The Need to Build a Market in Which Supply Exceeds Demand," *GMRB*, Dec. 27, p. 3.

Luo Shouchu and Pan Zhenmin. 1987. "On the Enterprise's Goal," *JJYJ*, No. 3, pp. 44–50.

Ma Hong. 1979. "Reform the Economic Management System and Expand Enterprise Autonomy," *HQ*, No. 10, pp. 50–8.

1981. "The Reform of the Economic System," *JJYJ*, No. 7, pp. 11–24.

1984. "China's Commodity Economy Under the Socialist System," *JJYJ*, No. 12, pp. 3–15.

Ma Jiantang. 1986. "Enterprise Behavior and Economic Mechanism," *JJYJ*, No. 2, pp. 12–17.

Makesi Engesi Quanji [Complete Works of Marx and Engels]. Beijing: People's Press, 1982, 49 volumes.

Makesi Engesi Xuanji [Selected Works of Marx and Engels]. Beijing: People's Press, 1972, 4 volumes.

Ouyang Sheng. 1979. "On Balancing Capital Goods and Consumer Goods," *JJYJ*, No. 6, pp. 13–19.

Pan Zhenmin, Luo Shochu, and Hua Min. 1987. "Socialist Enterprises' Behavior: The System of Control and Income Distribution," *JJYJ*, No. 7, pp. 61–7.

Qin Ming. 1980. "Remarks on the Development of Economic Advantages," *JJYJ*, No. 9, pp. 60–1.

Ren Zhongyi. 1980. "Socialist Construction Must Obey Basic Economic Laws of Socialism," *HQ*, No. 3, pp. 2–7.

Shen Shouye. 1987. "Enterprise Ownership Is a Vital Form of Public Ownership," *ZGJJWT*, No. 1, pp. 32–5.

Shi Xiaomin and Liu Jirui. 1989. "Economists Should First of All Respect History and Facts," *JJYJ*, No. 2, pp. 11–33.

Song Yangyan and Wang Haidong. 1988. "Correcting the Choices of the Relationship Between Prices and Wages," *JJRB*, July 19, p. 3.

Song Yingyu. 1988. "Economic Development Strategy, Industrial Structure, and Industrial Policy," *JJYJZL*, No. 5, pp. 20–5.

State Statistical Bureau. Various years. *Zhongguo Tongji Nianjian [China Statistical Yearbook]*. Beijing.

Sun Liancheng. 1987. "Socialism and the Open-Door Policy," *RMRB*, May 11, p. 5.

Sun Liancheng and Lin Huiyong. 1988. "How Did Marx and Engels Regard the Private Ownership System?" *GMRB*, Dec. 19, p. 3.

Sun Minghua. 1987. "Ownership Right, Control Right, and Management Right," *GMRB*, July 25, p. 3.

Sun Shangqing, Chen Jiyuan, and Zhang Er. 1979. "Some Theoretical Questions on Combining Planning with the Market in a Socialist Economy," *JJYJ*, No. 5, pp. 56–67.

Sun Yefang. 1959. "On Value," *JJYJ*, No. 9, pp. 42–69.

Tian Jianghai and Li Guang'an. 1981. "How Should an Overall Balance Be Attained in Planning the National Economy?" *SSC*, Vol. 2, No. 3, pp. 5–17.

Tian Jianghai and Liang Wensen. 1978. "There Should Not Be Gaps in Making Economic Plans," *RMRB*, Dec. 31, p. 3.

Tian Jianghai and Zhang Shuguang. 1981. "Organization, Planning, and Efficiency: An Enquiry into the Superiority of the Socialist Economic System," *SSC*, Vol. 2, No. 4, pp. 24–54.

Tian Jianghai and Zhong Hua. 1985. "Overall Balance in the National Economy," in *JJYJ* Editorial Department (ed.), pp. 622–56.

Tian Yuan et al. 1987. "Study and Application of Theoretical Prices," *SSIC*, Vol. 8, No. 4, pp. 71–86.

Wan Jieqiu. 1987. "The Challenge and Choices Facing the Sunan Model," *JJYJ*, No. 4, pp. 65–70.

Wang Bifeng. 1988. "A Survey of Discussions on Periodic Fluctuations in China," *JJLLJJGL*, No. 1, pp. 75–80.

Wang Cainan. 1983. "Exploring the Sellers' Market and the Buyers' Market," *CMJJ*, No. 5, pp. 26–8.

Wang Jian. 1988. "Selecting the Correct Long-Term Development Strategy," *JJRB*, Jan. 5, p. 3.

Wang Mengkui. 1987. "Some Thoughts on the Share Economy," *RMRB*, Apr. 6, p. 5.

Wang Senlin. 1986. "Study Marx's Approach Toward the Shareholding System," *GMRB*, Dec. 6, p. 3.

Wang Shaoqing and Xu Jingyi. 1984. "Prospects of Reforming the Distribution System of Producer Goods," *CMJJ*, No. 7, pp. 17–20.

Wang Yongzhi and Wang Zhenzhi. 1979. "Questions Concerning the Formation of Socialist Prices," *JJYJ*, No. 3, pp. 69–71.

1983. "Prices and Supply and Demand," *JJYJ*, No. 6, pp. 23–9.

Wang Zhenzhi. 1988. "Some Questions on Deepening the Price Reform," *CMJJ*, No. 7, pp. 30–4.

Wang Zhenzhi and Qiao Rongzhang. 1988. *Zhongguo Jiagegaige De Huigu Yu Zhanwang [Review and Prospect of China's Price Reform]*. Beijing: China Materials Press.

Wang Zhenzhi, Wang Yongzhi, and Jia Xiuyuan. 1982. "A Summary of the Discussions on Price Theory During the Past Few Years," *SSC*, Vol. 3, No. 3, pp. 16–34.

Wang Zhiyuan and Zeng Xingqun. 1988. "On the Development Strategy of Areas in China's Industrial Location," *JJYJ*, No. 1, pp. 66–74.

Wei Jie. 1986. "The Micro Foundation of Macro Control," *CMJJ*, No. 6, pp. 9–15.

1987. "Systematic Analysis of Indirect Macro Control Models," *JJLLJJGL*, No. 2, pp. 1–7.

Wei Xinghua, Hong Yinxing, and Wei Jie. 1986. "On Enterprise Vitality and Enterprise Behavior Constraints," *XSYK*, No. 4, pp. 1–5, 9.

1987. "Market Regulation Directed and Restrained by Plan Adjustment," *JJYJ*, No. 1, pp. 57–61.

Wen Qian. 1986. "On the Equilibrium Market," *CMJJ*, No. 7, pp. 33–8.

Wu Jinglian. 1988. " 'Rent–Seeking' Theory and Some Negative Phenomena in China's Economy," *JJRB*, Sept. 30, p. 3.

Wu Jinglian and Zhao Renwei. 1987. "The Dual Pricing System in China's Industry," *JCE*, Vol. 11, pp. 309–18.

Wu Jinglian and Zhou Xiaochuan. 1988. *Zhongguo Jingji Gaige De Zhengti Sheji [The Integrated Design of China's Economic Reform]*. Beijing: China Prospects Press.

Wu Jixue and Zhu Ling. 1986. "The Dual Structure and Operational Mechanism of Public Ownership," *ZGJJWT*, No. 6, pp. 9–14, 19.

Wu Renhong. 1988. "On the Particularity of China's Present Macroeconomic Functioning," *CMJJ*, No. 11, pp 3–8.

Wu Renjian and Li Xiuzhen. 1985. "Socialist Economic Accounting," in *JJYJ* Editorial Department (ed.), Vol. 1, pp. 546–87.

Wu Shuqing. 1987. "Share Issuing Is Not the Direction of Reform for Large and Medium-Sized State-Owned Enterprises," *RMRB*, Mar. 16, 1987, p. 5.

Wu Shuqing and Hu Renwu (eds.). 1987. *Moshi Yunxing Tiaokong [Models, Operations, Adjustment and Control]*. Beijing: People's University Press.

Wu Tongguang. 1979. "Socialist Economy and Competition," *GMRB*, Mar. 24, p. 4.

Xia Shen. 1988. "On the Choice of China's Externally Oriented Development Strategy," *CMJJ*, No. 9, pp. 11–16.

Xiang Qiyuan. 1987. "Discussions of Distribution According to Labor and Wage Reforms," *JJXWZ*, No. 4, pp. 4–6.

Xiao Zhuoji. 1988. "On the Shareholding System with the Dominance of Public Ownership," *JJRB*, Nov. 8, p. 3.

Xing Junfang. 1985. "Prices in Socialist Economy," in *Jingji Yanjiu* Editorial Department (ed.), pp. 499–545.

Xu Dixin. 1981. "On China's Socialist System," *JJYJ*, No. 7, pp. 3–9.

Xu Hua. 1988. "Agriculture in the Grand International Cycle," *ZGJJWT*, No. 3, pp. 1–5.

Xu Jiang'an. 1987. "The Stock–Share System: A New Avenue for China's Economic Reform," *JCE*, Vol. 11, pp. 509–14.

Xue Muqiao. 1980. "Reform of Economic Structure and Economic System," *HQ*, No. 14, pp. 6–15.

1981. *China's Socialist Economy* (in English). Beijing: Foreign Language Press.

1987. "Evolution of China's Ownership of the Means of Production," *JJYJ*, No. 2, pp. 15–28.

Yan Renchang. 1985. "Socialist Ownership of the Means of Production," in *JJYJ* Editorial Department (ed.), Vol. 1, pp. 149–95.

Yan Simao. 1984. "On The Socialist Stock Company," *JJYJ*, No. 12, pp. 33–6, 40.

Yang Fangxun. 1982. "Persist in Paying Attention to the State, the Collectives, and the Individuals and Stabilize the Prices of Agricultural Products," *JJYJ*, No. 4, pp. 27–9.

Yang Jingdong. 1988. "Wages Should Have a Soft Link with Prices," *JJGL*, No. 9, pp. 29–30.

You Lin. 1981. "Planned Production in the Main and Free Production as the Supplement," *JJYJ*, No. 9, pp. 3–9.

Yu Fengcun. 1962. "On the Commodity Economy," *JJYJ*, No. 10, pp. 48–54.

Yu Guangyuan. 1959. "On Commodity Production Under Socialism," *JJYJ*, No. 7, pp. 19–51.

1984. *Jingji Shehui Fazhan Zhanlue [Social and Economic Development Strategy]*. Beijing: China Social Science Press.

1986a. "Put Prices Ahead of Value," *JJYJ*, No. 5, pp. 25–35.

188   References

1986b. "China's Reform of the Socialist System and the Socialist Part of Political Economics," *JJYJ*, No. 8, pp. 3–8.

1987a. "Some Views on the System of Economics and on the Reform of the Economic System," *JJKX*, No. 1, pp 1–7.

1987b. "Socialist Primary Stage and Its Production Relations," *JJYJ*, No.7, pp. 3–9.

Yu Zuyao. 1988. "The Contradictions Between Reforms and Development and Their Countermeasures," *GMRB*, Jan. 16, p. 3.

Zeng Kanglin. 1985. "Establish and Develop the Relations of Commodity Economy within Enterprises," *CJKX*, No. 5, pp. 32–5, 40.

Zhang Bingguang. 1987. "Property Holding Rights of State-Owned Enterprises," *ZGJJWT*, No. 5, pp. 17–20, 7.

Zhang Chunyin. 1986. "On Measuring Theoretical Price," *JJYJ*, No. 4, pp. 66–7.

Zhang Chunyin and Zhan Junzhong. 1979. "Preliminary Inquiry Into the Formation of Socialist Prices," *JJYJ*, No. 8, pp. 65–9.

Zhang Lin. 1985. "Agricultural Modernization and Agricultural Development Strategy," in *JJYJ* Editorial Department (ed.), Vol. 2, pp. 1–27.

Zhang Shushan. 1981. "Clarifying the Concept of 'Supply Exceeding Demand,' " *GMRB*, Feb. 21, p. 4.

Zhang Weiying. 1987. "The System of Stock Financing and the Decomposition of Entrepreneur's Functions," *JJYJ*, No. 1, pp. 31–7.

Zhang Wenmin. 1985. "Distribution According to Labor," in *JJYJ* Editorial Department (ed.), Vol. 2, pp. 134–94.

1986. "Distribution According to Labor," in *JJYJ* Editorial Department (ed.), pp. 375–93.

Zhang Xianyang. 1988. "Some Views on the Unfairness of Society's Income Distribution," *GMRB*, July 2, p. 3.

Zhang Xiaoming. 1987. "Macro Coexistence and Micro Combination of Various Economic Elements," *GMRB*, Sept. 19, p. 3.

Zhang Yinggao. 1983. "A Brief Comment on Labor Accumulation Under Socialism," *JJYJ*, No. 5, pp. 48–51.

Zhang Zhuoyuan. 1987. *Shehuizhuyi Jiage Lilun Yu Jiage Gaige [Socialist Price Theory and Price Reform]*. Beijing: China Social Sciences Press.

1988a. "Recent Discussions on Price Reform Theory and Practice," *JJXWZ*, No. 4, pp. 4–7.

1988b. "Cure Inflation and Deepen Price Reform," *GMRB*, Nov. 19, 1988, p. 3.

Zhang Zhuoyuan and Bien Yongzhuang, 1987. "Price Reform Is Still the Key to the Reform of the Economic System," *SYYJ*, No. 2, pp. 3–8.

Zhang Zhuoyuan and Li Xiuzhen. 1985. "Socialist Commodity Production," in *JJYJ* Editorial Department (ed.), Vol. 1, pp. 365–416.

Zhao Lükuan and Yang Tiren. 1988. "Linking Enterprise Wages with Economic Results," *RMRB*, June 27, p. 5.

Zhao Renwei. 1985a. "The Plan and the Market Under Socialism," in *JJYJ* Editorial Department (ed.), Vol. 1, pp. 470–98.

1985b. "Trends in Laborers' Individual Income Distribution," *JJYJ*, No. 3, pp. 10–19.

1986. "The Dual System in China's Economic Reform," *JJYJ*, No. 9, pp. 12–23.
1987. "Comments on Discussions of Planning and the Market," *JJXWZ*, No. 9, pp. 4–7.
Zheng Bangcai. 1984. "Peasant Individual Ownership of the Means of Production on the Basis of Public Ownership," *CJKX*, No. 3, pp. 11–16.
1985. "Blindness in the Socialist Commodity Economy: Its Emergence and the Ways to Deal with It," *CJKX*, No. 6, pp. 4–7.
Zheng Hongqing and Liu Yenan. 1988. "Some Thoughts on the Economic Development and Reforms of the Western Region," *JJRB*, May 3, p. 3.
Zhou Shulian. 1981. "Theoretical Problems Concerning the Adjustment of the National Economy," *JJYJ*, No. 3, pp. 13–20.
1985. "Pay Attention to the Study of Enterprise Behavioral Laws," *RMRB*, Oct. 28, p. 5.
1986. "On Models of the Objectives of Socialist Enterprise Reforms," *JJGL*, No. 11, pp. 4–11.
Zhou Weimin and Ru Zhongyuan. 1986. "Giving Priority to Efficiency and Taking Account of Equity," *JJYJ*, No. 2, pp. 30–6.
Zhou Zhenhua. 1981. "Questions Concerning the Superiority of Socialist Economic System," *JJYJ*, No. 7, pp. 34–9.
1987. "Price and Nonprice Competition in the Socialist Market," *ZGJJWT*, No. 5, pp. 27–31.
1988. "The Characteristics, Stages, and Steps of Market Development in China," *JJLLJJGL*, No. 2, pp. 8–14.
Zhou Zhenhua, Liu Zhibiao, and Zhang Erzhen. 1986. "The Dynamic Analysis of Enterprise Behavior," *JJYJ*, No. 10, pp. 66–71.
Zhu Daohua. 1979. "Learn from Foreign Experience and Speed Up China's Agricultural Mechanization," *GMRB*, July 26, p. 1.
Zhu Jiaming. 1979. "Does the Socialist Economic System Absolutely Reject Competition?" *XSYK*, No. 7, pp. 28–31.
Zhu Tiezhen. 1980. "Taking a Dialectical View of the Superiority of the Socialist Economic System," *JJYJ*, No. 9, pp. 40–6.
Zuo Mu. 1987. "A Comment on the Alternative Way to Enliven the Enterprise," *JJYJ*, No. 6, pp. 65–70.

Secondary sources

Baark, Eric. 1981. "China's Technological Economics," *AS*, Vol. 21, No. 9, pp. 977–99.
Brodsgaard, Kjeld E. 1983a. "Paradigmatic Change: Readjustment and Reform in the Chinese Economy, 1953–1981, Part I," *MC*, Vol. 9, No. 1, pp. 37–83.
1983b. "Paradigmatic Change: Readjustment and Reform in the Chinese Economy, Part II," *MC*, Vol. 9, No. 2, pp. 253–72.
Brugger, Bill. 1985. *Chinese Marxism in Flux, 1978–84.* Armonk, N.Y.: M. E. Sharpe.
Burns, J., and Rosen, S. (eds.). 1986. *Policy Conflicts in Post–Mao China: A Documentary Survey with Analysis.* Armonk, N.Y.: M. E. Sharpe.

Chamberlain, Heath B. 1987. "Party–Management Relations in Chinese Industries: Some Political Dimensions of Economic Reform," *CQ*, No. 112, pp. 631–61.

Chen, Nai–Ruenn. 1966. "The Theory of Price Formation in Communist China," *CQ*, No. 27, pp. 33–53.

Chen, Nai-Ruenn, and Hou, Chi-ming. 1986. "China's Inflation, 1979–1983: Measurement and Analysis," *Economic Development and Cultural Change*, Vol. 34, No. 4, pp. 811–35.

Chenery, Hollis B. 1955. "The Role of Industrialization in Development Programming," *AER*, No. 2, pp. 40–57.

Chenery, Hollis B., Ahluwalia, Montek, S., Bell, C. L. G., Duloy John H., and Jolly, Richard. 1974. *Redistribution with Growth*. London: Oxford University Press.

Chow, Gregory C. 1987. "Money and Price Level Determination in China," *JCE*, Vol. 11, pp. 319–33.

Christensen, Peer M. 1983. "The Shanghai School and Its Rejection," in Feuchtwang and Hussain (1983), pp. 74–90.

Clausen, Soren. 1983. "Chinese Economic Debates After Mao and the Crisis of Official Marxism," in Feuchtwang and Hussain (1983), pp. 53–73.

Dernberger, Robert. 1982. "The Status of Economics in China," in U.S. Joint Economic Committee, *China Under the Four Modernizations*, Part I. Washington, D.C.: Government Printing Office, pp. 569–77.

Feuchtwang, S., and Hussain, A. 1983. *The Chinese Economic Reforms*. New York: St. Martin's Press.

Gillis, Malcolm, Perkins, Dwight, Roemer, Michael, and Snodgrass, Donald. 1987. *Economics of Development*, 2nd edition. New York: Norton.

Halpern, Nina P. 1985a. *Economic Specialists and the Making of Chinese Economic Policy, 1955–1983*. Ph.D. dissertation, Political Science Department, University of Michigan, Ann Arbor.

1985b."Learning from Abroad – Chinese Views of the East European Economic Experience, January 1977–June 1981," *MC*, Vol. 11, No. 1, pp. 77–109.

1986. "Making Economic Policy: The Influence of Economists," in U.S. Joint Economic Committee, *China's Economy Looks Toward the Year 2000*. Washington, D.C.: Government Printing Office, pp. 132–46.

Harding, Harry. 1987. *China's Second Revolution: Reform After Mao*. Washington, D.C.: Brookings Institution.

Hartford, Kathleen. 1985. "Socialist Agriculture Is Dead; Long Live Socialist Agriculture! Organizational Transformation in Rural China," in Perry and Wong (1985), pp. 31–61.

Heilbroner, Robert. 1980. *Marxism: For and Against*. New York: Norton.

Herschede, Fred. 1985. "Economics as an Academic Discipline at Nanjing University," *CQ*, No. 102, pp. 304–16.

Hirschman, Albert. 1958. *The Strategy of Economic Development*. New Haven, Conn.: Yale University Press.

Hsu, Robert C. 1982. *Food for One Billion: China's Agriculture Since 1949*. Boulder, Colo.: Westview Press.

1985. "Conceptions of the Market in Post–Mao China: An Interpretive Essay," *MC*, Vol. 11, No. 4, pp. 436–60.

1986. "The Political Economy of Guidance Planning in Post-Mao China," *Weltwirtschaftliches Archiv,* Vol. 122, No. 2, pp. 382–94.

1988. "Economics and Economists in Post–Mao China: Some Observations," *AS,* Vol. 28, No. 12, pp. 1211–28.

1989. "Changing Conceptions of the Socialist Enterprise in China, 1979–1988," *MC,* Vol. 15, No. 4, pp. 499–524.

Ignatius, Adi. 1988. "Beijing's Two Top Economic Thinkers Reflect Leadership's Broader Divisions," *WSJ,* Oct. 28, p. 10.

Knight, Frank H. 1921. *Risk, Uncertainty, and Profit.* Boston: Houghton Mifflin.

Kornai, Janos. 1980a. *Economics of Shortage.* 2 volumes. Amsterdam: North Holland.

1980b. "The Dilemmas of a Socialist Economy: the Hungarian Experience," *CJE,* Vol. 4, No. 2, pp. 147–57.

1980c. " 'Hard' and 'Soft' Budget Constraint," *Acta Oeconomica,* Vol. 25, No. 3–4, pp. 231–46.

1986. "The Hungarian Reform Process: Visions, Hopes, and Reality," *JEL,* Vol. 24, No. 4, pp. 1687–737.

Krueger, Anne O. 1983. *Trade and Employment in Developing Countries.* Vol. 3 *(Synthesis and Conclusions).* Chicago: University of Chicago Press.

Kuznets, Simon S. 1955. "Economic Growth and Income Inequality," *AER,* No. 1, pp. 1–28.

Lardy, Nicholas R. 1983. *Agriculture in China's Modern Economic Development.* New York: Cambridge University Press.

Lardy, Nicholas R., and Lieberthal, K. (eds.). 1982. *Chen Yun's Stragtegy for China's Development: A Non-Maoist Alternative.* Armonk, N.Y.: M. E. Sharpe.

Lin, Cyril L. 1981. "The Reinstatement of Economics in China Today," *CQ,* No. 85, pp. 1–48.

Lippit, Victor. 1982. "Socialist Development in China," in Selden and Lippit (1982), pp. 116–58.

1987. *The Economic Development of China.* Armonk, N.Y.: M. E. Sharpe.

Ma, Shu-yun. 1986. "Recent Changes in China's Pure Trade Theory," *CQ,* No. 106, pp. 291–305.

Naughton, Barry. 1985. "False Starts and Second Wind: Financial Reforms in China's Industrial System," in Perry and Wong (1985), pp. 223–52.

Nickum, James E. 1974. *A Collective Approach to Water Resource Development: The Chinese Commune System, 1962–1972.* Ph.D. dissertation, University of California, Department of Economics, Berkeley.

1978. "Labor Accumulation in Rural China and Its Role Since the Cultural Revolution," *CJE,* Vol. 2, pp. 273–86.

Nove, Alec. 1983. *The Economics of Feasible Socialism.* London: Allen & Unwin.

Nurkse, Ragner. 1953. *Problems of Capital Formation in Underdeveloped Countries.* Oxford: Oxford University Press.

Perkins, Dwight. 1988. "Reforming China's Economic System," *JEL,* Vol. 26, pp. 601–45.

Perroux, F. 1981. "Note on the Concept of 'Growth Poles'," in Ian Livingstone (ed.), *Development Economics and Policy.* London: Allen and Unwin, pp. 182–7.

192   References

Perry, Elizabeth J., and Wong, Christine, 1985. *The Political Economy of Reform in Post-Mao China*. Cambridge, Mass.: Harvard University Press.

Prybyla, Jan S. 1986. "From Mao to Market," *Problems of Communism*, Vol. 25, pp. 21–38.

Putterman, Louis. 1985. "The Restoration of the Peasant Household as Farm Production Unit," in Perry and Wong (1985), pp. 63–82.

Riskin, Carl. 1982. "Market, Maoism and Economic Reform in China," in Selden and Lippit (1982), pp. 300–23.

 1987. *China's Political Economy: The Quest for Development Since 1949*. New York: Oxford University Press.

Schram, Stuart R. 1984. "Economics in Command? Ideology and Policy Since the Third Plenum, 1978–84," *CQ*, No. 99, pp. 417–61.

Selden, Mark. 1988. *The Political Economy of Chinese Socialism*. Armonk, N.Y.: M. E. Sharpe.

Selden, Mark, and Lippit, V. 1982. *The Transition to Socialism in China*. Armonk, N.Y.: M. E. Sharpe.

Shirk, Susan. 1985. "The Politics of Industrial Reform," in Perry and Wong (1985), pp. 195–221.

Sicular, Terry. 1988. "Agricultural Planning and Pricing in the Post-Mao Period," *CQ*, No. 115, pp. 671–705.

Solinger, Dorothy J. 1983. "Marxism and the Market in Socialist China: The Reforms of 1979–1980 in Context," in V. Nee and D. Mozingo (eds.), *State and Society in Contemporary China*. Ithaca, N.Y.: Cornell University Press, pp. 194–219.

 (ed.). 1984. *Three Visions of Chinese Socialism*. Boulder, Colo.: Westview Press.

Stalin, Joseph. 1952. *Economic Problems in Socialism in the USSR*. New York: International Publishers.

Walder, Andrew G. 1983. "Organized Dependency and Cultures of Authority in Chinese Industry," *JAS*, Vol. 43, No. 1, pp. 51–76.

 1987. "Wage Reform and the Web of Factory Interests," *CQ*, No. 109, pp. 22–41.

Wong, Christine P. W. 1986. "The Economics of Shortages and Problems of Reform in Chinese Industry," *JCE*, Vol. 10, No. 4, pp. 363–87.

 1988. "Interpreting Rural Industrial Growth in the Post-Mao Period," *MC*, Vol. 14, No. 1, pp. 3–30.

Yang, Yongzheng, and Tyers, Rodney. 1989. "The Economic Costs of Food Self-Sufficiency in China," *World Development*, Vol. 17, No. 2, pp. 237–53.

Yotopoulos, P., and Lau, L. 1970. "A Test for Balanced and Unbalanced Growth," *Review of Economics and Statistics*, Vol. 52, No. 4, pp. 376–84.

Zimbalist, A., and Sherman, H. 1989. *Comparing Economic Systems* (2nd ed.). Orlando, Fla.: Academic Press.

Index